FRIDAY NIGHT
AND
BEYOND

FRIDAY NIGHT AND BEYOND

The Shabbat Experience Step-by-Step

Lori Palatnik

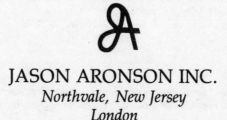

JASON ARONSON INC.
Northvale, New Jersey
London

This book was set in 11 pt. Palacio by Lind Graphics of Upper Saddle River, New Jersey, and printed by Haddon Craftsmen in Scranton, Pennsylvania.

Hebrew text reprinted with permission from *The NCSY Bencher*. Copyright © 1982 by the Union of Orthodox Jewish Congregations of America/National Conference of Synagogue Youth. English translations copyright © 1982 by David M. L. Olivestone, reprinted with permission from *The NCSY Bencher*.

Recipes and instructions on braiding *challah* from *The Taste of Shabbos: The Complete Cookbook*, copyright © 1987 by the Aish Ha'Torah Women's Organization, are used by permission of the Aish Ha'Torah Women's Division, Jerusalem.

Information on Beginners Services used by permission of National Jewish Outreach Program.

Library of Congress Cataloging-in-Publication Data

Palatnik, Lori
    Friday night and beyond : the Shabbat experience, step-by-step / by Lori Palatnik.
        p. cm.
    Includes index.
    ISBN 1-56821-035-3
    1. Sabbath (Jewish law)—Handbooks, manuals, etc. 2. Judaism—Customs and practices—Handbooks, manuals, etc. 3. Judaism—Liturgy—Handbooks, manuals, etc. 4. Jews—Interviews. I. Title.
BM685.P34 1994
296.4'1—dc20   93-26264 √

Manufactured in the United States of America. Jason Aronson Inc. offers books and cassettes. For information and catalog write to Jason Aronson Inc., 230 Livingston Street, Northvale, New Jersey 07647.

The Sabbath is a foundation stone of Jewish life, both spiritual and social. But the gap between those who have not tasted its sweetness and inspiration, and the mode of traditional Sabbath observance seems almost unbridgeable.

Friday Night and Beyond by Lori Palatnik provides such a bridge, for the uninitiated as well as the initiated. She does so painstakingly, engagingly, with an exaltation that hovers over every detail—and above all in both current idiom and profound love for both Sabbath and every Jew.

It is a pleasure to have read and to recommend *Friday Night and Beyond* to its potential readers.

Rabbi Nachman Bulman
Nachliel Institute
of Jewish Studies
Migdal Ha'emek, Israel

TO MY PARENTS, JOEL AND PHYLLIS ZELCER

You held my hand, so I could walk;
Let go, so I could run;
And cheered, so I could fly . . .

CONTENTS

Contents

ACKNOWLEDGMENTS

WITH MUCH THANKS . . .

To Rabbi Noah Weinberg, Rosh HaYeshiva and founder of Aish HaTorah International, for *everything*.

To Rebbetzin Dena Weinberg of EYAHT (Women's Aish HaTorah in Jerusalem), who told me to write five minutes a day, knowing that I would do more. . . . Thank you for setting your spiritual standards so high. (I'm still trying!)

To Richard Posluns, for inspiring the writing of this book ("If you write it, I'll read it"), talking me through the many ups and downs, encouraging me every step of the way, and reading and rereading every version. And to Cathy, for the suggestions and constant encouragement. This book is as much yours as it is mine. Both of you made it a reality.

To Rabbi Mitch Mandel of Aish HaTorah, Toronto ("the man of a thousand vorts"), who always had something beautiful and wise to say about every aspect of *Shabbat*. Your time and support are appreciated more than you can imagine. These pages are filled with your thoughts and wisdom.

To Rabbi Pinchas Winston, also of Aish HaTorah, who provided me with the initial *halachot* of *Shabbat*, and, as a fellow-writer, traded information on everything from publishers to computers. Thanks.

To Ron Dragushan of Sigma Star Research and Consulting Corporation, who did the impossible by teaching me how to *use* a computer. Your patience, generosity, and forever-positive feedback got me started and kept me going. This book would have taken forever without you.

To Allen Berg, for your generosity and computer support. You're the best!

To Sam Veffer, for convincing me to stay. A share of this is yours!

To all the people who gave me their time and their stories for the interview portions of the book. Your anecdotes, insights, humor, and feelings made this book human, warm, and real.

To the members of The Village Shul . . . this was written with all of you in mind . . . (Love you, Nancy!).

To Bev Benia, for "*Shabbat*-on-the-Go."

To Sarah Chana Radcliffe, author and friend-extraordinaire!

To my mother, Phyllis Zelcer, for the fabulous first edit.

To Linda Shapiro, for the fabulous *second* edit.

To David Himelfarb, my legal-eagle.

To Brenda Medjuck, Simone Bronfman, Robyn Daniels, Bev Benia, Sari Bensky Gorman, Riki Greenman, Rhonda "Fallen" Gourdji,

Rhona Hall, Cathy Posluns, and Sandra Herlick. "You learn more from your students than from your teachers. . . ."

To Arthur Kurzweil and the fabulous team at Jason Aronson. You made it a pleasure.

To my husband, Rabbi Yaakov Palatnik, for helping from the minute the idea for this book was conceived. Your ideas, wisdom, direction, encouragement, patience, and humor kept me on track and kept me going. Your love and faith in me never faltered and made it all possible. You know each word is also yours.

To my children, Shoshana Devorah and Zev Shmuel, who were endlessly patient while Ima was "writing her book." You are both too cute for words, and I love you whole bunches.

Special Thanks to Joe and Helen Berman. God created the world with both of you in mind. He knew what He was doing. With much love . . . Lori

---

To The Almighty, who was always there, even at 4 A.M. ESPECIALLY at 4 A.M. "Not for my sake, but for Yours . . ."

Note to reader: Generally, references to *halachah* (Jewish law), unless otherwise stated, have been seen and approved by Rabbi Yitzchak Berkowitz, Mashgiach of Aish HaTorah, Jerusalem. Any inadvertent errors are the sole mistake of the author and are no reflection on the rabbis and scholars who generously gave of their time to read and give guidance to the book *Friday Night and Beyond.*

The Reflections found throughout this book are taken from personal interviews with a wide variety of people who shared their feelings and thoughts about *Shabbat* with the author.

INTRODUCTION

I didn't discover *Shabbat* until I was about twenty-four. Before that, Friday and Saturday were days to shop, date, and catch a movie. My sister and brother didn't start "keeping" *Shabbat* (the term used to describe observing the Jewish Sabbath) until they were young adults. Actually, my brother was already married and had two children before deciding to "look into" *Shabbat*.

Most of my friends have similar stories: We all grew up in Jewish homes with good values, yet very little formal tradition. How we all started lighting candles, making *kiddush*, and going to *shul* could fill another book. Each story is unique and special. To give a blanket explanation as to why Jews are embracing Jewish traditions like *Shabbat* would do a disservice to the individuality of each journey.

Yet, it is happening. And this exciting resurgence of Judaism seems to be moving so quickly that resources to help guide people, both practically and philosophically, are just starting to catch up.

Friday Night and Beyond came about because of my current involvement in adult Jewish education. Both my husband and I help run The Village Shul, a small store-front synagogue in Toronto's Forest Hill that attracts Jews from all walks of life, united in their desire to grow Jewishly through understanding.

We have many guests on *Shabbat*, and often it is their first traditional *Shabbat* experience. We also have hundreds of people coming to classes and seminars to try and learn more about their heritage.

I wish I had a dollar for every time someone asked me if there was a book on *Shabbat* that they could get—something that would walk them through it step-by-step, with clear explanations and stories from people like them, who are just starting out. I didn't know of any such book, so I decided to put my background as a writer and my knowledge in Jewish education together and write one.

The result is *Friday Night and Beyond*.

It is the book I wanted to give my brother and sister-in-law when they first started testing the *Shabbat* waters. It is the book that I wanted to give all of those guests at my own *Shabbat* table. And it is the book that I wish *I* had had, when *I* was first starting out.

The people interviewed in the book are from the total spectrum of Jewish life: from the most unaffiliated to the most observant, and everyone in between. The stories they told and the feelings they shared continually inspired me. Some made me laugh, and others made me cry; all made me remember how personal *Shabbat* is to every individual, no matter what background or level of observance.

So here it is. I hope it is helpful to you. Please note that this is not

*To give a blanket explanation as to why Jews are embracing Jewish traditions like **Shabbat** would do a disservice to the individuality of each journey.*

offered as a complete and scholarly work. *Friday Night and Beyond* is a helpful hand; a place to start; a beginning. The *halachot* (laws) of *Shabbat* have been simplified in order to get you started. And if there is one thing that I would like to emphasize more than anything else, it is that *Judaism is not all or nothing.*

If you light *Shabbat* candles and then go to a movie, that *mitzvah* of lighting is not null and void. Every act of *Shabbat*, whether it be refraining from smoking for a day or making a Friday night *kiddush* is special and important unto itself.

Some people like to begin with Friday night, lighting candles, making *kiddush*, having a special meal, maybe a little song. Others try turning off the phones and the TV one *Shabbat* a month, gradually getting a taste of the tranquillity of *Shabbat* without making a drastic change in life-style. Everyone approaches it differently, and that's O.K. because, as you will see in the interviews of the book, *Shabbat* is a unique experience — unique to YOU. No one can tell you what you will feel and what it will add to your life, because it is different for everyone. For some, the blessing over the bread is the most spiritual moment of their week, filled with thoughts of God's outstretched hand leading the Jewish people out of Egypt and the blessings He bestows upon us every moment of the day. . . . For another, thoughts at that time are: "Boy, this looks yummy!"

And both are valid. Because *Shabbat* is filled with so much; and there is so much opportunity for each individual as a unique soul to understand why it was, and still is, one of the foundations of the Jewish people.

Shabbat should be one step at a time, done with understanding and joy. This is a process, one that takes a different amount of time for different people. If you are married, there is a special process of growing into *Shabbat* that takes place when you have two people proceeding in the same direction, each at his or her own pace.

With children, there has to be special concern for their needs and levels of understanding. A slow, gradual, and pleasurable introduction to *Shabbat* will be much more positive than any type of quick change and will ultimately stay with them longer.

Students and singles are challenged in a special way. They are often away from a family environment and must find friends with whom to share the *Shabbat* experience or try and connect with families in the community who love to have guests at their *Shabbat* table. I myself became close to many special families who were my "home-away-from-home" in town and abroad. No one likes to be an island, especially on *Shabbat*.

Shabbat is beautiful. It is not always easy (especially those long *Shabbat* days in July), but it is truly a gift, one that is for every Jew, no matter what your level of knowledge or observance. Open it up, and you will be amazed at its depth and touched by its warmth.

Good *Shabbos* . . . *Shabbat Shalom*.

When God announced that he was giving the Torah to the Jewish people, He said: "If you fulfill all these commandments, you will inherit heaven—the World to come.

The people asked: "Master of the Universe, won't you show us a sample of that World in THIS world?"

And so He replied: "Here is Shabbat. It will bring you a small taste of the pleasure and peace of the World to come."

Otiot D'Rabbi Akiva
(Second century)

xiv

WHAT IS *SHABBAT*?

Today we are witnessing something unique. Thousands of adults are taking a second look at what it means to be Jewish and, through learning, are beginning slowly to incorporate some of the beauty of their heritage into their lives. One of the first areas people approach is *Shabbat*. For, in *Shabbat* is found all the beauty, depth, and wisdom of what it means to be a Jew.

The Sabbath . . . *Shabbos* . . . *Shabbat*. What is so important about this special day? Is it simply a day of "rest" or is there a deeper and more profound reason for it to be one of the Ten Commandments given to us by God?

Shabbat does not actually mean "to rest," but rather "to cease," "to stop." On the seventh day, God stopped creating. Friday sundown until Saturday late evening is *Shabbat*.

During this time we refrain from certain activities and really get in touch with what life is all about.

On *Shabbat*, we take a step back and cease creating in order to recognize that there is indeed a Creator.

Throughout our week it is easy to get caught up in our accomplishments and projects. It is a natural outcome of the extremely busy lives we lead. Thus we were given a day to refocus and get back in touch with the meaning of it all and, most important, the Source of it all.

It is a time for love of God. It is peaceful, relaxing, but above all, connecting. This is your time to relate to your Creator, and all that He has given you.

We spend time with friends and family, for it is in the home that we see the true value of Judaism and a Jewish life. We dress in finery and bring to the table our best silver and china. Our homes take on a different quality. Our actions seem more refined and purposeful. We are in touch with something greater than ourselves.

Special *Shabbat* services at the synagogue connect us to community and, through prayer, help us to focus on our blessings.

As *Shabbat* approaches and the candles are lit, we begin a much-needed day that will give to all the spiritual and physical nourishment needed in order to grow as individuals and as unique beings connected to a people.

We enter *Shabbat* one way, and we leave another. When it is over, we have learned and grown, so that we can now give even more to our daily lives and to others.

Approach *Shabbat* slowly, one step—or one chapter—at a time. And know that by fulfilling this commandment from God, you are bringing that light of all that He gives into your home and into your heart.

> **On Shabbat**, *we take a step back and cease creating in order to recognize that there is indeed a Creator.*

CHAPTER ONE

Friday Night

Step-by-Step

Candlelighting

Synagogue (*Shul*)

Shalom Aleichem (Song Welcoming *Shabbat*)

Eishet Chayil (Song in Praise of Women)

Blessing of the Children

Kiddush

Washing for Bread

Ha-motzi (Blessing over the *Challah*)

Zemirot (*Shabbat* Songs)

Devar Torah (Torah Portion of the Week)

Shir Ha-maalot

Mayim Acharonim (Jewish "Fingerbowl")

Birkat Ha-mazon (Blessing after the Meal)

CANDLELIGHTING

*The **Shabbat** candles radiate peace.*

Sefer Ha-midot Le-Marahan

It seems there is something special about the act of lighting *Shabbat* candles. It is a touching picture: the woman bent over the flames in prayer, a kerchief covering her head.

One of the strongest symbols of the Jewish people, candlelighting encompasses what is central in Judaism: the Jewish home.

It is a moment steeped in tradition, as one may remember one's own mother lighting . . . a grandmother . . . or the Jewish women who have been lighting candles every Friday night for over 3,500 years. It is a powerful link to Jews everywhere; one that, until recently, remained unbroken in every home, in every land.

Customs vary, but in the family there are always at least two candles burning: one for her, and one for her husband—a symbol of *Shalom Bayit* (Peace in the House). Many add one for each child, as each is an additional blessing, each a source of new light coming into the world.

Lighting the *Shabbat* candles is one of the special *mitzvot* for women, although, as we will discuss, men are also obligated to light.

Why is this important *mitzvah* assigned to women? Because it is light, and that is the essence of a woman.

It is the woman who brings light into the home, providing the atmosphere in which she, her husband, and her children can live and prosper. The tone, the feel, the look . . . it is from her. When she is happy and positive, even the most depressed husband or tired child will absorb her energy and be lifted.

And, to the contrary, if she is unhappy and the home has a feeling of negativity, it can affect the whole family. She is the core of the family unit.

It is the power of the Jewish woman, for it is the woman who sanctifies space. Even if outside at the office, her presence makes a difference to the environment around her. There, and at home, she provides that unique quality of soul that lays the all-important foundation for everyone who comes into her world.

Historically, it was the Jewish women, not the men, who agreed to accept the Torah first at Mount Sinai. And today, it is the woman who transmits the essence of our Jewish heritage into every home.

So this is how the *Shabbat* begins, with special light; special understanding as to who we are and why we are here. For *Shabbat* is our time to connect with God; when we stop creating in order to recognize that there is a Creator. The entire week we are caught up in a hectic pace, where it is easy to think only of personal accomplishments and individual achievements.

3

Yet, once the candles are lit, it is time for love of God; remembering that everything is from Him.

It takes but a few seconds to do, but it is by far one of the deepest expressions of the Jewish soul: to recognize the Almighty and appreciate this special gift that He has given to us all—a gift we call *Shabbat*.

How To

1. Lighting time varies, depending on the time of year and city location, but must always be done before sunset. There are special calendars that you can buy at your local Jewish book store that will list all the candlelighting times for the year.

If you don't have such a guide, simply check your local newspaper for the time of sunset and subtract eighteen minutes. That is candlelighting time. It is best to light by that time, but if you cannot, just make sure you do so before the sun goes down. In other words, you have nearly 18 minutes in which to light, beginning with the time listed on your Jewish calendar.

2. It is customary to use white candles, although any can be used, as long as they will burn for two to three hours. Do not use Chanukah or birthday candles, for they burn too quickly.

3. The candles should be lit in an area where they can be seen, but not in a place where a breeze could extinguish the flames or cause them to burn faster, or where children could reach them. (There is more than one story of children innocently blowing out the candles, as if they were on the top of a birthday cake!)

4. Always let them burn naturally; never extinguish them yourself. If for some reason a candle does go out before completely burning down, do not be alarmed, you have already fulfilled the *mitzvah*.

5. Once lit, the candles should not be moved until after *Shabbat*.

6. Many have embraced the custom of depositing a few coins in a *tzedakah* box—charity box—just before candlelighting time.

7. In reverence for the moment, married women cover their hair, often with a kerchief, before lighting.

Questions and Answers

Who Lights?

A married woman usually lights candles on behalf of her whole family, unless for some reason she is unable to do so. Then her husband, or an older child, would light.

Single women and single men light candles on their own if their mothers do not light on their behalf.

It takes but a few seconds to do, but it is by far one of the deepest expressions of the Jewish soul: to recognize the Almighty and appreciate this special gift that He has given to us all—a gift we call **Shabbat.**

How Many Candles?

There are different customs. Some people light one candle while they are single, and then two once they are married. Others always light two, single or married. Parents often add one extra candle for each of their children. (Homes with lots of kids resemble a small bonfire!)

The most common is the lighting of two candles, one to fulfill the commandment to "remember" the *Shabbat* and one for the commandment to "guard" the *Shabbat* (which God commanded in one breath, see page 153).

What If We Won't Be Home for Dinner Friday Night?

Light your candles at your home if you will be returning to sleep there, as long as they will still be burning when you return home. Otherwise, light your candles at home and stay until after dark before leaving for your dinner "out."

(If you are lighting at home and are leaving and are afraid of candles burning unsupervised, simply light them in a sink that you won't be using through *Shabbat*!)

What If I Can't Get Home in Time to Light?

Some people may think that it is so important to light *Shabbat* candles that doing it late is better than not doing it at all. This is a mistaken idea. It is better not to light them at all than to transgress the prohibition of not making a fire on *Shabbat*. Just try and schedule Friday afternoons as best you can so that you will be home to light on time.

What About in the Summer When Candlelighting Is So Late? Are We Supposed to Have Our Friday Night Dinner at 9:30?

You are allowed to bring *Shabbat* in as early as 1¼ hours before sunset, and it is a common practice in the summer so that children can be at the Friday night table. Friday night services in the summer are often done in two shifts: one for those bringing it in early, and one for those bringing it in at sunset.

Remember: Once the candles are lit, even if it is an hour before sunset, it is *Shabbat*. This, however, does not mean that *Shabbat* can now *end* earlier. *Shabbat can begin early, but can never end early.* (For calculating the end of *Shabbat*, see page 90.)

What If I Don't Own Fancy Candlesticks?

Just melt a couple of candles onto a plate or tray covered with a piece of heavy-duty foil, and light them!

Why Can't I Move the Candlesticks after Lighting?

Things that have no use on *Shabbat* are not moved and fall under the category of *muktzah*, which means "set aside." This refers to objects whose handling are subject to restrictions of various kinds on *Shabbat* and on *Yom Tov*. Since we do not use matches, candles, or anything that

Some people may think that it is so important to light Shabbat candles that doing it late is better than not doing it at all. This is a mistaken idea.

5

involves starting or extinguishing a fire on *Shabbat*, these items are not moved at all, so make sure you light in a place where it will be convenient to leave the candlesticks for the whole *Shabbat*.

Blessing over the Candles

*Bringing the hands over the flames toward you signifies that you are drawing the spirituality and holiness of **Shabbat** into your home and into your life.*

Arms are motioned three times, hands drawing over the flames as if to bring the light in toward you,[1] at last covering your face[2] as the special blessing is said:

Baruch atah Adonai,   בָּרוּךְ אַתָּה יְיָ,
Eloheinu melech ha-olam,   אֱלֹהֵינוּ מֶלֶךְ הָעוֹלָם,
asher kideshanu be-mitzvotav   אֲשֶׁר קִדְּשָׁנוּ בְּמִצְוֹתָיו
ve-tzivanu lehadlik neir   וְצִוָּנוּ לְהַדְלִיק נֵר
shel Shabbat.   שֶׁל שַׁבָּת.

You are blessed, Lord our God, the sovereign of the world, who made us holy with His commandments and commanded us to kindle lights for *Shabbat*.

After the recitation, many take special time to thank God for the many blessings of health, prosperity, and joy in their lives. There is also a special prayer composed by women, for women, which many include at this time:

Yehi ratzon mi-lefanecha, Adonai   יְהִי רָצוֹן מִלְּפָנֶיךָ, יְיָ
Elohai veilohei avotai,   אֱלֹהַי וֵאלֹהֵי אֲבוֹתַי,
she-techonein oti (ve-et   שֶׁתְּחוֹנֵן אוֹתִי (וְאֶת־
ishi ve-et banai) ve-et kol   אִישִׁי וְאֶת־בָּנַי) וְאֶת־כָּל־
kerovai vetashlim bateinu.   קְרוֹבַי וְתַשְׁלִים בָּתֵּינוּ.
ve-sashkein shechinat'cha beineinu.   וְתַשְׁכֵּן שְׁכִינָתְךָ בֵּינֵינוּ.
Ve-zakeini legadeil banim u-vnay   וְזַכֵּנִי לְגַדֵּל בָּנִים וּבְנֵי
vanim chachamim umeirim   בָנִים חֲכָמִים וּמְאִירִים
et ha-olam ba-Torah   אֶת־הָעוֹלָם בַּתּוֹרָה
uve-ma'asim tovim ve-ha'eir   וּבְמַעֲשִׂים טוֹבִים וְהָאֵר
neireinu she-lo yichbeh le-olam   נֵרֵנוּ שֶׁלֹּא יִכְבֶּה לְעוֹלָם
va-ed. Ve-ha'eir panecha ve-nivashei'a   וָעֶד. וְהָאֵר פָּנֶיךָ וְנִוָּשֵׁעָה.
Amein.   אָמֵן.

May it be your will, Lord my God and God of my fathers, to be gracious to me (and to my husband and children)

---

[1]Bringing the hands over the flames toward you signifies that you are drawing the spirituality and holiness of *Shabbat* into your home and into your life. According to Jewish tradition, the number three represents commitment and strength. When a good act is performed three times, there is a sense of integration that takes place for the positive. And, conversely, when a transgression is made three times, there is a certain desensitization that takes place, numbing one to the negative.

[2]One usually recites a blessing and then performs the act (for example, saying *Kiddush*, and then drinking the wine), but in this case it is reversed. That is because once the blessing is said, one is accepting *Shabbat* to be in, and then no fire can be lit, and thus no match struck. So here we do the opposite, covering the eyes so that after the blessing we open them as if to see the fulfillment of the commandment for the very first time.

6

and to all my family, crowning our home with the feeling of your divine presence dwelling among us. Make me worthy to raise learned children and grandchildren who will dazzle the world with Torah and goodness and ensure that the glow of our lives will never be dimmed. Show us the glow of Your face and we will be saved. Amen.

It is a time to talk to God. So express anything that you wish, and ask for all that you desire. He wants to hear your prayers.

Reflections

When I was little, my mother never lit candles. Actually, no one I knew lit candles except for my friend's grandmother, so I guess I equated candlelighting with old people. Yet when I got married, a friend gave me beautiful antique wooden candlesticks, and I started lighting every Friday night.

I like doing it, and I found that as my family grew, so did my feeling for lighting.

I think it's because now I know what it means to have a home. Today, when I light, I take a moment to ask God to bless our home with peace, with special blessings for my entire family.

It is a time to talk to God. So express anything that you wish, and ask for all that you desire. He wants to hear your prayers.

The first time I lit *Shabbat* candles I was scared, feeling a sense of importance to it all. It's still an intense time, for that's when I really feel that God is there; that He is with me. It makes me a little nervous because it brings the *brachah*—the blessing—out from deep inside.

My little girl loves to light and has been since she was seven. Now we make sure we light them at the *Shabbat* table so that our evening meal is illuminated. It's so elegant.

As a little boy growing up in Russia, I had no idea that people actually lit candles and observed *Shabbat*. When we were allowed to leave we went to Israel, and there I saw the movie *Fiddler on the Roof*. In one scene the mother lights candles on the eve of the Sabbath.

Later I moved to Canada and began to be interested in *Shabbat*. Slowly, I began to observe it in my own fashion, first not working, then not traveling. And, since I didn't have a "woman in the house," I deduced that I should be the one to light the *Shabbat* candles. I liked it, especially the spirituality of it all. I would always take a few minutes and meditate on the candles. I enjoyed it so much that after I married, I was reluctant to let it go!

With the chicken soup cooking and the candles burning—it's such a nice feeling, as if we are all bonded. I love it.

My mother used to light candles on the back of a plate, put a kerchief over her head, and say a blessing. But to me it was weird because it didn't mean anything. Perhaps it's because she never explained it. I'm not sure. But it did make me feel Jewish, and strangely proud.

Later, when I married, I did a little reading on Judaism and began to study at a Jewish adult-education center.

It stirred up something inside me: a heritage, a desire to know where we come from and why we are here.

So I started lighting *Shabbat* candles. At first it felt strange, but good. Now it is more natural, and I enjoy saying the blessing and the special prayer for my son. My husband loves it, for it brings a sense of family and togetherness into the home.

With the chicken soup cooking and the candles burning—it's such a nice feeling, as if we are all bonded. I love it.

Here I was, this single guy living away from home, studying for my master's at a university out of town, and something made me light candles Friday night. Maybe it was because I had been learning about Judaism and it seemed time to put it into action.

I found it made Friday night very special, like a feeling of home and peace.

There is something about candles . . . it is light, and it makes me think about God. Growing up, it seemed Judaism was always filled with the lighting of candles: Chanukah, *yartzeits* . . . it made Judaism very visual.

Lighting candles Friday night gave me great pleasure and soon became a significant part of my relationship with God.

I think my mom lit candles when my brother had his *bar mitzvah*, but it didn't last long. Yet I was left knowing that Jewish women lit candles.

When I was twenty-nine years old, I traveled to Jerusalem as a journalist and began to take a second look at this thing called Judaism.

One weekend a friend and I went down to the Sinai and camped out on the beach. When Friday night came, I decided to light candles in the tent. I even made *kiddush* for everyone there.

After returning to the States I began to light on a regular basis. It seemed a simple enough thing to do, requiring very little commitment. Why not do such an easy *mitzvah*?

My mother lit candles until the divorce. I was about eight years old back then, but I still remember her covering her head and saying a special blessing over the candles. It was so nice. Many years later I traveled to Israel with my fiancé and spent some time in the Old City of Jerusalem with some good friends from back home. They had become observant and kept *Shabbat* in a very beautiful way.

We had already made plans to bring more Judaism into our new home, but it was this experience that made me want to start the process by keeping *Shabbat*.

Today I try and light my candles when the baby is quiet, and I consider it my special time to talk to God. I light one for each of us, one for my sister, and one in memory of my grandmother, who always lit candles. It makes me feel as if she's there.

It feels good to know that I am carrying on her tradition, because she was very, very special to me.

My mother has also been touched by my new observance and began to light candles again after all these years.

The year before I got married, I began to light candles. It came about after I began learning about what it means to be a Jew in today's world. My mom even started to light, and still does even though I am off and married with three little girls of my own.

I look forward every week to that moment when I bring in *Shabbat* by lighting my candles. If the kids are fighting or something, it's hard to concentrate.

But sometimes, when the mood is relaxed, I light, cover my eyes, and say special prayers for friends who are having difficulty getting pregnant or who are sick. When I take my hands away I see my kids all around me with their hands over their eyes, copying me. It is such a special moment, and I have to fight back the tears.

But sometimes, when the mood is relaxed, I light, cover my eyes, and say special prayers for friends who are having difficulty getting pregnant or who are sick. When I take my hands away I see my kids all around me with their hands over their eyes, copying me. It is such a special moment, and I have to fight back the tears.

Growing up, I had this vague awareness that Jewish women lit candles, although my own mother never did. During my travels as a young adult, I ended up in Israel, first living on a *kibbutz*, and then learning at a *yeshivah*.

Because I was a guy, I went to families for *Shabbat* and was included in the candlelighting done by the woman of the house.

On my own, I would often forget.

I don't always connect with this particular part of *Shabbat*, but I do know that it is an important *halachah*, and that was enough to keep me doing it.

Now my wife lights, and it's a lot more meaningful, because now I have a special woman who really brings light into our home.

It seems surprising that Jacob, grandson of Abraham and one of the fathers of the Jewish people, who fully understood the power of prayer, would not immediately *turn to God for help.*

In my house, my mom always lit, and to me it meant that this night was special. But I always identified it with family, so once I moved out on my own I never kept it up.

Then, when I got engaged my grandmother bought me beautiful candlesticks. I thought now that I was going to have my own family, it was time for me to begin to light. I did, but it was infrequent.

Then I began to take some classes and learned that, although simple, lighting candles was a very important thing to do and was filled with great meaning. I figured it was the least I could do.

Now I always light, and when I do I have a picture in my mind of my grandmother lighting, with a picture in her mind of her grandmother lighting.

FRIDAY NIGHT SYNAGOGUE (*SHUL*)

Prayer. How do you relate to prayer? Is it something only children do at bedtime? Is prayer reserved for services in *shul*? Why do we pray? Should we pray? Why is prayer considered one of the fundamental pillars of Judaism?

Many questions. Let's go to the Source and try to derive some answers.

In Genesis 32, we find Jacob, one of the fathers of the Jewish people, receiving the news that his wicked and vengeful brother, Esau, who had earlier threatened to kill him, is planning to arrive along with four hundred of his men.

Rashi, the eleventh-century scholar and foremost commentator on the Torah (Five Books of Moses), points out that, upon hearing the news, Jacob has three choices before him: appease Esau through gifts; fight him with a portion of his own men; pray.

Jacob chose to utilize all three options, but the order in which they were implemented is significant. Think—when is the best time for him to turn to prayer? At the beginning? In the end, as a last resort?

> Jacob was very frightened and distressed. He divided the people accompanying him into two camps (Genesis 30:8).
> Rescue me, I pray, from the hand of my brother (Genesis 30:12).
> He selected a tribute for his brother Esau from what he had with him (Genesis 30:14).

Rashi notes that, clearly, Jacob chose to prepare, first, by dividing his people for battle, *then* by praying, and, finally, by sending gifts.

It seems surprising that Jacob, grandson of Abraham and one of the fathers of the Jewish people, who fully understood the power of prayer, would not *immediately* turn to God for help.

And in this we find an important insight into prayer.

God responds to us based on our *choices*. Belief in the power of prayer is also belief in our *responsibility* to make the supreme effort. Prayers are meaningful and effective when preceded by serious intent and, in this case, action.

Prayer is also the confirmation of the Jewish view of the Almighty as a *personal* God. Relating to Him should be a daily part of one's life and should not be reserved just for a special occasion or a pressing situation.

Talk to God. It can be in English, Hebrew, Chinese, Spanish . . . or in whatever language you feel most comfortable. God understands every word and wants to hear your prayers.

Because through prayer we recognize our Creator and come close to Him. And being close to God is the ultimate pleasure.

When you pray, focus on the fact that God is our Father, Giver of all. Ask for whatever you aspire to in life, whatever you may need. If these things are not forthcoming, ask yourself, "What is God telling me? What am I to learn from this?"

Fill your prayers with praise and thanks for all that God gives you and ask for things for your own life, as well as for the lives of others.

But never forget the lesson of Jacob. Make efforts in your own life and know that God is there: protecting you, sustaining you, and watching over you with love.

When you are gearing up for *Shabbat*, Fridays can be a little . . . rushed. Everything has to be done in order to light those candles on time. For many, going to *shul* on Friday night really marks the beginning of *Shabbat*. You leave one plane and enter another. Seeing your friends and neighbors and wishing them a "Good *Shabbos . . . Shabbat Shalom*" connects you back to community and to being a Jew.

How To

1. Even those who do not formally pray during the week often attend services on *Shabbat*. The Friday night service contains three sections:

   Minchah (the afternoon service)
   Kabbalat Shabbat (literally, "receiving the Shabbat")
   Maariv (evening service)

2. *Minchah* consists primarily of the *Shemoneh Esrei* (the Silent *Amidah*), which literally means "eighteen," for it originally comprised eighteen blessings. It takes about 15 minutes to complete.

3. *Kabbalat Shabbat* is a special set of praises designed to create the proper atmosphere and attitude in preparation for *Shabbat*. In northern Israel centuries ago, Jewish mystics used to go into the fields as the sun set, singing the song *"Lechah Dodi"* to usher in the *Shabbat*. This section of the service also takes about 15 minutes.

*Prayer is also the confirmation of the Jewish view of the Almighty as a **personal** God. Relating to Him should be a daily part of one's life and should not be reserved just for a special occasion or a pressing situation.*

4. *Maariv* is special for *Shabbat* and includes the *Shema* and the Silent *Amidah*. The *Shema* is the ultimate in Jewish prayer, beginning with our credo:

> *Shema Yisrael, Adonai Eloheinu, Adonai Echad*
> Hear, O Israel, The Lord is God, The Lord is One

It is said in our prayers every morning and evening, and even young children are taught to recite it before bedtime.

In the event that one cannot make it to *shul*, most parts of the service can be said at home. The *ArtScroll Siddur* (see page 169) has laid out in great detail the procedure and explanation of prayer and can easily be followed, with or without a congregation.

Remember—prayer can be in any language, so choose one in which you feel most comfortable. However, try and brush up on the basics of Hebrew, as the songs and communal prayers can be even more inspiring when said as "one" with others.

Walking home from shul Friday night is the best—traffic is zooming all around you, and yet you, and the people you are walking home with, are in a different world.

Reflections

I'm usually halfway out the door when my wife is lighting the *Shabbat* candles, as it is always a rush to get to *shul* on time. So I don't get the "Whew—it's *Shabbat*" feeling until I get to our little synagogue, see everyone there, and begin singing the Friday night service. As I begin *"Lechah Dodi"* (the song welcoming *Shabbat*), my whole body begins to relax, and I feel the weekday pressures just slipping away.

After the service, there's a lot of Good *Shabbos* greetings, handshakes, and catching up. A lot of these people I see only on *Shabbat*, so when I see them Friday night, it's like my own kind of candlelighting.

———

Walking home from *shul* Friday night is the best—traffic is zooming all around you, and yet you, and the people you are walking home with, are in a different world. It's *Shabbat*, and all that rushing around is over. No more cars, no more phones, no more work.

———

Friday nights in the winter are my favorite, because I know that after that cold walk home from *shul*, I'm going to be greeted by my kids, all dressed up for *Shabbat*—and by that warm smell of chicken soup.

———

I'm not so "into" going to services, so after candlelighting, I just pick up my *siddur* and *daven* at home. Sometimes I even make up my own tunes, and my living room becomes my own private *shul*. The kids get into the act and imitate my swaying and singing. It's really rather fun.

Unless it's pouring, I always try to go to Friday night services, because seeing everyone around me dressed up and ready for *Shabbat* really puts me in the right frame of mind. Sometimes, especially if Friday was hectic at work, I just feel too tired to walk those few blocks. But if I just give myself a little push, I'm never sorry. By the time I come home I'm reenergized and ready for more.

SHALOM ALEICHEM

The table is set with the finest china, crystal, and silver. (When it comes to *Shabbat*, nothing is saved for "a special occasion," for this *is* the special occasion.) Those who went to *shul* have now returned, and the room is filled with the warm sounds of Good *Shabbos* greetings. Everyone is invited to the table, as we begin the meal with song.

Shalom Aleichem!—the traditional greeting used when two Jews meet, and the name of the song that begins the *Shabbat* meal Friday night. *Shalom Aleichem*—"May peace be upon you."

Shalom . . . peace . . . from the Hebrew word *shalei*, which means complete.

On the most basic level, by singing this song, we are asking God to bless our home with peace; that there should be no conflict between friends or family members, especially on *Shabbat*.

Yet, on another level, we are asking for completeness: that we should truly feel that we lack nothing—that the world is complete on *Shabbat*. We sit back in awe at this revelation. Our weekday work is done.

The only work now is the "work" of *Shabbat*, which is something much deeper and often much harder to attain, and that is working on oneself, on real completeness, which is the achievement of a more ideal sense of self.

This is achieved through the various aspects of *Shabbat*, which draw each part of the individual into an integrated whole, moving forward as a unit. There is an incredible power in this, as everything from speech to food is utilized for one purpose: the achievement of one's true potential.

On *Shabbat*, one is no longer split. During the week there is the working you, the family you, the day-to-day you. But on *Shabbat* you are focused, with everything in harmony: family, learning, joy of life . . .

Shalom Aleichem.

There are seven gates to the soul—two eyes, two ears, two nostrils, and a mouth.

The Creator blessed the seventh day of the week and sanctified it. It is therefore fitting that the mouth—which is the seventh gateway—give praise, through song, prayer and Torah learning all through the day.

Rabbi Moshe Azulai

Shalom Aleichem

Each verse is customarily sung three times:

Shalom aleichem malachei
ha-shareit malachei elyon,
mi-melech malchei ha-melachim
Ha-Kadosh Baruch Hu.

שָׁלוֹם עֲלֵיכֶם מַלְאֲכֵי
הַשָּׁרֵת מַלְאֲכֵי עֶלְיוֹן,
מִמֶּלֶךְ מַלְכֵי הַמְּלָכִים
הַקָּדוֹשׁ בָּרוּךְ הוּא.

Bo'achem le-shalom malachei
ha-shalom malachei elyon,
mi-melech malchei ha-melachim
Ha-Kadosh Baruch Hu.

בּוֹאֲכֶם לְשָׁלוֹם מַלְאֲכֵי
הַשָּׁלוֹם מַלְאֲכֵי עֶלְיוֹן,
מִמֶּלֶךְ מַלְכֵי הַמְּלָכִים
הַקָּדוֹשׁ בָּרוּךְ הוּא.

Barchuni le-shalom malachei
ha-shalom malachei elyon,
mi-melech malchei ha-melachim
Ha-Kadosh Baruch Hu.

בָּרְכוּנִי לְשָׁלוֹם מַלְאֲכֵי
הַשָּׁלוֹם מַלְאֲכֵי עֶלְיוֹן,
מִמֶּלֶךְ מַלְכֵי הַמְּלָכִים
הַקָּדוֹשׁ בָּרוּךְ הוּא.

Tzeitchem le-shalom malachei
ha-shalom malachei elyon,
mi-melech malchei ha-melachim
Ha-Kadosh Baruch Hu.

צֵאתְכֶם לְשָׁלוֹם מַלְאֲכֵי
הַשָּׁלוֹם מַלְאֲכֵי עֶלְיוֹן,
מִמֶּלֶךְ מַלְכֵי הַמְּלָכִים
הַקָּדוֹשׁ בָּרוּךְ הוּא.

Welcome, ministering angels, messengers of the Most High, of the Supreme King of Kings, the Holy One, blessed be He.

Come in peace, messengers of peace, messengers of the Most High, of the Supreme King of Kings, the Holy One, blessed be He.

Bless me with peace, messengers of peace, messengers of the Most High, of the Supreme King of Kings, the Holy One, blessed be He.

And may your departure be in peace, messengers of peace, messengers of the Most High, of the Supreme King of Kings, the Holy One, blessed be He.

Singing the praises of the Almighty is especially appropriate for **Shabbat.** *As it is written: "A psalm, a song for the* **Shabbat** *day. It is good to give thanks to the Lord and to sing to Your name, Most High."*

Psalm 92

Reflections

I remember a lot of things from my first *Shabbat* experiences, but the thing that stands out in my mind the most is the singing.

Back home, the only time I remember sitting around singing as a family was when a birthday cake was being brought in.

So when I sat at a *Shabbat* table and heard the singing of "*Shalom Aleichem*" with everyone, young and old, joining in, it brought tears to my eyes. I thought, I want this, too, one day at my own *Shabbat* table.

I really feel that music is the key to *Shabbat*. It opens up the heavens.

And you don't even have to know the words—just hum and sway along and you can feel the power of a *Shabbat* song.

EISHET CHAYIL

The Jewish woman.

If not for her, the Jewish people would still be enslaved in Egypt.[3]

The Jewish woman.

The one who was offered the Torah first from Moses.[4]

The Jewish woman.

Who, in the face of adversity, held steadfast to her trust in the Almighty, even when those around her did not.[5]

The Jewish woman.

Who time and time again saved the Jewish people through her insightfulness, virtue, and belief in God.[6]

The Jewish woman.

In whose merit will come the Messiah and the final redemption of the Jewish people.[7]

The Jewish woman, who today is the one entrusted with the responsibility of maintaining the three *mitzvot* central to the Jewish home: *kashrut*, *Shabbat*, and *mikvah*.

If not for her, where would we be? There would be no home, no family, . . . no Jewish people.

*When I was about nine years old, my father and my uncle used to rise at midnight on Friday night and learn [the Torah] together until it was time for the morning prayers. I, too, would learn part of the night with them, and my righteous mother got up and learned **Midrash** (oral tradition) and the weekly Torah portion with the commentaries of the Malbim (nineteenth-century Torah scholar and philosopher) and the Ramban (Nachmanides). When she joined us, I felt the festiveness of the occasion. She would serve us hot coffee and special oven-baked cakes, which were wondrously delicious. To be sure, the prime purpose of our early rising was to learn Torah, yet I cannot deny that those cakes played an important part in my eagerness to jump out of bed!*

Rabbi Dessler
Michtav Me'Eliyahu
Memory from Pre–World
War II

---

[3]When Pharaoh decreed that all first-born Jewish males should die, the men decided to refrain from relations with their wives so as not to bring any more children into this world. The women realized that God would indeed save them and bring them out of Egypt, so they went to their husbands in order to bring more Jewish children into the world. Their faith and foresight were said to have merited the redemption from Egypt of the entire Jewish people.

[4]After Moses received the Torah from God at Mount Sinai, he offered it first to the Jewish women, for he knew that if they accepted it, it would become part of the Jewish people for all time.

[5]While the Jewish people wandered through the desert, the men repeatedly complained to Moses and even asked to go back to Egypt. And, when Jewish spies were sent in to the Land of Israel and came back with reports of great dangers, it was the men who refused to enter. Forty years later, only the women of that generation merited entering the Land.

[6]There are many examples, one being Rebecca, who helped disguise her son Jacob so that her husband, Isaac, would bestow a blessing upon him and not upon Jacob's brother, Esau. She knew that it was Jacob who had the character to become the father of the Jewish people. Later, it was his twelve sons who led the twelve Tribes of Israel.

[7]*Sotah* 11.

On Friday night, she sits as the queen of her table, while all those around her sing her praises. And rightly so.

She is the *Eishet Chayil*, the Woman of Valor, who sets the tone of love, spirituality, and personal growth for all those around her.

To know her is to appreciate her strength and talents. And, just in case you might happen to forget, *Eishet Chayil* is there as a weekly reminder.

It is found in the Book of Proverbs and is widely accepted as being composed by King Solomon. But some say it dates as far back as Abraham, who is said to have composed it as a eulogy for his wife, Sarah. In fact, upon closer scrutiny, one can see deep allusions to Sarah's life and contribution to the Jewish people in its lines.

Sing it with feeling for your own *Eishet Chayil*, or to the *Eishet Chayils* that were the foundation of the Jewish people for thousands of years and continue to be so today.

On Friday night, she sits as the queen of her table, while all those around her sing her praises. And rightly so.

How To

1. Although only a custom, *Eishet Chayil* is sung at every *Shabbat* table throughout the world.

2. If no women are present, *Eishet Chayil* is still sung in praise of Jewish women everywhere.

3. If no men are present, the women sing it in praise of Jewish womanhood.

In other words, no matter what, sing *Eishet Chayil*!

Eishet Chayil

Eishet chayil mi yimtza	אֵשֶׁת־חַיִל מִי יִמְצָא
ve-rachok mi-peninim michrah.	וְרָחֹק מִפְּנִינִים מִכְרָהּ.
Batach bah leiv ba'alah	בָּטַח בָּהּ לֵב בַּעְלָהּ
ve-shalal lo yechsar.	וְשָׁלָל לֹא יֶחְסָר.
Gemalat'hu tov ve-lo ra kol	גְּמָלַתְהוּ טוֹב וְלֹא־רָע כֹּל
yemei chayeha. Darshah tzemer	יְמֵי חַיֶּיהָ. דָּרְשָׁה צֶמֶר
u-fishtim va-ta'as be-cheifetz	וּפִשְׁתִּים וַתַּעַשׂ בְּחֵפֶץ
kapeha. Haitah ko-oniyot	כַּפֶּיהָ. הָיְתָה כָאֳנִיּוֹת
socheir mi-merchak tavi	סוֹחֵר מִמֶּרְחָק תָּבִיא
lachmah. Va-takam beod	לַחְמָהּ. וַתָּקָם בְּעוֹד
lailah va-titein teref le-veitah	לַיְלָה וַתִּתֵּן טֶרֶף לְבֵיתָהּ
ve-chok le-na'aroteha. Zamemah	וְחֹק לְנַעֲרֹתֶיהָ. זָמְמָה
sadeha va-tikacheihu mi-pri	שָׂדֶה וַתִּקָּחֵהוּ מִפְּרִי
chapeha natah karem. Chagrah	כַּפֶּיהָ נָטְעָה כָּרֶם. חָגְרָה
ve-oz motneha va-te'ameitz	בְעוֹז מָתְנֶיהָ וַתְּאַמֵּץ
zero'oteha. Ta'amah ki tov	זְרוֹעֹתֶיהָ. טָעֲמָה כִּי־טוֹב

sachrah lo yichbeh ba-lailah	סַחְרָהּ לֹא־יִכְבֶּה בַלָּיְלָה
neirah. Yadeha shilchah	נֵרָהּ. יָדֶיהָ שִׁלְּחָה
va-kishor ve-chapeha tamchu	בַכִּישׁוֹר וְכַפֶּיהָ תָּמְכוּ
falech. Kapah parsah le-oni	פָלֶךְ. כַּפָּהּ פָּרְשָׂה לֶעָנִי
ve-yadeha shilchah la-evyon.	וְיָדֶיהָ שִׁלְּחָה לָאֶבְיוֹן.
Lo tira le-veitah mi-shaleg	לֹא־תִירָא לְבֵיתָהּ מִשָּׁלֶג
ki chol beitah lavush shanim.	כִּי כָל־בֵּיתָהּ לָבֻשׁ שָׁנִים.
Marvadim astah lah sheish	מַרְבַדִּים עָשְׂתָה־לָּהּ שֵׁשׁ
ve-argaman levushah. Noda	וְאַרְגָּמָן לְבוּשָׁהּ. נוֹדָע
ba-she'arim ba'alah be-shivto	בַּשְּׁעָרִים בַּעְלָהּ בְּשִׁבְתּוֹ
im ziknei aretz. Sadin	עִם־זִקְנֵי־אָרֶץ. סָדִין
astah va-timkor va-chagor	עָשְׂתָה וַתִּמְכֹּר וַחֲגוֹר
natnah la-kena'ani. Oz ve-hadar	נָתְנָה לַכְּנַעֲנִי. עֹז־וְהָדָר
levushah va-tischak le-yom	לְבוּשָׁהּ וַתִּשְׂחַק לְיוֹם
acharon. Piha patchah	אַחֲרוֹן. פִּיהָ פָּתְחָה
ve-chochmah ve-torat chesed al	בְחָכְמָה וְתוֹרַת־חֶסֶד עַל
leshonah. Tzofiyah halichot	לְשׁוֹנָהּ. צוֹפִיָּה הֲלִיכוֹת
beitah ve-lechem atzlut lo	בֵּיתָהּ וְלֶחֶם עַצְלוּת לֹא
tocheil. Kamu vaneha	תֹאכֵל. קָמוּ בָנֶיהָ
va-ye'ashruha ba'alah va-yehalelah	וַיְאַשְּׁרוּהָ בַּעְלָהּ וַיְהַלְלָהּ.
Rabot banot asu chayil	רַבּוֹת בָּנוֹת עָשׂוּ חָיִל
ve-at alit al kulanah.	וְאַתְּ עָלִית עַל־כֻּלָּנָה.
Sheker ha-chein ve-hevel ha-yofi	שֶׁקֶר הַחֵן וְהֶבֶל הַיֹּפִי
ishah yirat Adonai hi	אִשָּׁה יִרְאַת־יְיָ הִיא
tithalal. Tenu lah mi-pri	תִתְהַלָּל. תְּנוּ־לָהּ מִפְּרִי
yadeha vi-haleluha ba-she'arim	יָדֶיהָ וִיהַלְלוּהָ בַשְּׁעָרִים
ma'aseha.	מַעֲשֶׂיהָ.

A Woman of Valor, who can find? She is more precious than corals. Her husband places his trust in her and profits only thereby. She brings him good, not harm, all the days of her life. She seeks out wool and flax and cheerfully does the work of her hands. She is like the trading ships, bringing food from afar. She gets up while it is still night to provide food for her household, and a fair share for her staff. She considers a field and purchases it and plants a vineyard with the fruit of her labors. She invests herself with strength and makes her arms powerful. She senses that her trade is profitable; her light does not go out at night. She stretches out her hands to the distaff and her palms hold the spindle. She opens her hands to the poor and reaches out her hands to the needy. She has no fear of the snow for her household, for all her household is dressed in fine clothing. She makes her own coverlets; her clothing is of fine linen and luxurious cloth. Her husband is known at the gates, where he sits with the elders of the land. She makes and sells linens; she supplies the merchants with sashes. She is robed in strength and dignity, and she smiles at the future. She opens her mouth with wisdom and the teaching of kindness is on her tongue. She looks after the conduct of her household and never tastes the

A Woman of Valor, who can find? She is more precious than corals. Her husband places his trust in her and profits only thereby.

bread of sloth. Her children rise up and make her happy; her husband praises her: "Many women have excelled, but you outshine them all!" Grace is elusive and beauty is vain, but a woman who fears God—she shall be praised. Give her credit for the fruit of her labors and let her achievements praise her at the gates.

Reflections

The first time I went to someone's *Shabbat* table, the husband sang this song, but no one explained it to me, so it could have been Happy Birthday for all I knew. After a friend told me what it was about I thought it was such a beautiful custom.

There's one family I spend *Shabbat* with a lot, and Friday night the wife always says, "You'd better sing my song."

Anyway, I think *Eishet Chayil* is very cool, except the part about never tasting the bread of sloth.

I hope the men know that honoring their wives is not just for one song, it's for a whole week. Maybe it's there as a reminder.

Grace is elusive and beauty is vain, but a woman who fears God—she shall be praised.

I think some of our guests think it's strange that my husband sings to me on Friday night at the *Shabbat* table. No one else usually knows the words because none of our friends are as observant as we are yet (though a lot are on their way), so there's this unbelievable silence surrounding him while he sings.

In addition, he doesn't have the greatest voice, and it's kind of a hard tune.

When we're alone he always ends the song by saying, "Good *Shabbos*, I love you." Isn't that just so sweet?

I always have a lot of friends over Friday night, just a bunch of men and women who are starting to get into the idea of *Shabbat*. Some of them are friends of mine whom I got involved in learning and practicing being Jewish, and others are singles whom we've all met at classes and different downtown *shuls*.

Everyone sings *Eishet Chayil* together, but it's a pretty sad rendition, as the tune is unusually hard to grasp. I always get kidded by the girls because they claim the reason I've never gotten married is because I can't sing *Eishet Chayil* on key.

18

A friend of mine who has a beautiful voice recorded the song on a cassette for me, so now I've been secretly practicing, playing it in my car to and from work. I'm waiting for my next Friday night get-together to surprise everyone. I'll never be a cantor, but I think I at least deserve an A for effort.

It is beautiful to bless your children every Friday night; it's a moment filled with love and meaning, especially when you understand the source behind such a tradition.

My husband always tells any bachelors at the table that they can't get married until they learn this song. They always laugh kind of nervously and quickly try to hum along.

I've been divorced a few years, and it made some of the *Shabbat* rituals a little tough. I got used to saying my own *kiddush*, instead of my husband, but for years I just skipped *Eishet Chayil*. Then one Friday night I had a girlfriend over who just naturally began singing it at the appropriate time. I found myself singing, too, and liking it. Now I sing it no matter who is there, and my kids have really picked up the tune. *Eishet Chayil* is now a fixture at our Friday night table, and I'm really glad. I missed it.

BLESSING OF THE CHILDREN

It is beautiful to bless your children every Friday night; it's a moment filled with love and meaning, especially when you understand the source behind such a tradition.

The Blessing for One's Sons

One of the Fathers of the Jewish people was Jacob, who had twelve sons who were to grow to become the leaders of the twelve tribes of Israel. The next-to-youngest son was Joseph, who was judged evil by his brothers and ended up in Egypt, later to be reunited with his family after they realized their judgment was wrong.

Joseph had two sons, Ephraim and Menasha.

Just before Jacob, our father, dies, he calls all of his sons to him for a final blessing that will recognize their essence, award each a portion of the Land of Israel, and indicate what role they will play in the future of the Jewish people.

As a special reward to Joseph, who remained righteous throughout his ordeal of exile, he calls forward Joseph's two sons,

19

Ephraim and Menasha, and gives them a special blessing, as well as two portions of the Land of Israel:

> On that day Jacob blessed them. He said, "In time to come, Israel (the Jewish people) will use you as a blessing. They will say, 'May God make you like Ephraim and Menasha.' "
>
> Genesis 48, *Parshat Vayechi*

Jacob's blessing was that they should *be* a blessing, an example to the Jewish people for all time. From that day forward, they would become role models for Jewish children everywhere, as they represented qualities to emulate eternally.

What were these qualities?

Ephraim and Menasha were the first brothers among our forefathers to live without rivalry. Before them came Isaac and Ishmael, Jacob and Esau, and, of course, the brothers and Joseph—all relationships fraught with conflict and competition.

Ephraim and Menasha were brothers who lived in harmony, for their life focus was the highest example of working for good for their community and people. Decisions were not based on, What is good for me? but on, What is good for the Jewish people? Petty concerns of ego were cast aside in favor of something greater.

In addition, of the twelve sons and their families, these two were the only ones to grow to maturity outside of the Land of Israel. Yet, they still remained steadfast in their commitment to Judaism.

Thus the qualities exhibited by these two young men, that of being united in their quest for the good of all, as well as possessing the strength of character to maintain Jewish values in a non-Jewish environment, became the benchmark for raising Jewish children even millenia later.

Ephraim and Menasha were brothers who lived in harmony, for their life focus was the highest example of working for good for their community and people.

The Blessing for One's Daughters

Sarah, Rebecca, Rachel, and Leah . . . the mothers of the Jewish people. Each one possessed unique qualities that played essential roles in the strength and future of the nation. Yet there was something that they all shared, something that Jewish women for all time would strive to emulate.

Each one lived a life in recognition that the ultimate in fulfillment is enabling others to realize their potentials as individuals and as members of the Jewish people. They recognized that in the power of relationship comes the ultimate in life's purpose.

The Torah is filled with accounts of these women, recording their insight, their giving nature, and their sensitivity, leadership, and special ability to inspire others. One example of this is the story of Rachel and Leah.

Rachel and Leah were sisters, and one day into their lives stepped Jacob, destined to be one of the fathers of the Jewish people.

Jacob fell in love with Rachel and asked her father, Laban, for her hand in marriage. Laban promised it, and yet, at the last minute told his daughters that it would be Leah who would marry Jacob instead.

Rachel could have reacted with resentment and jealousy, but

instead she helped Leah to marry Jacob, for she recognized that her sister needed to do this in order to fulfill her life's purpose and to become one of the mothers of the Jewish people.

This act of selfless giving, where the other person's needs (which may be just as important as our own) take priority, is the quality that Rachel and the other mothers of the Jewish people truly exemplified.

But it wasn't all so self-sacrificing, for Rachel knew that doing the right thing, enabling Leah to step into her place, was the ultimate in her *own* fulfillment. For when we give to others who need us and help them to realize their potentials, it fulfills our own needs and our own desires to grow.

We see this in our relationships today, whether it be with friends, family, partners, or children. When the needs of others are our priority, our own sense of self is heightened immeasurably, and our relationships become worlds of giving, where love and self-esteem flourish.

These women, sensitive, insightful, and self-sacrificing, all shared a special relationship with the Almighty and used the gifts that He gave them for the good of others and for the Jewish people.

When we bless our daughters on Friday night, we are asking God to endow them with the qualities of their foremothers, and we remind ourselves what real giving is all about.

When the needs of others are our priority, our own sense of self is heightened immeasurably, and our relationships become worlds of giving, where love and self-esteem flourish.

How To

1. There are different customs in different homes. Some people get up and go to their children's place, others have the children come to them. In some homes the father gives the blessing to each child, in others it is both parents. (If the child is not present, the blessing is still recited, as one does not have to be there to be blessed.)

2. In either case, the hands are placed on the child's head and the following blessing is recited, appropriate for the girl or boy:

Blessing of the Children

For a son:

Yesimcha Elohim　　　　　　　　　יְשִׂמְךָ אֱלֹהִים
ke-Efrayim vechi-Menasheh　　　כְּאֶפְרַיִם וְכִמְנַשֶּׁה.

May God make you like Ephraim and Menasha.

For a daughter:

Yesimeich Elohim ke-Sarah,　　　יְשִׂמֵךְ אֱלֹהִים כְּשָׂרָה,
Rivkah, Racheil ve-Lei'ah　　　　רִבְקָה, רָחֵל וְלֵאָה.

21

May God make you like Sarah, Rebecca, Rachel and Leah.

For both, continue:

Yevarechecha Adonai ve-yishmerecha.   יְבָרֶכְךָ יְיָ וְיִשְׁמְרֶךָ.
Ya'eir Adonai panav eilecha viy-chuneka.   יָאֵר יְיָ פָּנָיו אֵלֶיךָ וִיחֻנֶּךָּ.
Yisa Adonai panav eilecha,   יִשָּׂא יְיָ פָּנָיו אֵלֶיךָ,
ve-yaseim lecha shalom.   וְיָשֵׂם לְךָ שָׁלוֹם.

May the Lord bless you and watch over you. May the Lord shine His face toward you and show you favor. May the Lord be favorably disposed toward you and may He grant you peace.

Afterward, it's nice to whisper something personal into the child's ear, praising some accomplishment in his or her week, such as a good mark on a test or playing nicely with a kid brother. It's your moment with your child, use it as a way of connecting in your own personal way.

Reflections

My brother became observant years ago, and some of the traditions and practices started rubbing off. Now my wife and I go to my parents' home about three out of four *Shabbats* a month.

My father has been giving a blessing to my wife and to myself every Friday night for a long time now, and yet when my own son was born, I didn't do it to him. I think I just felt uncomfortable doing it in front of everyone.

A couple of months ago I started sneaking the *brachah* to him when everyone got up to wash. The first time I did it, it felt *amazing*. So gradually I started building up my strength, and at last I did it at the appropriate point, with everyone at the table.

Now it's an honor to do it, and my one-year-old son sits there as I place my hands on his head and give him his *brachah*.

It feels so good. I can't believe how good it makes me feel.

I didn't raise my children in a traditional home environment, so it was pretty surprising—to put it mildly—that they grew to become very observant.

There are still a lot of issues that we disagree on, but it's mostly intellectual sparring.

But my favorite part is the point where my grandchildren go to each of their parents to receive their blessing.

My husband and I love to spend Friday nights in their homes, with the whole family gathered around, everyone dressed in their *Shabbat* best, the table glittering with silver and crystal. . . . But my favorite part is the point where my grandchildren go to each of their parents to receive their blessing.

It's so touching—and so healthy! No matter what conflicts occurred during the week, at that moment the child cannot help but feel very special and very loved.

No doubt that they will grow with fond memories of those Friday night blessings, truly the building-blocks of self-esteem.

FRIDAY NIGHT *KIDDUSH*

Act I, Scene I. *Kiddush*.

This is where it all begins, with the First Meal, and the first blessing over the wine. These words, more than any others, are going to set the pace for *Shabbat*.

And what is it that we say—

". . . so the heavens and the earth were finished . . . ."

God is Creator.

And since part of our definition of God being One is that He has no needs, then this act of creation must be one with no desire for return. It is an act of giving based on the purest love.

We get a taste of it in our own lives when we give to a newborn baby. In the first stages, there is nothing the baby can give back to us (except spit-up and dirty diapers), and yet we continue to give, and our love continues to grow.

If you give charity anonymously, helping others who will never know that it came from you gives you a similar feeling of giving without any agenda, without ever expecting anything in return.

And then the *kiddush* continues:

". . . (He) made us holy . . . favored us . . . gave us His holy Shabbat . . . marking the exodus from Egypt . . . ."

Who is this Creation for? It is for us.

He created the world for us, gave us *Shabbat*, took us out of Egypt, and made us special.

The message is clear: God loves us. God created the world for our benefit.

The word *kiddush* is from the same root as *kedushah* or *kodesh*—to make holy; to elevate the physical to a level of spirituality. It is part of our challenge in this world to take the physical pleasures that the Almighty has provided and use them for a higher purpose.

Let's face it, we can use the physical or abuse it. We can drink wine to excess and fall down drunk, or we can take it, pour it into a silver cup, and say a blessing over it, designating that the next 24 hours are special; 24 hours of experiencing the more refined things in life: friends, nature, singing, discussion, prayer . . .

We use wine to not only intellectually and emotionally "taste" the words that we're speaking but to also physically "taste."

Sanctify the Sabbath by choice meals, by beautiful garments, delight your soul with pleasure, and I will reward you for this very pleasure.

Devarim Rabbah

And wine brings joy. What greater joy could there possibly be than knowing that God is there, watching over all that He created with love.

The curtain is rising, and *Shabbat* begins.

The curtain is rising, and **Shabbat** *begins*.

How To

Kiddush does not have to be said in Hebrew. Whoever is making *kiddush* should know that it is perfectly acceptable to say it in English or any other language, although Hebrew is preferred.

From the time the sun sets (or, for a woman, once the candles are lit), until after *kiddush* is made, one should not eat or drink anything.

The procedure is as follows:

1. The table should be set with both *challahs* on the table, covered on top and below. (For example, *challah* cover on top, *challah* board below, see page 37.)

2. A special cup (or any cup, as long as it is not disposable, like Styrofoam), holding at least 4½ ounces (most *kiddush* cups hold at least 5 ounces), should be used and filled to the rim (our joy should be "full").

Any *kosher* wine or grape juice (considered as wine) can be used.

3. The one making *kiddush* should have in mind that the others present are being included in all the blessings; thus *kiddush* is being made on their behalf. Likewise, those present should have in mind the same. It is proper to also keep in mind that, by reciting *kiddush*, one is fulfilling a Torah commandment.

4. There are different customs regarding whether one stands or sits while making *kiddush*. If you don't have a family custom, the choice is yours! Just be consistent from week to week, and all those present will do a little "Simon Says" and follow your lead.

5. Those being included in *kiddush* should be sure to answer "Amen" after the blessing of the wine ("*borei peri ha-gafen*") *and* after the concluding blessing that follows.[8]

6. When the blessings are complete, everyone should be seated (if they weren't already). The one who led the blessings then drinks at least 2 ounces of the wine or grape juice in one

---

[8]We do not speak between the saying of a blessing and the fulfillment of the blessing. Thus each person present refrains from speaking until they taste a sip of the wine or grape juice. The person making *kiddush* should remind everyone of this beforehand, to avoid uncomfortable nodding and shaking of heads when someone asks a question or makes a comment.

or two gulps (this is no time to savor and sip). The balance of the *kiddush* wine or grape juice is then distributed in little glasses, or cups, to all those who were included in *kiddush* (they need have only a taste).[9]

Questions and Answers

I've Seen People Standing for Kiddush on Friday Night and Sitting on Shabbat Day. What Should I Do?

Standing and sitting for *kiddush* is all custom. Some people stand on Friday night while making *kiddush* because, Friday night, we are like witnesses to the "coming in" of *Shabbat*. And just as witnesses stand when giving testimony, so do we stand when making *kiddush*. On *Shabbat* day there is no "coming in" to witness, so some people choose to make *kiddush* while seated.

Other people sit both Friday night *and Shabbat* day.

You can adopt whatever custom you feel comfortable doing. Just be consistent and don't change from week to week.

I Don't Think People Feel Comfortable Drinking Wine from the Glass That I Just Drank from. What Should I Do?

To avoid germs, try this method:

The person making *kiddush* should recite all the blessings, but before drinking at the end, spill about four ounces of the liquid into another cup or wine glass; then drink from that new cup. Take the original liquid from the first cup and pour some into smaller cups to pass around. (If there isn't enough, add more wine or grape juice before pouring.)

I Want to Have a Lot of Friends over Friday Night and It Would Take Forever to Pass Around Kiddush, Let Alone Wait All That Time Without Talking.

When there are a lot of people present, prepour wine into everyone's glass. After *kiddush* is said by the host or hostess, everyone drinks from his or her own glass.

Why Does the Person Making Kiddush Have to Drink So Much After Making the Blessing?

The two ounces should be swallowed right after making the blessing in order to fulfill the commandment of "drinking" *kiddush* wine. Drinking, according to the Talmud, constitutes at least a "cheekful," or approximately two ounces. Only the person making *kiddush* on behalf of everyone present need do this.

I Don't Think People Feel Comfortable Drinking Wine from the Glass That I Just Drank from. What Should I Do?

---

[9]If there are many people at your *Shabbat* table, you can add grape juice or wine to the remaining liquid in the original *kiddush* cup and then distribute it.

You gave us Your holy Shabbat, in love and favor, as our heritage.

Friday Night *Kiddush*

(The first line is recited quietly to one's self.)

Va-yehi erev va-yehi voker
yom ha-shishi.

וַיְהִי־עֶרֶב וַיְהִי־בֹקֶר
יוֹם הַשִּׁשִּׁי.

Va-yechulu ha-shamayim ve-ha-aretz
ve-chol tzeva'am. Va-yechal
Elohim ba-yom ha-shevi'i
melachto asher asah,
va-yishbot ba-yom ha-shevi'i
mi-kol melachto asher
asah. Va-yevarech Elohim
et yom ha-shevi'i va-yekadeish
oto, ki vo shavat mi-kol
melachto asher bara
Elohim la'asot.

וַיְכֻלּוּ הַשָּׁמַיִם וְהָאָרֶץ
וְכָל־צְבָאָם. וַיְכַל
אֱלֹהִים בַּיּוֹם הַשְּׁבִיעִי
מְלַאכְתּוֹ אֲשֶׁר עָשָׂה,
וַיִּשְׁבֹּת בַּיּוֹם הַשְּׁבִיעִי
מִכָּל־מְלַאכְתּוֹ אֲשֶׁר
עָשָׂה. וַיְבָרֶךְ אֱלֹהִים
אֶת־יוֹם הַשְּׁבִיעִי וַיְקַדֵּשׁ
אוֹתוֹ, כִּי בוֹ שָׁבַת מִכָּל־
מְלַאכְתּוֹ אֲשֶׁר בָּרָא
אֱלֹהִים לַעֲשׂוֹת.

It was evening and it was morning, the sixth day. So the heavens and the earth were finished, with all their complement. Thus, on the seventh day, God had completed His work which He had undertaken, and He rested on the seventh day from all His work which He had been doing. Then God blessed the seventh day and made it holy, because on it He ceased from all His creative work, which God had brought into being to fulfill its purpose.

Savri maranan ve-rabanan ve-rabotai:

סָבְרִי מָרָנָן וְרַבָּנָן וְרַבּוֹתַי:

Baruch atah Adonai,
Eloheinu melech ha-olam,
borei peri ha-gafen.

בָּרוּךְ אַתָּה יְיָ,
אֱלֹהֵינוּ מֶלֶךְ הָעוֹלָם,
בּוֹרֵא פְּרִי הַגָּפֶן.

(Those present respond, "Amen.")

You are blessed, Lord our God, the sovereign of the world, creator of the fruit of the vine.

You gave us Your holy *Shabbat*, in love and favor, as our heritage. You are blessed, Lord, who sanctifies *Shabbat*.

Baruch atah Adonai,
Eloheinu melech ha-olam,
asher kideshanu be-mitzvotav
ve-ratzah banu, ve-Shabbat kodesho
be-ahavah uve-ratzon hinchilanu,
zikaron le-ma'aseh vereishit.
Ki hu yom techilah
le-mikra'ei kodesh, zeicher
litziat mitzrayim. Ki vanu
vacharta ve-otanu kidashta
mi-kol ha-amim, ve-Shabbat
kodshecha be-ahavah uve-ratzon
hinchaltanu. Baruch atah Adonai,
mekadeish ha-Shabbat.

בָּרוּךְ אַתָּה יְיָ,
אֱלֹהֵינוּ מֶלֶךְ הָעוֹלָם,
אֲשֶׁר קִדְּשָׁנוּ בְּמִצְוֹתָיו
וְרָצָה בָנוּ, וְשַׁבַּת קָדְשׁוֹ
בְּאַהֲבָה וּבְרָצוֹן הִנְחִילָנוּ,
זִכָּרוֹן לְמַעֲשֵׂה בְרֵאשִׁית.
כִּי הוּא יוֹם תְּחִלָּה
לְמִקְרָאֵי קֹדֶשׁ, זֵכֶר
לִיצִיאַת מִצְרָיִם. כִּי־בָנוּ
בָחַרְתָּ וְאוֹתָנוּ קִדַּשְׁתָּ
מִכָּל־הָעַמִּים, וְשַׁבַּת
קָדְשְׁךָ בְּאַהֲבָה וּבְרָצוֹן
הִנְחַלְתָּנוּ. בָּרוּךְ אַתָּה יְיָ,
מְקַדֵּשׁ הַשַּׁבָּת.

("Amen")

You are blessed, Lord our God, the sovereign of the world, who made us holy with his commandments and favored us, and gave us His holy *Shabbat*, in love and favor, to be our heritage, as a reminder of the Creation. It is the foremost day of the holy festivals marking the exodus from Egypt. For—out of all the nations—You chose us and made us holy, and You gave us Your holy *Shabbat*, in love and favor, as our heritage. You are blessed, Lord, who sanctifies *Shabbat*.

Reflections

When my father made *kiddush* it seemed like a ritual, and one that I didn't understand. When I began to study, I learned that *kiddush* was my connection to creation and the Jews who were enslaved in Egypt. It kind of places a Jew in history.

During the week it is easy to get caught up in the hectic pace of the business world. But when I stand up to make *kiddush*, I am totally tuned into being a Jew. It brings everything into focus.

I use the 30 seconds as a moment of intensity and try and concentrate on the words and what it means to be a Jew.

My father never made *kiddush* when I was growing up, but I do remember one time that his friend did. We were at his house one Friday night and he made *kiddush*, but his family didn't seem to be listening. Later, as a young adult, I went to the home of a rabbi who made *kiddush* with such concentration and feeling that it took 20 minutes to say it!

Well, I guess I have achieved something in between.

Today, I have a personal connection with this *mitzvah*, as it helps me focus on gratefulness; that The Almighty is the Creator of the world; that He has given me so much to be thankful for: my wife, my children . . .

One of my all-time favorite *kiddushes* was the Friday night my daughter was born. We brought in *Shabbat* in the hospital, and my *kiddush* was filled with a feeling of gratefulness that I had never experienced before.

*We brought in **Shabbat** in the hospital, and my **kiddush** was filled with a feeling of gratefulness that I had never experienced before.*

I spent about six weeks in Israel, part of the time learning at a *yeshivah*. Afterwards, I went traveling through Europe and tried to keep a semblance of *kosher* and *Shabbat*.

I'll never forget my first Friday night on my own in a little cheap hotel in Paris, making *kiddush* over wine I had brought from Jerusalem.

27

My *Shabbat* meal was bread, vegetables, and cheese, but to me it was a banquet.

———————

My father used to make *kiddush* every Friday night. We grew up very Zionistic, so *kiddush* was more of a Jewish identification thing, as opposed to a religious experience. After a while we just stopped doing it.

But when I was about twenty I started to learn more about Judaism, and spent a *Shabbat* with a traditional family. The father encouraged me to say *kiddush*, so I did. But I really didn't understand what I was saying.

Now that I am married it has become tremendously more meaningful, for I've really made an effort to understand the words. After all, it's not just me anymore—now I am including my wife in my blessing.

I like to concentrate on the words, especially the part about God giving us *Shabbat*. There is also an element of this being my special thing to do—to bring in *Shabbat*, helping to make my house a home.

———————

After traveling to South Africa to attend my best friend's wedding, I decided to have a little adventure and go on safari with some local Jewish guys my age.

We went to this remote reserve and stayed in a cabin. The guys in this group were more likely to be in a nightclub than a synagogue on a Friday night, yet when I poured the wine for *kiddush*, everyone gathered around.

Now you must keep in mind that we were in the middle of a jungle, and when night falls the animal sounds become very loud and quite ferocious.

But as I began the blessing, a hush seemed to fall, as if nature were allowing me to bring in *Shabbat* with a special peace, even in the wild. Definitely my most exciting *Shabbat*!

———————

The guys in this group were more likely to be in a nightclub than a synagogue on a Friday night, yet when I poured the wine for **kiddush**, *everyone gathered around.*

———————

My father used to make a kind of *Reader's Digest* version of *kiddush*, but my grandfather taught me the full *kiddush* when I was just a little boy. He had me memorize the Hebrew, although I had no idea what I was saying. But something stayed with me.

When I grew up, I started learning more, and began attending traditional *Shabbat* meals with families in a nearby neighborhood. Still, *kiddush* was something you heard in other people's homes.

One time I arrived late for the meal and missed *kiddush*. You're really not supposed to eat until you hear *kiddush*, so I had to make my own. I was so nervous. But I said it quietly to myself and then just joined the rest of the festivities.

After I got married, I really felt the responsibility of making *kiddush* for my wife and guests, so I really stopped to think about the significance of the day and what the words really mean.

Now I try and work on not losing the freshness of *kiddush*, for I would hate for it to become a tired ritual, instead of the special moment that it is in our lives.

To help me in that, I always try and think of my grandfather, and how he patiently taught a little boy a Hebrew prayer that would come to mean so much.

I always try and think of my grandfather, and how he patiently taught a little boy a Hebrew prayer that would come to mean so much.

As I began learning more about what it means to be a Jew, I decided it was about time to put it into action. So I started to make *kiddush*. The food I was eating afterward wasn't *kosher*, but I was taking it all one step at a time.

At one point I stopped because I was confused and didn't understand what *Shabbat* was really all about. I decided to learn more, then begin again, this time doing it right.

So we designated Friday night as special, stopped driving, and my wife began lighting candles. I started to go to *shul* and making *kiddush* again. And even though I had officially brought *Shabbat* in at *shul*, I felt that it really began when I made *kiddush*. I was ushering in the *Shabbat*, and we were doing it together.

Today my Hebrew skills are not so great. I try and use a *siddur* with Hebrew and English, so that when I'm saying the Hebrew I can glance over and understand what I am saying.

I was learning at a school for women in Jerusalem when a friend invited me to spend *Shabbat* with her at her uncle's place on a settlement town in the north of Israel.

The town happened to be hosting a group from North America that weekend, and when it came time for *Shabbat* to begin, they asked me to say *kiddush* for everyone, because very few of the visitors spoke Hebrew, and the settlers were not religious.

I was so nervous and thought, "Who am I to be saying this for everyone?" But I did it.

Today I will often make my own *kiddush Shabbat* morning if my husband is delayed at *shul*. It always feels so special, like a feeling of power, connecting with God, one-to-One.

After traveling through Europe, I landed in Israel and spent a traditional *Shabbat* with a family in the Old City of Jerusalem. When the man made *kiddush*, something in me connected with the familiarity of it, for, as a little girl, I had remembered listening to my brother practice *kiddush* for his *bar mitzvah*.

As I began experiencing *Shabbat*, I enjoyed hearing the different tunes you would hear at different people's homes. If I wasn't a guest, I made sure that I still made *kiddush* on my own.

When I met my husband, he was making *kiddush* in English, so I taught him how to do it in Hebrew, and now he's even added a tune of his own!

———

I'm fifty-eight years old, and I never learned how to read Hebrew. My *bar mitzvah* was totally phonetic, I memorized what I could, and read the English transliteration for the rest. And all these years I just faked it in *shul*.

After thirty-five years, of marriage (and a long time after my *bar mitzvah*!), my wife started asking me to make *kiddush* on Friday night. This was something very new, but it seemed important to her. So I did it by using the English phonetics.

My wife's interest in Judaism became so keen that she convinced me to go to Israel with her for six weeks to study. I agreed, and soon I found myself sitting in a *yeshivah* in the Old City of Jerusalem with a rabbi half my age. We learned the Five Books of Moses, the weekly Torah Portion, the laws of *Shabbat*, and a host of other things. Finally, one day he asked me what else I'd like to learn, and I told him Hebrew.

He taught me to read in one afternoon.

I was a new person, sounding out the ads on the Egged bus, reading the street signs, and the restaurant menus. O.K., I didn't know what everything meant, but I could *read*!

When we got home, we invited all of our grown sons for Friday night dinner, and I stood up and sounded out every Hebrew word of *kiddush*. It took me a long time, but I did it. Afterward, my wife told me my sons sat so amazed, you could have heard a pin drop. All I remember is sweating through it, but at the end feeling like a million bucks, especially when the whole table answered with a resounding "Amen!"

———

Years ago my wife and I traveled to China when they were just opening the doors to visitors. Our tour group was made up mostly of North Americans, and we all experienced the wonder and excitement of this mysterious land.

One of the most memorable parts of the trip was a cruise we took down one of their rivers. We all set sail one Friday morning for a four-day adventure on the Chinese waters.

I'm fifty-eight years old, and I never learned how to read Hebrew.

Sometime in the afternoon I asked the captain if it was all right if I made *kiddush* for me and my wife and another Jewish couple we had met on the tour. He said it was fine.

Well, within a matter of an hour, word had spread throughout the boat, and people were coming up to us—Jewish people we hadn't even known were Jewish—asking to participate.

The captain was most accommodating and invited our growing group to perform this "Sabbath ritual" on the highest deck near his quarters.

It was quite an event as Jews from all over gathered round while I brought in *Shabbat*.

WASHING FOR BREAD

The candles are flickering, *Shalom Aleichem* and *Eishet Chayil* have been sung, and *kiddush* has been made for all those gathered around the beautiful Sabbath table.

Now it is time to begin the meal. But first, we are invited by the host to step into the kitchen to wash our hands in preparation for the eating of the *challah*.

No, this is not a call for cleanliness, but an important step that will lead us to *ha-motzi*, the blessing that is said over the bread.

Before explaining this simple action, we need to understand some Jewish symbolism:

Water—symbolic of Torah; wisdom. Water is the essence of physical life, for without it we would die; whereas wisdom is the essence of spiritual life, the foundation of self-growth and self-realization.

Hands—symbolize our interaction in the physical world.

Bread—(the *challahs*) symbolizes physical sustenance; the staff of life.

Judaism is based on the principle that actions are rooted in understanding, and the combination results in the pleasure of positive and meaningful interaction.

On *Shabbat*, the action of washing to begin the meal achieves just that—an action that connects us to ourselves, to others, and to our understanding of life.

We take the water and pour it twice over each hand (see "How To" to follow)—that's the action. The understanding is that I want all my interactions in the physical world—creative or destructive—to be done with wisdom.

Everything I do with my hands: to write; to touch; to communicate—should be done in a wise, meaningful way. I should have "wise" hands.

And it is a reminder that tonight our table is holy, like an altar. Just as the Priests in the Temple so long ago prepared themselves for eating by washing, so do we wash before our meal.

The concept of holiness appears first in the Torah with reference to Shabbat. This is to teach us that Shabbat is the root and foundation of all holiness in the world.
    Be'er Moshe

It is a unique pleasure to perform a simple act that represents something so meaningful.

How To

Having made *kiddush*, it is time to "break bread" and begin the *Shabbat* meal. The first stage is to perform the special washing necessary for eating bread:

1. Before washing, make sure the *challahs*, *challah* knife, *challah* cover, and salt are all on the table.

2. In the kitchen, hand towels should be laid out for guests to dry their hands after washing.

3. Use either a special washing cup: a large, two-handled cup or a regular glass without handles, providing the top rim has no indentations or spout and holds at least 5 ounces.

4. Remove any rings from your fingers. Hold the cup in your right hand while filling it with water from the tap.

5. Pass the cup to your left hand and then pour a good amount of water over the right, so that you're able to soak the hand on both sides from the wrist down. You want every area of the hand to be wet.

6. Now pass the cup to your right hand and repeat on the left side. (Refill the cup if necessary.)

7. After the hands have been washed, they should be held upward, so that the water drips toward the wrist and not the fingers. The blessing is then recited:

It is a unique pleasure to perform a simple act that represents something so meaningful.

Blessing over the Washing of the Hands

Baruch atah Adonai,	בָּרוּךְ אַתָּה יְיָ,
Eloheinu melech ha-olam,	אֱלֹהֵינוּ מֶלֶךְ הָעוֹלָם,
asher kideshanu be-mitzvotav	אֲשֶׁר קִדְּשָׁנוּ בְּמִצְוֹתָיו
ve-tzivanu al netilat yadayim.	וְצִוָּנוּ עַל נְטִילַת יָדָיִם.

You are blessed, Lord our God, the sovereign of the world, who made us holy with his commandments and commanded us in the washing of the hands.

---

8. The hands are dried, and one returns to the table, careful not to speak until *ha-motzi* is recited and the bread is passed and eaten (see page 24, footnote 8 for explanation).

Questions and Answers

Why Do We Pour Water on the Right Hand First?

According to Jewish tradition, the right means "straight," as in heading in the right direction. You will notice many other areas where this comes up, including the custom of a bride and groom beginning their walk down the aisle with their right feet.

When we are washing, we begin by pouring water over our right hand. This indicates that we are beginning the night directed, with a desire to stay on track toward our goals for the Sabbath.

Why Do We Raise Our Hands After Washing, Letting the Water Drip toward Our Wrists?

In the blessing for the washing it says, ". . . *al netilat yadayim,*" which literally means " . . . in the raising up of the hands." We are elevating our hands spiritually. Thus, when we recite the blessing, we customarily elevate our hands physically in order to get in touch with this concept.

Reflections

I was attending a beautiful luncheon in honor of one of the leaders of my Jewish community when suddenly one of the organizers came over to my table and asked me if I would please do the honors and make *ha-motzi* for everyone at the function.

Now, I am no rabbi, but I was one of the few *kippah*-laden Jews there, so I accepted the invitation and waited for them to announce *ha-motzi* and introduce me.

Suddenly a horrible thought came to mind: I could say *ha-motzi* only if I washed, and this being a secular function (although *kosher*), there seemed to be no washing stations in sight.

I quickly raced through the options in my head: politely refuse the honor . . . feign sickness at the last moment and race from the room . . . or frantically try and find a washroom where I could wash.

Although not the ideal, I decided to choose the last, but before I could even stand to look, I heard from the microphone: ". . . who will now honor us with *ha-motzi.*"

Panic. In a second that seemed like an eternity, I somehow had the presence of mind to act.

In one deft move I grabbed my glass of ice water, brought it under the table, threw water over my hands (creating icy puddles on the floor below), and strode confidently to the head table, reciting the *"al netilat yadayim" brachah* quietly to myself.

Now I couldn't talk, so I ceremoniously nodded to the guest of

Panic. In a second that seemed like an eternity, I somehow had the presence of mind to act.

33

honor and his entourage and reached for the large braided *challah* laid out before me.

Before I could even say the *brachah*, someone tapped me on my shoulder. It was a waiter who had just wheeled in a tray with a large bowl and a pitcher . . . full . . . of . . . water.

They had planned for me to wash all along. And now I was really up a creek because I wasn't sure what to do—wash again? Wave it away??

Well, to make a long story short, I washed again and only pretended to say the *brachah*, picked up the *challah*, said the *ha-motzi* into the microphone with as much *kavanah* (intent) as I could muster, cut the *challah*, and ate a piece.

Then I returned to my seat, and put my feet into the puddles.

I like *Shabbat*. I like the food. I like the company. I like the whole idea. But I can't seem to be able to stop talking between washing my hands and eating the *challah*!

I remember one of my first *Shabbat* experiences as if it were yesterday. I was at this rabbi's house on a Friday night and after *kiddush* it was announced that it was time to "wash."

Then I heard all this clinking. It was the women taking off their rings and putting them on their plates.

I remember feeling so embarrassed thinking that I hadn't worn any rings for this ceremony so that I could remove them too.

It was three or four more *Shabbats* before I realized that you take off your rings to wash only if you happened to be wearing any.

Live and learn.

I don't relate to the idea of washing so much, so it's not exactly the most elevating experience. I guess I do it because I feel I have to. There are other parts of *Shabbat* that I feel much closer to, but I've come to realize that it's all a package; even if I don't feel deeply about everything inside, that's O.K. The things I enjoy, I enjoy. The things I don't feel close to probably help me, in some way, to enjoy the others.

Washing, to me, means elevating the meal. It is saying, "I am not an animal . . . this table is my altar . . . and this meal is from God."

Washing, to me, means elevating the meal. It is saying, "I am not an animal . . . this table is my altar . . . and this meal is from God."

The meal then becomes more satisfying, for it nourishes you, both physically and spiritually.

It seemed so strange not to talk after washing, everyone waiting to make *ha-motzi*. I think the first time I went through it, no one explained to me the whole concept, so I of course started gaily chatting away by myself, oblivious to the fact that my hosts were just answering with "Uh huh" and "Hmmmm."

Now I have the protocol down, but it's still hard for me to relate to the whole ritual. It's not as if I connect with it or anything. For me, just getting the mechanics secured is enough. For spirituality, I'll take candlelighting every time.

I like having to wash my hands before the blessing of *ha-motzi*. It slows me down and makes me realize that there is sanctity in food. It separates us from animals and reminds me that I was created with a soul. It makes a statement that this is special.

Nourishment is a gift, not a right. And that gift is from God; a God who is there keeping the whole thing in motion.

To me it makes sense, all the preparation and specialness of washing and *ha-motzi*, because bread is not an apple. It is the result of a long and involved process that can come only from civilized man. It is a statement that man has to be involved in his own existence, and yet bread is the culmination; for when God is the partner in all of this, it is like taking creation and making it even better.

I like having to wash my hands before the blessing of **ha-motzi**. *It slows me down and makes me realize that there is sanctity in food.*

I always remembered something being said over a big braided *challah* at all the weddings I went to as a kid. But I didn't connect the loudspeaker blessing to the little cubes of raisin bread that were passed around.

When I was traveling through Israel, I spent a *Shabbat* with a family in the Old City of Jerusalem. They explained what was going to happen with the washing and not talking and everything. Someone said something about the *Bais Ha-Mikash*[10] but I didn't understand what even that was . . . What? *Bais* a what?

It's funny, I didn't think twice about following and participating. It seemed like a cultural, fun thing to do and it was done in a very tasteful way.

----

[10]The holy Temple that used to stand in Jerusalem. Today's Western Wall was its outer gateway.

I wasn't embarrassed about not knowing the blessing, because none of the guests seemed to know it.

HA-MOTZI—BLESSING OVER THE BREAD

And it came to pass that on the sixth day they gathered twice as much bread [lechem mishneh], two omers for each person, and all the rulers of the congregation came and told Moses. And he said to them, "This is what the Lord said, 'Tomorrow is the rest of the holy Shabbat of the Lord. Bake that which you will bake [today], cook that which you will cook [today], and that which remains leave over until the morning.'"

And they left it over until the morning, as Moses commanded, and it did not spoil. And Moses said, "Eat it today for today is the Sabbath of the Lord. Today you shall not find it in the field. Six days shall you gather it but the seventh day is Shabbat—there shall be none"

Exodus 16

At each *Shabbat* meal, we place on the table two whole loaves of bread, covered with a cloth.

It is called *lechem mishneh* (two breads). Their place at our meal reminds us of where we come from, why we are here, and where we are going.

All this from two loaves of bread?

When God brought the Jewish people out of Egypt thousands of years ago, they spent many years in the desert on their way to the Land of Israel.

Their survival during this time was totally from the Almighty. He made sure there would always be water (from Miriam's well), and protection (they were surrounded by Clouds of Glory and a wall of fire). And for food there was manna, a crystal-like substance that fell from the heavens each day.

The Jews had simply to scoop it up and eat it, and it is said that it had the taste of whatever the person desired.

And there was a promise: So that there would be no need to gather the manna on *Shabbat*, God said that on Friday afternoon—*erev Shabbat*—a double portion would fall. And so it did.

This is where we come from. Go back enough generations, and your ancestors and mine were wandering the desert toward Mount Sinai, readying themselves to receive the Torah from God. Before the great event could even occur, they were receiving God's goodness each day as He provided manna for each person; double portions for every *Shabbat*.

All this took place in the desert, a place of emptiness. At each *Shabbat* meal, we, too, begin with a sense of emptiness. Not the emptiness of having nothing, but the emptiness of being ready to receive everything—food for physical sustenance and words of wisdom for spiritual fulfillment.

It is why we are here: to receive everything that is good. On *Shabbat* we focus on that and make sure that we try and make each moment, each word, each thought the finest possible in order to fill the desert, to see our personal deserts bloom.

And where are we going?

During the six days of the week we are involved with the physical world, and our sense of future or of security is often manifested in the physical, in things that are temporal.

Shabbat is a day detached from the physical (as an end). It is a day attached to eternity, to permanence . . . to God.

And, just as we had to trust that God would provide for us in the desert at Sinai, today we have to learn to trust again. We have to know that it is God who is providing for us every day and that if we get in touch with that, we will know that our futures are also in His hands.

And why do we cover the *challahs* atop a *challah* board? Because, in the desert, the manna fell with a covering of dew, on top and below. The dew was a sort of preservative, as well as an insurance that the freshness would be intact so that the taste would be new and stimulating.

The three meals on *Shabbat* are each special, each able to achieve something unique. When we make *ha-motzi* with the *challah* cover draped over the two loaves, we remind ourselves that we need to instill into our consciousness a sense of wonder and freshness that the morning dew represents.

I am awakening.

Enjoy the special hush that falls over the table as the covered *challahs* are lifted, the blessing is recited, and once again, the physical and spiritual are one.

*When we make **ha-motzi** with the **challah** cover draped over the two loaves, we remind ourselves that we need to instill into our consciousness a sense of wonder and freshness that the morning dew represents.*

I am awakening.

How To

1. Everyone, having washed for bread, is now seated at the table. Just as in *kiddush*, the leader, and all those at the table, should have in mind that the leader is making the blessing for all those listening.

2. The *challahs* on the table should be covered on top and below (for example, *challah* board on bottom, *challah* cover on top).

3. The leader picks up both *challahs*. They should be held back-to-back, with the bottom one slightly closer to the person. Some leave the *challah* cover on during the blessing, while others remove it at this point.

4. The following blessing is recited. Upon saying God's name (*Adonai*), the *challahs* are raised slightly:

Ha-motzi—Blessing over the Bread

Baruch atah Adonai,　　　　　　　　בָּרוּךְ אַתָּה יְיָ,
Eloheinu melech ha-olam,　　　　אֱלֹהֵינוּ מֶלֶךְ הָעוֹלָם,
ha-motzi lechem min ha-aretz　הַמּוֹצִיא לֶחֶם מִן הָאָרֶץ.

("Amen")

You are blessed, Lord our God, sovereign of the world, who brings forth bread from the earth.

---

5. Cut or tear the *challah* into pieces. Each slice or piece should be equivalent to about one full slice of regular bread.

6. The person who recited the blessing should take a slice first, dip it in some salt,[11] take a bite, dip the other slices in salt, and pass them around for others to follow.

Just as in *kiddush*, we do not speak until we swallow a bite of bread, so there is no interruption between the blessing and what the blessing was intended for.

One should eat at least the equivalent of one slice of bread in order to be able to *bentch* (say the Grace after the Meal, see page 51).

Note: If you do not have two *challahs*, two whole "loaves" of anything can be used. For example, you could use two whole bagels, two whole *matzot*, two whole rolls. Or try a combination: one bagel and one *challah* . . . one *matzah* and one roll . . . and so on.

Questions and Answers

Why Does One Lift the Challahs *during the Blessing?*

Upon saying God's name (*Adonai*), we lift both *challahs*, for the blessing is about recognizing the source of this bread, and of all our blessings. The source is God, and we emphasize it by lifting the bounty that He provides (in this case the *challahs*) when reciting His name.

Reflections

When I am at the head of the table making *ha-motzi*, I try and concentrate on gratefulness—that God is providing this food for me and my family. I will be able to eat and be full, and it's all from Him.

The Sabbath reunites body and soul because physical gratification and enjoyment enter the realm of **mitzvah**. *The struggle between the spiritual and the physical ceases on the day of rest.* **Shabbat** *is the great peacemaker between body and soul; therefore we say* "**Shabbat Shalom**"—*a* **Shabbat** *of Peace.*
Ben Ish Chai

I'm trying to incorporate *Shabbat* into my life, but I still have to balance family obligations. So right now I've found a compromise:

At my parent's home we make *kiddush*, but never *ha-motzi*. So when the *challah* is passed around, I say the *brachah* quickly under my breath and pop it into my mouth.

No one feels uncomfortable, and I fulfill the *mitzvah*.

Now if I can just figure out how to wash without anyone seeing.

---

[11]Your *Shabbat* table is considered the same as your own personal altar. And, just as the altar in the Temple in Jerusalem was used for offerings to God, so do we laden our table with the finest in honor of God's presence. And, just as the offerings were salted before being eaten, we dip our bread in salt on *Shabbat*. The only exception is during the weeks from Rosh Ha-Shanah to the end of Sukkot. Then the bread is dipped in honey, for a sweet New Year.

That moment of concentration said it all. This was not just something ceremonial, this was something that held great meaning.

I was raised as a Christian, so I didn't see the *ha-motzi* ceremony until I was an adult attending a Jewish *simchah*. It reminded me of a more physical manifestation of "grace." It didn't seem out of context, for even a secular humanist has regard for food on the table.

But I got the feeling that this respectful "break in the action" held little meaning for the people around me. It was something that you did, even if you didn't know why.

Years later I was privileged to be at a Friday night table of a teacher of mine. There was a whole ceremony leading up to the *ha-motzi*, with everyone washing, saying a blessing, and staying quiet until the *challahs* were passed around and eaten.

I liked having that time during the process of preparation. It allowed me to take the whole thing in and take it seriously.

And when it was time for *ha-motzi*, my teacher lifted the two covered *challahs*, closed his eyes, and paused. That moment of concentration said it all. This was not just something ceremonial, this was something that held great meaning.

And so we asked: "Why two *challahs*? Why the salt? Why the no talking after washing?"

For when it's done right, it should provoke questions.

After my conversion, making *ha-motzi* at my table helped me to really connect. Images fly through my head as I utter the *brachah*—God's hand leading us out of the desert to freedom . . . my *Shabbat* table, where I have the freedom to live and express myself as a Jew . . . the sanctity of *Shabbat* where God is total Provider.

I take great pleasure, now, in explaining to *my* guests the meaning behind all the steps. But the greatest pleasure is that they ask questions. I'm glad I can be the teacher now.

It's hard to concentrate during *ha-motzi*, because all I can think about is DID THE CHALLAH TURN OUT??!

The first time I was exposed to the *mitzvah* of *ha-motzi* was at a Zionist summer camp. I thought it was cute.

I wish I could say that I make *ha-motzi* now with great concentration and meaning, but what I'm usually thinking as I lift the warm *challahs* up to recite the blessing is, "This looks yummy!"

What do I think about when I make *ha-motzi*? That I'm blessed.

When my husband is making *ha-motzi* I always think about my guests. How do they feel? I always hope that the fact that I made homemade *challah* will make them feel warm and cozy, taken care of, like a taste of home. That's how it makes me feel, and I just hope everyone else will feel the same.

When I came home from Israel with my newfound observances, I decided to spend *Shabbat* at home with my family and show them what I had learned.

When I sang, they sang. When I stood up to make *kiddush*, they stood up. When I washed, they washed. When I didn't talk, they didn't talk. When I ate *challah*, they ate *challah*. Then I coughed, and my brother coughed. I scratched my head, my brother scratched his head . . .

Then we all laughed, together.

ZEMIROT—SONGS FOR *SHABBAT*

One should sing and rejoice in the Sabbath as it says, "The statutes of the Almighty are just, gladdening the heart." Therefore it has become customary to sing songs and praises at the Shabbat meals. Certainly this honors Shabbat, as it is befitting to rejoice with royalty as it arrives and departs.

Commentary on
Yeish Nochalim

Let's face it, unless it's somebody's birthday, when do people sit around singing together?

Yet singing is fun, kids love it, and for everyone it's a real release. And when it's done on *Shabbat*, it can be another extension of the tremendous pleasure that *Shabbat* has to offer.

We can even understand the pleasure of singing from a look at the Hebrew language. *Lezamer* means "to sing," sharing the same root as the word *lizmor* which means "to prune." The fact that they come from the same word is no accident.

When we prune a bush we are removing old, dead growth that is inhibiting its growth; we're shaping the bush to bring out its own beauty. The same thing happens to us with song.

When we sing, we "prune" away the excess baggage that we carry around, revealing our essence. The harmony of music releases the disharmony within us.

Thus we fill *Shabbat* with song. We revel in the pleasure of getting rid of the excess, the disharmonious things that have accumulated during the past six days, leaving us, as *Shalom Aleichem*, the first song of *Shabbat* says, with a feeling of *shalom*—peace.

Shabbat Songs

Eitz Chayim

(This is also sung in *shul* when the Torah is returned to the ark.)

Eitz chayim hi la-machazikim
bah ve-tomcheha me'ushar.
Deracheha darchei noam ve-chol
netivoteha shalom.
Hashiveinu Hashem eilecha
ve-nashuvah, chadeish yameinu
ke-kedem.

עֵץ חַיִּים הִיא לַמַּחֲזִיקִים
בָּהּ וְתֹמְכֶיהָ מְאֻשָּׁר.
דְּרָכֶיהָ דַרְכֵי נֹעַם וְכָל־
נְתִיבוֹתֶיהָ שָׁלוֹם.
הֲשִׁיבֵנוּ ה' אֵלֶיךָ
וְנָשׁוּבָה, חַדֵּשׁ יָמֵינוּ
כְּקֶדֶם.

May you live to see your children's children. May Israel have peace!

It is a tree of life to those who grasp it, and its supporters are happy. Its ways are pleasant and its paths are peaceful. Bring us back, Lord, to You, and we will return; renew our days as of old.

David Melech

David melech Yisrael
chai ve-kayam.

דָּוִד מֶלֶךְ יִשְׂרָאֵל
חַי וְקַיָּם.

David, King of Israel, lives forever.

Hineih Mah Tov

Hineih mah tov u-mah naim
shevet achim gam yachad.

הִנֵּה מַה טּוֹב וּמַה נָּעִים
שֶׁבֶת אַחִים גַּם יָחַד.

How good and pleasant it is when brothers live together in harmony.

U-re'eih Vanim (also sung at a *brit* or baby naming)

U-re'eih vanim le-vanecha,
shalom al Yisrael.

וּרְאֵה בָנִים לְבָנֶיךָ,
שָׁלוֹם עַל יִשְׂרָאֵל.

May you live to see your children's children. May Israel have peace!

Tov Lehodot

Tov lehodot lashem u-lezameir
le-shimcha elyon. Le-hagid
ba-boker chasdecha ve-emunatcha
ba-leilot.

טוֹב לְהוֹדוֹת לַה' וּלְזַמֵּר
לְשִׁמְךָ עֶלְיוֹן. לְהַגִּיד
בַּבֹּקֶר חַסְדֶּךָ וֶאֱמוּנָתְךָ
בַּלֵּילוֹת.

It is good to give thanks to the Lord, to sing praises to Your name, Exalted One; to tell of Your kindness in the morning and of Your steadfastness by night.

Koh Amar Hashem

Koh amar Hashem: matzah chein
ba-midbar, am seridei charev,
halach le-hargio Yisrael.

כֹּה אָמַר ה': מָצָא חֵן
בַּמִּדְבָּר, עַם שְׂרִידֵי חָרֶב,
הָלוֹךְ לְהַרְגִּיעוֹ יִשְׂרָאֵל.

41

Thus says the Lord: The people who survived the sword have found grace in the wilderness; now I go to give Israel rest.

Kol Ha-Olam

Kol ha-olam kulo gesher tzar meod veha-ikar lo lefacheid kelal.

כָּל הָעוֹלָם כֻּלּוֹ גֶּשֶׁר צַר מְאֹד וְהָעִיקָר לֹא לְפַחֵד כְּלָל.

The whole wide world is a very narrow bridge, but the main thing to recall is to have no fear at all.

Le-Shanah Ha-Baah

Le-shanah ha-baah bi-yerushalayim ha-benuyah.

לְשָׁנָה הַבָּאָה בִּירוּשָׁלַיִם הַבְּנוּיָה.

Next year may we be in rebuilt Jerusalem.

Siman Tov

(This is also sung at other Jewish celebrations, such as weddings.)

Siman tov u-mazal tov yehei lanu u-lechol Yisrael, amein.

סְמָן טוֹב וּמַזָּל טוֹב יְהֵא לָנוּ וּלְכָל יִשְׂרָאֵל, אָמֵן.

May we and all of Israel have a good omen and good luck.

Ivdu

Ivdu et Hashem be-simchah, bo'u lefanav bi-renanah.

עִבְדוּ אֶת־ה׳ בְּשִׂמְחָה, בֹּאוּ לְפָנָיו בִּרְנָנָה.

Serve the Lord with joy, come before Him with happy singing.

Od Yishama (also a traditional wedding song)

Od yishama be-arei yehudah uve-chutzot Yerushalayim, kol sason ve-kol simchah, kol chatan ve-kol kalah.

עוֹד יִשָּׁמַע בְּעָרֵי יְהוּדָה וּבְחוּצוֹת יְרוּשָׁלַיִם, קוֹל שָׂשׂוֹן וְקוֹל שִׂמְחָה, קוֹל חָתָן וְקוֹל כַּלָּה.

May there still be heard in the cities of Judea and in the streets of Jerusalem, the sound of joy and the sound of celebration, the voice of the bridegroom and the voice of the bride.

Am Yisrael Chai

Am Yisrael chai, od avinu chai.

עַם יִשְׂרָאֵל חַי, עוֹד אָבִינוּ חַי.

The people of Israel lives; our Father still lives!

May there still be heard in the cities of Judea and in the streets of Jerusalem, the sound of joy and the sound of celebration, the voice of the bridegroom and the voice of the bride.

Shema Yisrael

Shema Yisrael Hashem Elokeinu
Hashem echad.

שְׁמַע יִשְׂרָאֵל ה' אֱלֹקֵינוּ
ה' אֶחָד.

Hear, Israel, the Lord is our God, the Lord is one.

Torat Hashem

Torat Hashem temimah,
meshivat nafesh. Eidut Hashem
ne'emanah, machkimat peti.

תּוֹרַת ה' תְּמִימָה,
מְשִׁיבַת נָפֶשׁ. עֵדוּת ה'
נֶאֱמָנָה, מַחְכִּימַת פֶּתִי.

The Lord's Torah is perfect; it restores the soul. The Lord's testimony is reliable; it makes the simple person wise.

For more traditional *Shabbat Zemirot* please see *The NCSY Bencher* (see For Further Reading, p. 169).

Reflections

When I was single and first went to people's homes on *Shabbat*, I thought that the singing part of the meal was really beautiful. It was something I never really had in my home—the idea of song and the joy that it brings. In fact, it was so nice that it almost made me embarrassed and uncomfortable. I kept trying to picture my own family singing, and just couldn't imagine.

Today, my husband and I almost always sing, especially when we have guests. Everyone gets into it, even if the songs are new to them. We have three NCSY[12] bentchers,[13] which transliterate all the songs. The tunes continually repeat, so people catch on quite quickly.

My kids love it, and every *Shabbat* they say, "Daddy, sing us wild songs!" My husband will break out into a really lively one, and the kids will dance around, doing cartwheels and flips.

Once you have kids and they're old enough to join in, it's just incredible. I love that they know the songs, and that *Shabbat* for them is such a joyful experience.

I love a lot of the songs, but my favorite is *Eitz Chaim*. The tune is very slow and moving, and sometimes makes me feel like crying.

———

My favorite song? *Kol Ha-Olam* (see page 42). It focuses your attention: Yes, there is difficulty in life, and six days a week we work and experience that. But the seventh day—that's when we're not afraid of anything, because that's the day we know what's important; that's the day God is really in your life.

But the seventh day—that's when we're not afraid of anything, because that's the day we know what's important; that's the day God is really in your life.

---

[12]National Conference of Synagogue Youth (an organization that promotes Judaism to pre-teens and teens through social and educational programs).
[13]Booklet of blessings. (*Bentch* is the Yiddish word for "bless.")

———

Everyone at the *Shabbat* table has a favorite song, and we all vie for the chance to sing ours first. Even the little ones have favorites and light up and clap their hands when they're sung.

I have a daughter who remembers which ones were her favorites as she was growing up. She says, "When I was a baby and Daddy was carrying me around, this was the song he sang to me," and she would sing one of the slow ones, and she would be right! Now she's three and loves the peppy tunes, because for her, *Shabbat* is dancing around the table. I can imagine her one day all grown up, sitting around her own *Shabbat* table, saying to her own children, "This is the one my father sang to me, when I was a baby."

———

Sometimes, when I spend *Shabbat* at home with my parents—who don't observe *Shabbat*—singing the songs from my *bentcher* really helps me feel the *Shabbat* spirit, even when the TV is going in the background, and the phones are ringing. When I sing, no matter what's going on around me, it's *Shabbat*.

———

Although I didn't come from an observant home, my husband did. Recently he told me a story that had a real impact on me and made me appreciate what singing at the *Shabbat* table can really mean.

Last year my father-in-law took ill and was dying. His four grown children went to his bedside to say good-bye and to try and offer him some comfort in his last hours. What did they do? Together they sang him *Shabbat zemirot*—all the songs they had shared together as a family growing up.

It was so beautiful and gave him great joy, even at the end. Can you imagine? To me it said so much about their bond and what their family stood for.

That's what I want for my children. I want them to have sweet memories of sitting around the *Shabbat* table and singing. I want them to know the tremendous pleasure that it gives their parents.

And I think they will. After all, it's their *Zaidy's* legacy.

———

Shabbat *is especially condu-cive to teaching Torah, since the Torah was given by God to Israel on* **Shabbat.**
The Skulener *Rebbe*

DEVAR TORAH—A WORD OF TORAH

Imagine someone walking into your dining room at this moment. With *kiddush* and *ha-motzi* complete, how would that person know that this meal was more than just a dinner party?

They wouldn't, if it were not for two important elements: the singing, as discussed in the previous section, and the *devar Torah*—the "Word of Torah."

Shabbat is the celebration of creation. It is a day when we recognize that the Almighty has given us a wondrous gift—a world filled with pleasure.

The challenge of humanity is, How does one extract this pleasure for the ultimate life experience?

By reading the manual.

A pilot does not jump into the cockpit of a 747, turn the keys, and fly. He studies, reads the manual, slowly absorbs the material, tests it out, and eventually reaches tremendous heights.

So, too, it is with life. God did not create the world, throw us into the "driver's seat," and then neglect to give us the instructions on how to drive.

The word *Torah means* "instructions." It is referred to as *Torat Chayim*—"Instructions for Living." It is not just a history of our people, or a meaningless bunch of stories. It is the instruction manual that, read properly, can give us the key to all the pleasures of life.

It is a book of wisdom that has application to our lives *today*; to help us be better people, better spouses, friends, children, parents. To help us get the most out of this world, we look into something timeless, something practical and relevant. We look to the Torah.

How To

Devar Torah literally means the "Word of Torah" and is usually a short talk on the *parshah*—Torah portion of the week,[14] though it can be about anything meaningful and Jewish. Perhaps a holiday is approaching, or a significant Jewish celebration, such as a wedding or a *brit*. Discuss the meaning and traditions of the event and how we can appreciate and grow from it.

If chosen well, it should be the springboard to a lively discussion at the table, with questions welcome from everyone, young and old. You will often see people pulling reference books from the shelves to find passages to back up their opinions.

Children who attend Jewish school will often bring home *parshah* sheets, with questions concerning the week's Torah portion. It can turn the table into a quiz show, with parents asking the questions, giving out prizes of sweets for correct answers or "good tries" from the kids *and* the guests. Everyone can get into the act, and everyone is bound to learn something.

To know which *parshah* of the week it happens to be, ask

> **Shabbat** *is the celebration of creation. It is a day when we recognize that the Almighty has given us a wondrous gift—a world filled with pleasure.*

---

[14]The Torah is divided into fifty-four portions, each called a *"parshah,"* with one portion read each week in synagogue on *Shabbat* morning. Occasionally, there are weeks with double portions.

your local rabbi or teacher, or simply look on a Jewish calendar. Along with candlelighting times, these calendars (available at your local Jewish bookstore, or free from some Jewish grocers and butchers), also list the name of each week's *parshah*.

Try and read the *parshah* every week in Hebrew or in English. Many people experience an incredible feeling of strength, knowing that thousands upon thousands of Jews all over the world are reading that same *parshah*. An excellent translation of the Torah (The Five Books of Moses) is *The Living Torah* by Rabbi Aryeh Kaplan. It is written in relatable English, without all the "thees" and "thous." (For more information see For Further Reading, page 167.)

There are a number of excellent books available that give some relevant thoughts on the *parshah* of the week. Reading a paragraph or two aloud at the table is a good way to spark conversation, or just read ahead yourself and present the ideas informally to your family and guests. A very good book to start with is *Growth Through Torah* by Rabbi Zelig Pliskin (see page 168).

Reflections

Sometimes I feel if it weren't for the *devar Torah*, the *Shabbat* meal would just be a get-together. Going to someone's home for *Shabbat* would be just like eating out.

At our home, my husband usually jumps in with a *devar Torah* just when the conversation starts getting kind of "ordinary." He always makes it relevant to the people at the table and directs the focus to more meaningful things. Our guests always seem to love it. It's as if they *wanted* it to be like that all along, but were too timid to bring up something heavy. So we do, and they just join in.

———

At our *Shabbat* table, the *devar Torah* is always about life: character development, the *Shabbat* experience, and our relationship to God. It's anything but a bunch of stories, and people are continually amazed at how relevant the Torah is. They always walk away with "food for thought" and a piece of wisdom to apply to their lives.

———

Many people experience an incredible feeling of strength, knowing that thousands upon thousands of Jews all over the world are reading that same parshah.

When I first heard people giving *devar Torahs* at *Shabbat* tables, I immediately filed them into one of two categories: those given because that's what you're supposed to do, so let's get it done; and those given with thought and heart. The former was empty, and the latter was real. The ones that stayed with me in a positive way were the ones when, I could honestly say, the persons really believed what they said.

I always felt a little awkward when people started into a *devar Torah*. It was so . . . heavy. But then I began to feel that something was missing if nothing was said, to the point where today, if I have a meal with family or friends during the week, I feel that someone should say something! Eating and talking about current events just doesn't cut it anymore. . . . I suppose you can say the most substantial part of the meal are the words of Torah, not the brisket.

I suppose you can say the most substantial part of the meal are the words of Torah, not the brisket.

It takes me about 15 or 20 minutes to prepare a *devar Torah*. Usually it's simply a matter of reading through the *parshah* (Torah portion of the week), and picking out one or two lines that seem to be making sense of what's going on in the world today. Then I just relay my thoughts at the *Shabbat* table and open it up for discussion.

The best *Shabbats* are the ones where the *devar Torah* really hits a chord with people and opens them up to experience ideas. The table seems almost transformed and unified in thought. It's as if something "clicked" and everyone gets into it.

I must admit that I put more time into preparing something when we have guests. If it's just the family, I try and say something meaningful, but it doesn't have the same amount of thought and energy behind it.

When I start my *devar Torah*, my guests kind of freeze and have that "What's this going to be?" look on their faces. But when they find out that I'm not preaching fire and brimstone and I'm just talking about issues relevant to all of us, they relax, ask questions, and contribute ideas; and the whole *Shabbat* table experience becomes much more meaningful. I really think it's the basis for the whole meal.

I enjoy speaking, because it's exhilarating to be responsible for bringing insight; to be the catalyst to opening people up, so that they can speak about things that are important.

The *devar Torah* I remember the most stands out in my mind because it was funny—I mean, *really* funny. I learned that humor is an important element in giving over ideas because it relaxes people and makes the ideas human, not distant or ethereal. It was *so* funny . . .

Our family always had a Friday night *Shabbat* meal, but we never had a *devar Torah*. The first time I ever experienced such a thing was, as an adult, at the home of one of my teachers. He told a charming story, related it to the upcoming Jewish holiday or the *parshah* that week and left me with such a sweet feeling. The whole thing was just so friendly, warm, and . . . relevant. I liked it.

Now that I'm married, I try and make sure the topics at the table are somewhat meaningful and Jewish, without there being a formal break in the action with a *devar Torah*. It's just not my style.

However, I do see that, without that break, all too often we look back and say. "Hey, we forgot it was *Shabbat*. We slowed down from our busy week, but we didn't stop."

Our meals Sunday through Thursday are so hectic, what with us both working, that part of "hitting on the brakes" has to be talking about something meaningful, not just what movies everyone's seen.

We usually spend *Shabbat* meals with family, so the conversation is very much a "catch-up" on our week. I try and say something that I've heard or read that's in the spirit of *Shabbat*, but not always. Putting the "*Shabbat*" into the *Shabbat* meal takes a little bit of preparation . . . and, more than anything, a conscious effort. I've got to try harder.

I'm not so observant, so hearing a *devar Torah* on a Friday night really depends on whose home I'm at. If it's my brother-in-law's house, there's a real emphasis on the *devar Torah*, and even my nephew, who is twelve, says something about the *parshah* at the table.

But if we're at my in-laws, although we make *kiddush*, wash, sing, and all the other *Shabbat* things, we rarely have a *devar Torah*.

If one of us happened to take a class that week or heard something interesting in *shul*, we may share it with everyone there, so I guess that's like a *devar Torah*, isn't it?

Our meals Sunday through Thursday are so hectic, what with us both working, that part of "hitting on the brakes" has to be talking about something meaningful, not just what movies everyone's seen.

When I go to a rabbi's house and he gives a *devar Torah*, I think it's very nice. But when I go to "Joe Schmo," the businessman's house, I'm blown away that he actually finds time to learn and wants to share it with others. The rabbi is supposed to do it, but Joe Schmo *chose* to do it. It really floors me, because I don't expect it from someone like him, a guy in business, who is not a big talmudic scholar. It makes me realize that the Torah is for everyone, even me.

Do I ever give a *devar Torah*? No. Do I shy away from ever giving one? Yes.

You see, I've just started getting into *Shabbat*, and I suppose I'm a little intimidated if I'm at a rabbi's table. Sometimes they ask me to say a little something—because I am learning more and more during the week—but I always decline. I guess I just don't feel I can contribute anything that would be meaningful. I would rather just listen to someone who knows so much more, and then ask questions. Although, if they don't ask for questions, I don't ask.

I think I'm still confused as to what is the role of the guest. Am I supposed to just passively listen, or is it proper to interject? Until I'm sure, I'll just keep quiet and contribute if the table is open and I feel comfortable with those around me.

My favorite *Shabbat* table was one where everyone was new at all of this, like me, and the host gave a *devar Torah* that brought out ideas that everyone wanted to comment on. I think the whole discussion lasted about 45 minutes, which to me was amazing. Everyone gave input, and I know it was because the host set such a relaxed, such an open atmosphere.

One day, when I become a host, I'll be sure and make the *devar Torah* an involved process—always practical and relevant, avoiding any "this is what you should do" laws.

But remember, although Hebrew is preferred God understands English and all languages. So feel free to express your thanks in the language in which you feel most comfortable.

SHIR HA-MAALOT—SONG PRECEDING GRACE AFTER MEALS

On *Shabbat* and *Yom Tov*, and other occasions of celebration, we begin with the singing of *Shir Ha-maalot* just before the *bentching* (Grace after Meals). This psalm was composed by King David and speaks of the Jewish people's return from exile to the Land of Israel.

There are many tunes to *Shir Ha-maalot*, and if you're not familiar with them, try just about any tune. It's one of those songs that works with just about anything. *Hatikvah* (Israel's national anthem) is perfect!

There is also a traditional tune for the rest of the *bentching* that helps people familiarize themselves with the Hebrew (see page 170 on how to order tapes). But remember, although Hebrew is preferred God understands English and *all* languages. So feel free to express your thanks in the language in which you feel most comfortable.

Shir Ha-Maalot

Shir ha-maalot, beshuv Adonai	שִׁיר הַמַּעֲלוֹת, בְּשׁוּב יְיָ
et shivat tziyon hayinu	אֶת־שִׁיבַת צִיּוֹן הָיִינוּ
ke-cholmim. Az yimalei	כְּחֹלְמִים. אָז יִמָּלֵא
sechok pinu u-leshoneinu rinah,	שְׂחוֹק פִּינוּ וּלְשׁוֹנֵנוּ רִנָּה,
az yomru va-goyim higdil	אָז יֹאמְרוּ בַגּוֹיִם הִגְדִּיל

When the Lord brought Zion out of captivity, we were like people in a dream.

Adonai la'asot im eileh.
Higdil Adonai la'asot imanu
hayinu semeichim. Shuvah Adonai
et sheviteinu ka-afikim
ba-negev. Ha-zorim be-dimah
be-rinah yiktzoru. Haloch yeileich
u-vachoh nosei meshech ha-zara,
bo yavo ve-rinah nosei
alumotav.

יְיָ לַעֲשׂוֹת עִם־אֵלֶּה.
הִגְדִּיל יְיָ לַעֲשׂוֹת עִמָּנוּ
הָיִינוּ שְׂמֵחִים. שׁוּבָה יְיָ
אֶת־שְׁבִיתֵנוּ כַּאֲפִיקִים
בַּנֶּגֶב. הַזֹּרְעִים בְּדִמְעָה
בְּרִנָּה יִקְצֹרוּ. הָלוֹךְ יֵלֵךְ
וּבָכֹה נֹשֵׂא מֶשֶׁךְ הַזָּרַע,
בֹּא־יָבֹא בְרִנָּה נֹשֵׂא
אֲלֻמֹּתָיו.

A Song of Ascents. When the Lord brought Zion out of captivity, we were like people in a dream. At the time, our mouth was filled with laughter and our tongue with cries of joy; at the time it was said among the nations, "The Lord has done great things for them." The Lord had done great things for us; we were happy. Let our captivity, Lord, be a thing of the past, like dried-up streams in the Negev. Those who sow in tears shall reap in joy. The man who weeps as he trails the seed along will return with cries of joy, carrying his sheaves.

MAYIM ACHARONIM—"FINAL WATERS"

With the meal at a conclusion, it is time to thank God for our sustenance and for all the blessings in our life.

Yet, before the saying of the Grace after Meals, we clean our fingertips. This is a small ceremony called *Mayim Acharonim*, which literally means "final waters," or, as some call it, a "Jewish fingerbowl."

If one is attending a *Shabbat* meal at a traditional home, there will be other customs apparent at this point. Men who have removed their jackets during the meal will often put them back on, for there is a general feeling of formality about the next step.

Our blessings and thanks at the end of the meal are directed toward God. He is King, and just as one would dress in one's best if going before royalty, so does one act appropriately when addressing the Almighty.

Before we handle anything physically precious—a silver goblet, a newborn baby, a priceless artifact, we make sure our hands are clean. It is a recognition that physical objects can have tremendous value.

Mayim Acharonim recognizes the tremendous value of the spiritual. Thus, before we approach God and get in touch with all that He has given us; we clean our hands, respectfully don our jackets, and give thanks.

How To

After the singing of *Shir Ha-maalot*, one of the hosts will go to the kitchen and fill a small container with water. There are beautiful sets that can be purchased for this purpose, coming in a wide variety of styles—a wishing well with the water held in a little bucket . . . silver cup and saucer sets . . . those made of brass . . .

But all that is really needed is a simple cup and small bowl.

1. Fill the cup with water, set it in a small bowl and bring it to the table.

2. Pass it around to those present, with each person pouring a little bit of water over their fingertips (from the middle knuckle down), over the bowl.

3. When everyone has washed, remove the cup and bowl filled with used water from the table before *bentching*.

Reflections

Long before I began keeping *Shabbat*, I went to a three-week summer "camp" for guys in their twenties who were interested in learning more about Judaism.

I had only one quick *Shabbat* experience previously, so I was surprised at some of the customs at the camp's *Shabbat* table.

When we had finished the meal, I saw a cup being passed around from man to man, somewhere way down the table. Before I knew it, someone was passing it to me. I figured this must be another kind of after-meal *kiddush*, so I went to pick it up and drink.

Before I barely had lifted it off the table, the guy next to me grabbed my arm and motioned for me to just pass it on.

Later, I realized that this was *Mayim Acharonim*—water to wash your fingertips with—and that the guy next to me had just saved me from tremendous embarrassment.

We became instant friends, and to this day I will always be grateful to him for "showing me the ropes."

———

I don't always do *Mayim Acharonim*; perhaps it's because I don't know much about it. Last *Shabbat* we all got into a discussion about it, and it was agreed that hardly *anyone* knew much about it. It's kind of a mystery . . . or maybe just a "Jewish fingerbowl" exercise. The main thing to remember is just to rinse your fingertips. If you do your whole hand someone will inevitably say, "Hey, what, are you taking a bath??"

Appreciation brings joy.

———

BIRKAT HA-MAZON—GRACE AFTER MEALS

Appreciation brings joy. When someone gives you a present, the appreciation of the gift is directly linked to how much you know about it. What is it, where is it from, how was it made, and who is giving it to you?

51

Someone gives you a sweater. Beautiful. The wool is from Ireland. Stunning. It was made by hand. Amazing. The person giving it to you is the one who made it, and that person is your best friend.

You can imagine how much this sweater would be appreciated.

The more knowledge you have about the source of the gift, the more it can be appreciated and the more joy it will bring.

And that is why, in Judaism, we take the time to say blessings.

Baruch atah . . . is the familiar start to the many blessings that we say. *Baruch* is Hebrew for "blessed," so it seems that we are continually blessing God. Does God really need our blessings?

Baruch is from the same root as *bereichah*, which means spring, where water comes from. Their connection is that they are both about "source."

When we say a *brachah*, a blessing, we are acknowledging that everything has a source, and that source is God. We are thanking Him, for He is the source of everything.

When we recite the Grace after Meals (also referred to as *bentching*, meaning "to bless"), we are appreciating that this food came from Him, and that gives the enjoyment of the meal a whole new meaning. We recognize that we are truly blessed and give thanks. The act of thanking helps us to recognize the source of this blessing. This recognition brings appreciation, and appreciation brings joy.

God does not need our blessings. *We* need our blessings, for they get us back in touch with the root of it all. That knowledge of source is the foundation for the ultimate in happiness.

A good meal now becomes a connection to the Eternal.

God does not need our blessings. We need our blessings, for they get us back in touch with the root of it all.

A good meal now becomes a connection to the Eternal.

How To

When three or more men have eaten together, one invites the others to join him in the Blessing after the Meal:

(To begin, sing *Shir Ha-maalot*, p. 49.)

Rabotai nevareich.

רַבּוֹתַי נְבָרֵךְ.

My friends, let us say the blessing.

The others answer

Yehi sheim Adonai mevorach mei-atah ve-ad olam.

יְהִי שֵׁם יְיָ מְבֹרָךְ מֵעַתָּה וְעַד־עוֹלָם.

May the name of the Lord be blessed from now and forever more.

The leader repeats

Yehi sheim Adonai mevorach mei-atah ve-ad olam.

יְהִי שֵׁם יְיָ מְבֹרָךְ מֵעַתָּה וְעַד־עוֹלָם.

May the name of the Lord be blessed from now and forever more.

and he continues

Bireshut   בִּרְשׁוּת

If he is a guest at someone else's table he adds

ba'al ha-bayit   בַּעַל הַבַּיִת

maranan ve-rabanan ve-rabotai nevareich   מָרָנָן וְרַבָּנָן וְרַבּוֹתַי נְבָרֵךְ

If there are ten men present he adds

Eloheinu   אֱלֹהֵינוּ

she-achalnu mishelo   שֶׁאָכַלְנוּ מִשֶּׁלוֹ.

With the consent of (my honored father and) (our host and) all present, let us bless Him (our God) whose food we have eaten.

The others say

Baruch (Eloheinu) she-achalnu   בָּרוּךְ (אֱלֹהֵינוּ) שֶׁאָכַלְנוּ
mishelo uve-tuvo chayinu.   מִשֶּׁלוֹ וּבְטוּבוֹ חָיִינוּ.

Blessed is He (our God) whose food we have eaten and through whose goodness we live.

Individuals begin here:

Baruch atah Adonai, Eloheinu   בָּרוּךְ אַתָּה יְיָ, אֱלֹהֵינוּ
melech ha-olam, ha-zan et   מֶלֶךְ הָעוֹלָם, הַזָּן אֶת־
ha-olam kulo be-tuvo be-chein   הָעוֹלָם כֻּלוֹ בְּטוּבוֹ בְּחֵן
be-chesed uve-rachamim hu   בְּחֶסֶד וּבְרַחֲמִים הוּא
notein lechem le-chol basar, ki   נוֹתֵן לֶחֶם לְכָל־בָּשָׂר, כִּי
le-olam chasdo. Uve-tuvo   לְעוֹלָם חַסְדּוֹ. וּבְטוּבוֹ
ha-gadol tamid lo chasar   הַגָּדוֹל תָּמִיד לֹא־חָסַר
lanu ve'al yechsar lanu mazon   לָנוּ וְאַל־יֶחְסַר לָנוּ מָזוֹן
le-olam vaed. Ba'avur shemo   לְעוֹלָם וָעֶד. בַּעֲבוּר שְׁמוֹ
ha-gadol ki hu Eil zan   הַגָּדוֹל כִּי הוּא אֵל זָן
u-mefarneis la-kol u-meitiv la-kol   וּמְפַרְנֵס לַכֹּל וּמֵטִיב לַכֹּל
u-meichin mazon le-chol beriyotav   וּמֵכִין מָזוֹן לְכָל־בְּרִיּוֹתָיו
asher baro. Baruch atah   אֲשֶׁר בָּרָא. בָּרוּךְ אַתָּה
Adonai, ha-zan et ha-kol.   יְיָ, הַזָּן אֶת־הַכֹּל.

You are blessed, Lord our God, the sovereign of the world, who provides food for the entire world in his goodness, with grace, kindness, and mercy; He supplies bread for all living beings, for His kindness is everlasting. Because of His great goodness, we have never lacked food, nor will we ever lack it—on account of His great name—since He is God who feeds and provides for all and is good to all, and who supplies food for all His creatures which He brought into being. You are blessed, Lord, who provides food for all.

He supplies bread for all living beings, for His kindness is everlasting.

53

Nodeh lecha Adonai Eloheinu al
she-hinchalta la-avoteinu eretz
chemdah tovah u-rechavoh,
ve-al she-hotzeitanu Adonai
Eloheinu mei-eretz mitzrayim
u-feditanu mi-beit avadim,
ve-al beritcha she-chatamta
bi-vesareinu, ve-al Toratcha
she-limadetanu, ve-al chukecha
she-hodatanu, ve-al chayim chein
va-chesed she-chonantanu, ve-al
achilat mazon sha-atah zan
u-mefarneis otanu tamid
be-chol yom uve-chol eit
uve-chol sha'ah.

נוֹדֶה לְךָ יְיָ אֱלֹהֵינוּ עַל
שֶׁהִנְחַלְתָּ לַאֲבוֹתֵינוּ אֶרֶץ
חֶמְדָּה טוֹבָה וּרְחָבָה,
וְעַל שֶׁהוֹצֵאתָנוּ יְיָ
אֱלֹהֵינוּ מֵאֶרֶץ מִצְרַיִם
וּפְדִיתָנוּ מִבֵּית עֲבָדִים,
וְעַל בְּרִיתְךָ שֶׁחָתַמְתָּ
בִּבְשָׂרֵנוּ, וְעַל תּוֹרָתְךָ
שֶׁלִּמַּדְתָּנוּ, וְעַל חֻקֶּיךָ
שֶׁהוֹדַעְתָּנוּ, וְעַל חַיִּים חֵן
וָחֶסֶד שֶׁחוֹנַנְתָּנוּ, וְעַל
אֲכִילַת מָזוֹן שָׁאַתָּה זָן
וּמְפַרְנֵס אוֹתָנוּ תָּמִיד
בְּכָל־יוֹם וּבְכָל־עֵת
וּבְכָל־שָׁעָה.

We thank You, Lord our God, for having given the heritage of a lovely, fine and spacious land to our fathers, and for having brought us out, Lord our God, from Egypt, and for rescuing us from slavery, and also for Your covenant which You sealed in our flesh, as well as for Your Torah which You taught us, and Your laws of which You told us, and for the life, grace and kindness You have granted us, and for the food which You supply and provide for us constantly, every day, all the time, and at every hour.

Ve-al ha-kol Adonai Eloheinu
anachnu modim lach
u-mevarchim otach yitbarach
shimcha be-fi kol chai tamid
le-olam va-ed. Ka-katuv,
ve-achalta ve-savata u-veirachta
et Adonai Elohecha al ha-aretz
ha-tovah asher natan lach.
Baruch atah Adonai, al ha-aretz
ve-al ha-mazon.

וְעַל הַכֹּל יְיָ אֱלֹהֵינוּ
אֲנַחְנוּ מוֹדִים לָךְ
וּמְבָרְכִים אוֹתָךְ יִתְבָּרַךְ
שִׁמְךָ בְּפִי כָּל־חַי תָּמִיד
לְעוֹלָם וָעֶד. כַּכָּתוּב,
וְאָכַלְתָּ וְשָׂבָעְתָּ וּבֵרַכְתָּ
אֶת־יְיָ אֱלֹהֶיךָ עַל־הָאָרֶץ
הַטֹּבָה אֲשֶׁר נָתַן־לָךְ.
בָּרוּךְ אַתָּה יְיָ, עַל־הָאָרֶץ
וְעַל־הַמָּזוֹן.

So for everything, Lord our God, we thank You and bless You—may Your name be blessed in the speech of all living beings, constantly, for all time. For it is written: "And you shall eat, and be satisfied, and bless the Lord your God for the good land He gave you." You are blessed, Lord, for the land and for the food.

Racheim Adonai Eloheinu al
Yisrael amecha ve-al
Yerushalayim irecha ve-al tziyon
mishkan kevodecha ve-al
malchut beit David meshichecha
ve-al ha-bayit ha-gadol
veha-kadosh she-nikra shimcha
alav. Eloheinu avinu re'einu

רַחֵם יְיָ אֱלֹהֵינוּ עַל־
יִשְׂרָאֵל עַמֶּךָ וְעַל
יְרוּשָׁלַיִם עִירֶךָ וְעַל צִיּוֹן
מִשְׁכַּן כְּבוֹדֶךָ וְעַל
מַלְכוּת בֵּית דָּוִד מְשִׁיחֶךָ
וְעַל הַבַּיִת הַגָּדוֹל
וְהַקָּדוֹשׁ שֶׁנִּקְרָא שִׁמְךָ
עָלָיו. אֱלֹהֵינוּ אָבִינוּ רְעֵנוּ

We thank You, Lord our God, for having given the heritage of a lovely, fine and spacious land to our fathers, and for having brought us out, Lord our God, from Egypt.

54

zuneinu parneseinu ve-chalkeleinu	זוּנֵנוּ פַּרְנְסֵנוּ וְכַלְכְּלֵנוּ
ve-harvicheinu ve-harvach lanu Adonai	וְהַרְוִיחֵנוּ וְהַרְוַח־לָנוּ יְיָ
Eloheinu meheirah mi-kol	אֱלֹהֵינוּ מְהֵרָה מִכָּל־
tzaroteinu. Ve-na al	צָרוֹתֵינוּ. וְנָא אַל־
tatzricheinu Adonai Eloheinu lo	תַּצְרִיכֵנוּ יְיָ אֱלֹהֵינוּ לֹא
lidei matnat basar va-dam	לִידֵי מַתְּנַת בָּשָׂר וָדָם
ve-lo lidei halva'atam, ki	וְלֹא לִידֵי הַלְוָאָתָם, כִּי
im le-yadcha ha-melei'ah	אִם לְיָדְךָ הַמְּלֵאָה
ha-petucha ha-kedoshah	הַפְּתוּחָה הַקְּדוֹשָׁה
veha-rechavah, she-lo neivosh	וְהָרְחָבָה, שֶׁלֹּא נֵבוֹשׁ
ve-lo nikaleim le-olam vaed.	וְלֹא נִכָּלֵם לְעוֹלָם וָעֶד.

For this is indeed a great and holy day for You; to rest and be at ease, with loving concern for the command of Your will.

    Have mercy, Lord our God, on Israel Your people, on Jerusalem Your city, on Zion the home of your glory, on the kingdom of the house of David, Your anointed one, and on the great and holy house which is called by Your name. Our God, our Father—look after us and feed us, give us a livelihood and support us, and provide a respite for us—a respite for us, Lord our God, soon, from all our troubles. And please, let us not be dependent, Lord our God, neither on a gift, nor on a loan from a human being, but rather on Your full, open, holy and generous hand, so that we should never feel embarrassed or ashamed.

    Special paragraph for *Shabbat*:

Retzeih ve-hachalitzeinu Adonai	רְצֵה וְהַחֲלִיצֵנוּ יְיָ
Eloheinu be-mitzvotecha	אֱלֹהֵינוּ בְּמִצְוֹתֶיךָ
uve-mitzvat yom ha-shevi-i	וּבְמִצְוַת יוֹם הַשְּׁבִיעִי
ha-Shabbat ha-gadol veha-kadosh	הַשַּׁבָּת הַגָּדוֹל וְהַקָּדוֹשׁ
ha-zeh. Ki yom zeh gadol	הַזֶּה. כִּי יוֹם זֶה גָּדוֹל
ve-kadosh hu lefanecha	וְקָדוֹשׁ הוּא לְפָנֶיךָ
lishbot ba ve-lanuach ba	לִשְׁבָּת־בּוֹ וְלָנוּחַ בּוֹ
be-ahavah ke-mitzvat retzonecha.	בְּאַהֲבָה כְּמִצְוַת רְצוֹנֶךָ.
Uvi-retzoncha haniyach lanu Adonai	וּבִרְצוֹנְךָ הָנִיחַ לָנוּ יְיָ
Eloheinu she-lo tehei tzarah	אֱלֹהֵינוּ שֶׁלֹּא תְהֵא צָרָה
ve-yagon va-anachah be-yom	וְיָגוֹן וַאֲנָחָה בְּיוֹם
menuchateinu. Ve-hareinu Adonai	מְנוּחָתֵנוּ. וְהַרְאֵנוּ יְיָ
Eloheinu be-nechamat tziyon	אֱלֹהֵינוּ בְּנֶחָמַת צִיּוֹן
irecha uve-vinyan Yerushalayim	עִירֶךָ וּבְבִנְיַן יְרוּשָׁלַיִם
ir kodshecha ki atah hu	עִיר קָדְשֶׁךָ כִּי אַתָּה הוּא
baal ha-yeshuot u-vaal	בַּעַל הַיְשׁוּעוֹת וּבַעַל
ha-nechamot.	הַנֶּחָמוֹת.

    Be pleased, Lord our God, to strengthen us through Your commandments, especially the commandment of the seventh day, this great and holy *Shabbat*. For this is indeed a great and holy day for You; to rest and be at ease, with loving concern for the command of Your will. So may it please You to grant us rest, Lord our God, with no trouble, or unhappiness, or weeping on our day of rest. And let us witness, Lord our God, the consolation of Zion, Your city, and the building up

of Jerusalem, Your holy city, for you are the Lord of redemption, and the Lord of consolation.

And may You build up Jerusalem, the holy city, rapidly in our lifetimes.

U-veneih Yerushalayim ir	וּבְנֵה יְרוּשָׁלַיִם עִיר
ha-kodesh bi-meheirah ve-yameinu.	הַקֹּדֶשׁ בִּמְהֵרָה בְיָמֵינוּ.
Baruch atah Adonai, boneih	בָּרוּךְ אַתָּה יְיָ, בּוֹנֵה
ve-rachamav Yerushalayim. Amein.	בְרַחֲמָיו יְרוּשָׁלָיִם. אָמֵן.

And may You build up Jerusalem, the holy city, rapidly in our lifetimes. You are blessed, Lord, who in His mercy, builds up Jerusalem. Amen.

Baruch atah Adonai, Eloheinu	בָּרוּךְ אַתָּה יְיָ, אֱלֹהֵינוּ
melech ha-olam, ha-Eil avinu	מֶלֶךְ הָעוֹלָם, הָאֵל אָבִינוּ
malkeinu adireinu boreinu	מַלְכֵּנוּ אַדִּירֵנוּ בּוֹרְאֵנוּ
goaleinu yotzreinu kedosheinu	גֹּאֲלֵנוּ יוֹצְרֵנוּ קְדוֹשֵׁנוּ
kedosh Ya'akov, ro'einu ro'eih	קְדוֹשׁ יַעֲקֹב, רוֹעֵנוּ רוֹעֵה
Yisrael ha-melech ha-tov	יִשְׂרָאֵל הַמֶּלֶךְ הַטּוֹב
veha-meitiv la-kol shebechol yom	וְהַמֵּטִיב לַכֹּל שֶׁבְּכָל-יוֹם
va-yom hu heitiv hu	וָיוֹם הוּא הֵטִיב הוּא
meitiv hu yeitiv lanu.	מֵטִיב הוּא יֵטִיב לָנוּ.
Hu gemalanu hu gomleinu	הוּא גְמָלָנוּ הוּא גוֹמְלֵנוּ
hu yigmeleinu la-ad lechein	הוּא יִגְמְלֵנוּ לָעַד לְחֵן
le-chesed ule-rachamim ule-revach	לְחֶסֶד וּלְרַחֲמִים וּלְרֶוַח
hatzalah ve-hatzlachah berachah	הַצָּלָה וְהַצְלָחָה בְּרָכָה
viyshuah nechamah parnasah	וִישׁוּעָה נֶחָמָה פַּרְנָסָה
ve-chalkalah ve-rachamim ve-chayim	וְכַלְכָּלָה וְרַחֲמִים וְחַיִּים
ve-shalom ve-chol tov, umi-kol	וְשָׁלוֹם וְכָל-טוֹב, וּמִכָּל-
tuv le-olam al yechasreinu.	טוּב לְעוֹלָם אַל-יְחַסְּרֵנוּ.

You are blessed, Lord our God, the Sovereign of the world—God who is our Father, our King, our Mighty One, our Creator, our Redeemer, our Maker, our Holy One—the Holy One Jacob; our Shepherd—the Shepherd of Israel; the King who is good and does good to all, who each and every day has been good, is good and will be good to us. He gave, gives, and will always give us grace, kindness, and mercy, and respite, deliverance, and success, blessing and salvation, comfort, a livelihood and sustenance, and mercy and life and peace and everything that is good—and may He never let us lack anything that is good.

The following are additional blessings, including blessings for your family, that are added by many at each meal.

Ha-rachaman hu yimloch aleinu	הָרַחֲמָן הוּא יִמְלֹךְ עָלֵינוּ
le-olam va'ed. Ha-rachaman hu	לְעוֹלָם וָעֶד. הָרַחֲמָן הוּא
yitbarach ba-shamayim uva-aretz.	יִתְבָּרַךְ בַּשָּׁמַיִם וּבָאָרֶץ.
Ha-rachaman hu yishtabach	הָרַחֲמָן הוּא יִשְׁתַּבַּח
le-dor dorim ve-yitpa'eir banu	לְדוֹר דּוֹרִים וְיִתְפָּאַר בָּנוּ
le-neitzach netzachim ve-yit'hadar	לְנֵצַח נְצָחִים וְיִתְהַדַּר
banu la'ad ule-olmei	בָּנוּ לָעַד וּלְעוֹלְמֵי
olamim. Ha-rachaman hu	עוֹלָמִים. הָרַחֲמָן הוּא

yefarneseinu be-chavod. Ha-rachaman	יְפַרְנְסֵנוּ בְּכָבוֹד. הָרַחֲמָן
hu yishbor uleinu mei'al	הוּא יִשְׁבֹּר עֻלֵנוּ מֵעַל
tzavareinu ve-hu yolicheinu	צַוָּארֵנוּ וְהוּא יוֹלִיכֵנוּ
komemiyut le-artzeinu.	קוֹמְמִיּוּת לְאַרְצֵנוּ.
Ha-rachaman hu yishlach	הָרַחֲמָן הוּא יִשְׁלַח
berachah merubah ba-bayit ha-zeh	בְּרָכָה מְרֻבָּה בַּבַּיִת הַזֶּה
ve-al shulchan zeh she-achalnu	וְעַל שֻׁלְחָן זֶה שֶׁאָכַלְנוּ
alav. Ha-rachaman hu yishlach	עָלָיו. הָרַחֲמָן הוּא יִשְׁלַח
lanu et Eiliyahu ha-navi	לָנוּ אֶת־אֵלִיָּהוּ הַנָּבִיא
zachur la-tov viyvaser lanu	זָכוּר לַטּוֹב וִיבַשֶּׂר־לָנוּ
besorot tovot yeshuot	בְּשׂוֹרוֹת טוֹבוֹת יְשׁוּעוֹת
venechamot.	וְנֶחָמוֹת.

The Merciful One—He will rule over us forever. May the Merciful One be blessed in heaven and on earth. May the Merciful One be praised for generation upon generation, and may He be glorified through us forever and ever, and may He be honored through us eternally. May the Merciful One grant us an honorable livelihood. May the Merciful One break the yoke from our neck and lead us upright to our land. May the Merciful One send a plentiful blessing on this house and on this table at which we have eaten. May the Merciful One send us Elijah the prophet—who is remembered for good—who will bring us good tidings of salvation and comfort.

These personal blessings are added according to the individual circumstances:

Ha-rachaman hu yevareich	הָרַחֲמָן הוּא יְבָרֵךְ

May the Merciful One bless

for one's parents:

et avi mori (ba'al	אֶת־אָבִי מוֹרִי (בַּעַל
ha-bayit ha'zeh) ve-et imi	הַבַּיִת הַזֶּה) וְאֶת־אִמִּי
morati (ba'alat ha-bayit	מוֹרָתִי (בַּעֲלַת הַבַּיִת
ha-zeh), otam ve-et beitam	הַזֶּה), אוֹתָם וְאֶת־בֵּיתָם
ve-et zaram ve-et kol	וְאֶת־זַרְעָם וְאֶת־כָּל־
asher lahem,	אֲשֶׁר לָהֶם,

my honored father (the man of this house) and my honored mother (the woman of this house)—them, together with their household, their children and everything that is theirs.

for oneself and one's own family:

oti ve-et ishti (ba'ali)	אוֹתִי וְאֶת־אִשְׁתִּי (בַּעֲלִי)
ve-et zari ve-et kol asher	וְאֶת־זַרְעִי וְאֶת־כָּל־אֲשֶׁר
li,	לִי,

me, my wife (my husband), together with everything that is mine,

May the Merciful One be praised for generation upon generation, and may He be glorified through us forever and ever, and may He be honored through us eternally.

for one's hosts:

et ba'al ha-bayit ha-zeh,	אֶת־בַּעַל הַבַּיִת הַזֶּה
ve-et ba'alat ha-bayit ha-zeh,	וְאֶת־בַּעֲלַת הַבַּיִת הַזֶּה,
otam ve-et beitam ve-et	אוֹתָם וְאֶת־בֵּיתָם וְאֶת־
zaram ve-et kol asher	זַרְעָם וְאֶת־כָּל־אֲשֶׁר
lahem,	לָהֶם,

the man of this house and the woman of this house— them, together with their household, their children and everything that is theirs,

for others present:

ve-et kol ha-mesubin kan,	וְאֶת־כָּל־הַמְסֻבִּין כָּאן,

and all who are seated here,

—otanu ve-et kol asher	— אוֹתָנוּ וְאֶת־כָּל־אֲשֶׁר
lanu, kemo she-nitbarchu	לָנוּ, כְּמוֹ שֶׁנִּתְבָּרְכוּ
avoteinu Avraham Yitzchak	אֲבוֹתֵינוּ אַבְרָהָם יִצְחָק
ve-Ya'akov ba-kol mi-kol kol, kein	וְיַעֲקֹב בַּכֹּל מִכֹּל כֹּל, כֵּן
yevareich otanu kulanu yachad	יְבָרֵךְ אוֹתָנוּ כֻּלָּנוּ יַחַד
biverachah sheleimah, ve-nomar	בִּבְרָכָה שְׁלֵמָה, וְנֹאמַר
amein.	אָמֵן.

May a plea be heard on high, for them and for us, which will result in the security of peace.

—us, together with all that is ours, just as our fathers, Abraham, Isaac and Jacob, were blessed—totally—so may He bless us, all of us together, with a complete blessing, and let us say, Amen.

Ba-marom yelamdu aleihem	בַּמָּרוֹם יְלַמְּדוּ עֲלֵיהֶם
ve-aleinu zechut she-tehei	וְעָלֵינוּ זְכוּת שֶׁתְּהֵא
le-mishmeret shalom. Ve-nisa	לְמִשְׁמֶרֶת שָׁלוֹם. וְנִשָּׂא
verachah mei-eit Adonai u-tzedakah	בְרָכָה מֵאֵת יְיָ וּצְדָקָה
mei-Elohei yisheinu. Ve-nimtza	מֵאֱלֹהֵי יִשְׁעֵנוּ. וְנִמְצָא־
chein ve-seichel tov be-einei	חֵן וְשֵׂכֶל טוֹב בְּעֵינֵי
Elohim ve-adam.	אֱלֹהִים וְאָדָם.

May a plea be heard on high, for them and for us, which will result in the security of peace. So may we receive a blessing from the Lord and righteousness from the God of our salvation. So may we find favor and understanding in the sight of God and man.

On *Shabbat*:

Ha-rachaman hu yanchileinu yom	הָרַחֲמָן הוּא יַנְחִילֵנוּ יוֹם
she-kulo Shabbat u-menuchah	שֶׁכֻּלּוֹ שַׁבָּת וּמְנוּחָה
le-chayei ha-olamim.	לְחַיֵּי הָעוֹלָמִים.

May the Merciful One bring us the day that will be totally *Shabbat* and rest, in everlasting life.

Ha-rachaman hu yezakeinu liymot	הָרַחֲמָן הוּא יְזַכֵּנוּ לִימוֹת
ha-moshiach ule-chayei ha-olam	הַמָּשִׁיחַ וּלְחַיֵּי הָעוֹלָם
ha-ba.	הַבָּא.

May the Merciful One make us worthy of experiencing the days of the Messiah and the life of the world to come.

Stand in awe of the Lord, you who are His holy ones, for there is nothing lacking to those who stand in awe of Him.

Migdol	מִגְדּוֹל
yeshuot malko ve-oseh	יְשׁוּעוֹת מַלְכּוֹ וְעֹשֶׂה
chesed li-meshicho le-David	חֶסֶד לִמְשִׁיחוֹ לְדָוִד
ule-zaro ad olam. Oseh	וּלְזַרְעוֹ עַד־עוֹלָם. עֹשֶׂה
shalom bi-meromav hu	שָׁלוֹם בִּמְרוֹמָיו הוּא
ya'aseh shalom aleinu ve-al	יַעֲשֶׂה שָׁלוֹם עָלֵינוּ וְעַל
kol Yisrael, ve-imru amein.	כָּל־יִשְׂרָאֵל, וְאִמְרוּ אָמֵן.

He brings about great victories for His king and shows kindness to his anointed one—to David and to his descendants forever. He who makes peace in His high places, may He bring about peace for us and for all Israel, and say, Amen.

Yeru et Adonai kedoshav ki	יְראוּ אֶת־יְיָ קְדֹשָׁיו כִּי
ein machsor liyrei'av.	אֵין מַחְסוֹר לִירֵאָיו.
Kefirim rashu ve-ra'eivu	כְּפִירִים רָשׁוּ וְרָעֵבוּ
ve-dorshei Adonai lo yachseru chol	וְדֹרְשֵׁי יְיָ לֹא־יַחְסְרוּ כָל־
tov. Hodu ladonai ki tov ki	טוֹב. הוֹדוּ לַייָ כִּי־טוֹב כִּי
le-olam chasdo. Potei'ach	לְעוֹלָם חַסְדּוֹ. פּוֹתֵחַ
et yadecha u-masbia le-chol	אֶת־יָדֶךָ וּמַשְׂבִּיעַ לְכָל־
chai ratzon. Baruch ha-gever	חַי רָצוֹן. בָּרוּךְ הַגֶּבֶר
asher yivtach badonai ve-hayah Adonai	אֲשֶׁר יִבְטַח בַּייָ וְהָיָה יְיָ
mivtacho. Na'ar hayiti	מִבְטַחוֹ. נַעַר הָיִיתִי
gam zakanti ve-lo ra'iti	גַּם־זָקַנְתִּי וְלֹא־רָאִיתִי
tzaddik ne'ezav ve'zaro	צַדִּיק נֶעֱזָב וְזַרְעוֹ
mevakeish lachem. Adonai oz le-amo	מְבַקֶּשׁ־לָחֶם. יְיָ עֹז לְעַמּוֹ
yitein Adonai yevareich et amo	יִתֵּן יְיָ יְבָרֵךְ אֶת־עַמּוֹ
va-shalom.	בַשָׁלוֹם.

Stand in awe of the Lord, you who are His holy ones, for there is nothing lacking to those who stand in awe of Him. Even young lions suffer want and hunger, but those who seek the Lord will not lack any good thing. Give thanks to the Lord, for He is good, for His kindness is everlasting. You open Your hand and satisfy the desire of all living. Blessed is the man who trusts in the Lord, and who makes the Lord the object of his trust. I was young and I have become old, and yet I never overlooked a deserving man who was destitute, with his children begging for bread. May the Lord give strength to His people; May the Lord bless his people with peace.

You shall lack nothing on the Sabbath. Eat, be satisfied, and bless your God whom you love, because He has blessed you beyond all nations.

Zemirot (a *Shabbat* song)

Reflections

When I was a little girl growing up, I remember my grandmother used to go and sit to one side after the meal and sing the *bentching* to herself.

I didn't even know she was *bentching* until I grew up and started experiencing traditional Judaism as an adult. After the Friday night meal where I was a guest, people passed around little books (*bentchers*), and began singing that familiar tune!

That's what she was doing all those years ago!

But why didn't she tell me? Why didn't she teach it to me?

Perhaps she knew that I wouldn't appreciate it or embrace it. Not then . . . but now.

How wise she was. I know somewhere in heaven she is listening with great *nachas* everytime I sing that song of thanks.

My oldest, who is five and a half, can say most of the **bentching** *herself, in and out. That's a lot further ahead than I was at twenty-seven, that first Friday night with my favorite teacher.*

I love *bentching* at the *Shabbat* table because it always evokes an emotion in me, as memories of my first *Shabbat* come flooding back.

There was a particular teacher that I had become close to through the learning that I was doing in the evening. He invited me for *Shabbat* to his home for a Friday night.

I didn't know what to expect, but it was beautiful. To teach his children the importance of *bentching* after the meal, he would always sing the *bentching* out loud, slowly, so that everyone could follow.

(Since I was such a beginner, I was probably at the same stage as the three or four year old at the table.)

It was such a warm feeling, seeing him take his little daughter onto his lap, swaying with her as he *bentched*, all of the kids joining in.

Now I watch as my own husband holds our littlest one, carefully singing each word clearly, so that all our little girls can keep up and learn it properly.

My oldest, who is five and a half, can say most of the *bentching* herself, in and out. That's a lot further ahead than I was at twenty-seven, that first Friday night with my favorite teacher.

What do I think about when I *bentch*? Probably how much more I have to *bentch* to get good at it.

Seriously though, I find that *bentching* has two qualities—physical and spiritual.

The spiritual aspect has to do with the words themselves. I find that just saying them has an effect, as if the Hebrew is magical and can bring holiness to your table.

But hey—after a big meal, you feel full, and you don't always feel like thanking God. All you want to do is get into your pj's and go to bed.

That's where the physical stuff comes in. It's the time you have to go that extra mile, even if you're not in the mood. It's called discipline. And I suppose it's good for me too.

I was studying in Israel when my parents asked me to meet them in Turkey, as they were traveling together for business.

I hadn't been keeping *Shabbat* for very long, but there were some basic components that I was determined to keep, and one was *bentching*.

In Turkey, you don't exactly advertise that you are Jewish, so I kept my head covered with the ol' baseball cap, and *bentching* . . . well, let's just say that I said it quietly. Very, very quietly.

CHAPTER TWO

Shabbat Morning and Midday Meal

Step-by-Step

Synagogue (*Shul*)

Kiddush

Washing for Bread

Ha-motzi (Blessing over the *Challah*)

Zemirot (*Shabbat* Songs)

Devar Torah (Torah Portion of the Week)

Mayim Acharonim (Jewish "Fingerbowl")

Birkat Ha-mazon (Blessing after the Meal)

Shabbat Day Activities

SYNAGOGUE (*SHUL*)—*SHABBAT* MORNING

When people are united behind something and share a common cause, there is a wonderful energy and power to it. It is the feeling that anything can be accomplished. It happens in sports, in school, in politics. It is a wonderful feeling, and sharing it with those around you who feel exactly the same is truly exciting and binds you together as nothing else can.

Yet, when the activity or cause is over, the game is won, or the election lost, that feeling of unity and brotherhood all but disappears.

But with the Jewish people it is different; for that which binds us is something so powerful and so eternal that we feel an almost unexplainable link to one another because of it.

The Talmud says that when we stood at the foot of Mount Sinai, we were one people, and the Torah actually refers to us in the singular. We looked to one another as if we were standing beside ourselves. We were one person with one goal: to receive the Torah from God.

It says that we were united at Mount Sinai to get a Torah, and *then* God gave us the Torah. The order here is important, for it shows that when people come together, that coming together *causes* great events to happen.

When we gather together each week at *shul*, we are making a statement that these are my brothers and sisters; these services are in fact a weekly family reunion.

Commentators say at Mount Sinai we were "one people, one heart," and the Talmud asks, what is the work of the heart? The answer— prayer.

Shabbat morning is the public reading of the Torah. When we gather as a community to hear it, it reminds us that this is our common heart.

When we talk to God we want to be all there, to be whole. A Jew being with fellow Jews means that wholeness is much easier to achieve, for the power of what we share is so awesome.

Gathering together does have a power, and it is a power that can make things happen—a united people, a world of values . . . *anything* is possible.

Shul and Prayer

There are a lot of people who have a very hard time relating to the concept of prayer in synagogue.

Perhaps you've found yourself in the position where you were standing while everyone else was sitting, or you were sitting while everyone else was standing. Even if you were in sync with those around you, why was everyone standing and sitting in the first place?

> When one visits a friend on Shabbat *morning, one should not greet the friend with "good morning," as one does during the week, but rather with "Shabbat Shalom," or "Good Shabbos," to fulfill the* mitzvah *of remembering the Sabbath.*
>
> Shaloh

65

The structure, the movements, the rituals . . . it can be pretty confusing. And, in many synagogues, worship has evolved into a kind of "spectator sport," with people in the audience watching the "show." There is also a language barrier. For many, Hebrew is as foreign as Greek.

Remember, we go to *shul* to talk to God. Being with other Jews, singing the songs, hearing the reading of the Torah—all this helps us to achieve this goal of having an active relationship with our Creator.

The fact is, you can talk to God anytime. He is always there, ready to hear from you. For many, being in *shul* inspires these words and feelings. For others, it does not.

The right *shul* should bring out this connection with God.

Search for the right *shul*; perhaps you just haven't found the one for you yet. Also, remember that going to *shul* is a good way to connect to community, which is very important for a Jew. And last, but certainly not least, work on talking to God. Whether you are in *shul* or on your back porch—take time to talk, in an audible whisper, to the Source of all your blessings.

Recognize Him, thank Him for all that He gives you, and ask for all that you desire.

And if the standing, sitting, Hebrew, and responsive readings are getting you down—then find someone or some place to teach you the basics of being in *shul*. (See page 171 for Beginner's Services and international teaching contacts.) Sometimes it's just a matter of 1–2–3, and a whole new world can open up before you.

How To

A detailed breakdown of what goes on in *shul* is beyond the scope of this book. Try *To Pray as a Jew* by Rabbi Hayim Halevy Donin for more depth and explanation. (See For Further Reading, Appendix B).

But, just to get a quick feel for the schedule of a typical service, here is what goes on at The Village Shul, the storefront synagogue where my husband is the rabbi.

Shabbat Morning

9:00–9:35 A.M.—Morning Blessings and *Pesukei De-zimrah*. Attended by those who are more knowledgeable and want the full prayer experience.

(You can arrive at any time, so don't stay home just because you may be a mid-morning attendee.)

9:35–9:45 A.M.—*Barchu*, blessings from *Shema Yisrael*, *Shema Yisrael* itself, and blessings after *Shema Yisrael*. Includes some nice singing.

9:45–10:00 A.M.—Silent *Amidah*. People will be standing and perhaps swaying in more introspective prayer. Followed by the leader's repetition aloud.

10:00–10:55 A.M.—The Torah is taken out, and the Torah

Remember, we go to **shul** *to talk to God.*

66

portion of the week is read out loud in Hebrew. The Torah is then returned to the ark.

At The Village Shul, we have an alternative program during the Torah reading, which is held downstairs from the regular service. Called "Be Cool in Shul," it is a class that explains the ins and outs of prayer, as well as a meaningful and relevant discussion of the Torah portion of the week. Everyone joins the regular service at 10:55 A.M.

10:55–11:10 A.M.—The rabbi speaks.

11:10 A.M.—*Musaf*, which is a second silent *Amidah* and is also again repeated aloud by the leader.

11:25 A.M.—*Aleinu* and closing songs are sung together.

11:30 A.M.—*Shul* announcements.

11:35 A.M.—*Kiddush* and socializing for about an hour.

Reflections

I never went to *shul* growing up, because my family just didn't belong to one. I knew they existed, and by about ten years old I even had a desire to go. Don't ask me why, there was absolutely no connection with *shul* . . . so I didn't even bother asking my parents to take me. I was a little Jewish girl who never went to *shul* . . . no big deal.

Later, about my third year in university, I met a girl in one of my classes who was from a similar background but had become observant. We connected, and she invited me for *Shabbat*.

For services we went to a downstairs *minyan* at the Hillel House. Everything was so foreign to me; I didn't know Hebrew, and there seemed to be a whole new etiquette to learn. I remember feeling as if I wanted to hold her hand.

After a few visits, my friend taught me Hebrew, and I started to catch on to the do's and don't's of the service.

Shul began to give me a feeling of beauty of place. Everyone was together, singing songs. . . . It was a wonderful atmosphere of community, with a special power in everyone just doing the same thing.

It's funny, now that I am married with kids, I hardly go now. It's hard to sit and *daven*, and the big *shul* in our neighborhood just doesn't have that same quality I had experienced so long ago in the basement of that Hillel House.

Still, I should go more often. I feel more connected with God when I'm in *shul*.

———

The Temple that we went to on the High Holidays relied heavily on organ music and choral singing. To me, it was a church.

I didn't mind having to go, but the whole experience was devoid of meaning; just a lot of ornament and ceremony.

The responsive reading, using flowery English prose, was so repetitive.

I was a little Jewish girl who never went to shul *. . . no big deal.*

I believed in God, I just didn't feel that Temple brought me close to Him.

When I grew a little bit older, I actually tried a more traditional synagogue, but I was lost because I didn't understand the Hebrew.

It was pretty depressing to think that my choices were something I considered a mockery and something that was too foreign.

That was before I discovered a Jewish educational center that followed traditional practices with a lot of clear explanation in English for those of us who were "novices" (which was most of us).

It made Judaism so accessible. There was always enough time to go through everything at my own pace, and it instilled a sense of community. Because it was small and so genuine, it took away any thoughts of being intimidated by atmosphere or ritual. It was just so laid back!

On Rosh HaShanah and Yom Kippur, I found myself *davening* for hours on end, and it seemed like just a half an hour had gone by!

Now that I am at home with a child, it's harder to get to services. I suppose I should open my *siddur* at home, but I need the people around me and the sound of the singing too much.

So instead I just talk to God, informally. I thank Him and ask Him to help me understand things. I feel the most important thing is to have an ongoing relationship with God.

After finishing my master's in education, I took some time off to travel and ended up in Israel.

Someone invited me into one of the rabbinical schools for lunch, and I was hungry, so I went. Afterwards they began *davening Minchah*, praying the afternoon service. Yikes—it reminded me of being forced to go to Temple on *Shabbat* back home when I was a kid, so I quickly got up and left.

Growing up it was the dreaded Junior *Minyan*. Mom would dress me up in a suit and make me go by myself. My family didn't even go!

By the age of ten, I got smart and began wearing my gym clothes underneath my suit and went to play basketball in the nearby schoolyard, always keeping one eye open to see when services were getting out.

Then I quickly got dressed and went on home, no one the wiser.

So what happened in Israel? Well, the next day I went back for a class and was pretty impressed. So I stayed on and got into the learning, but still never connected with *davening* in a deep way. For me, it always went too long.

Today, if it wasn't such an important commandment, I probably would go only occasionally. Yet, every once in a while, I'll feel much more connected with *Shabbat* and the Almighty just by being in the *shul* atmosphere.

Maybe if the service was just a little bit shorter . . .

---

*Growing up it was the dreaded Junior **Minyan**. Mom would dress me up in a suit and make me go by myself. My family didn't even go!*

Growing up we went to *shul* as a family, and I just loved it—being with all the people, watching my father *daven* all day long on the High Holidays. . . . You know, being Jewish.

I remember sitting there thinking about God and feeling close to Him. It was really very meaningful, and I look back at it as being one of the warmest parts of my life.

Today it is much deeper. During *Shemoneh Esrei*—the silent meditation—I take the time to really *daven*. During the repetition I cry, as the *chazzan's* voice lifts me even higher.

The whole experience now is much more real, as I have matured and studied more. God is not only in *shul* for me now, but a real part of my life.

As a family we went to *shul* only on the High Holidays and for *bar mitzvahs*. But there was a time that I went myself, because in grades three and four, our Sunday school teacher would give us gold stars if we had gone to *shul* the day before. I wanted those stars.

But *shul* was basically a bore; no one understood what was going on, even though it was supposed to be a youth service.

Today, I found a much smaller *shul* that was founded on the premise of learning and understanding, so a lot of the service is explained, and, most important, made relevant to my life today.

Yet it's still sometimes an effort to get up early and go—just laziness I guess. When I do make it, I really like it and am glad I'm there.

What do I think about in *shul*? Mostly about if my being there is making a difference to me and God. I also think about Jews all over the world doing exactly the same thing. I like the continuity of that thought, as it links me to thousands of years of unbroken tradition.

When it's a nice day, I love the slow walk home.

Oh yeah—and don't forget the honey cake!

We were your classic High Holiday/*Simchah shul* go-ers. I remember sitting there listening to a service I didn't understand, topped by a sermon about Israeli politics, and wondering why no one ever talked about God.

Playing with the fringes on my brother's *tallit*, I would take in the whole "scene": people seemed focused on what everyone was wearing or driving that year; talk all around me was either gossip or business.

This was Judaism??

I had a sense that there had to be more, and I was right.

Later I began learning more about our heritage and tradition and became exposed to a whole different world where people seemed to really care about prayer and their relationship with God.

> *I remember sitting there listening to a service I didn't understand, topped by a sermon about Israeli politics, and wondering why no one ever talked about God.*

69

However, I'll be the first to admit that my thoughts in *shul* are not always so spiritual. Sometimes I really connect, but sometimes I just enjoy the feeling of being together, the *kiddush*, and the "Good *Shabbos*" greetings.

———

To me *shul* is community, and my enjoyment of prayer is directly affected by the people around me. If I identify with them, my *davening* is much more relaxed and intimate. If I feel apart from them, my thoughts are much more detached.

It took me awhile to find a congregation that was "just right"—not too religious, not too secular. I've found a traditional *minyan* now that satisfies most of my needs, but, most important, it attracts people just like me: down-to-earth, genuine, and open to personal growth through Judaism. It's a small place, so everyone is friendly; yet it is a "serious" *minyan*, so there's no chitchat during the service to distract me.

I think it's important that people try out different places until they find one that suits them best. I think there's a danger when the first place you try just isn't for you. It's not Judaism that's at fault, just the place you happen to be in—whether it's the physical layout of the place, the rabbi, the community . . . whatever.

I was lucky because I had a variety of places to choose from. But the one I settled on was a unique place in that it wasn't an established synagogue, but a brand-new storefront that was started by six people just like me—people who didn't fit into any other congregation, who wanted a small, family-based *shul*.

———

AFTER *SHUL*—THE SECOND MEAL

The First Meal of *Shabbat*, the Friday night meal, is always filled with great joy, for it is the start of the Sabbath. Everything is fresh, and the air is filled with anticipation. It is the beginning.

Later, we will see that *Seudah Shelishit*, the Third Meal, held near sunset, is the completion: a time to reflect on the achievements of *Shabbat*. It is the end, the attainment of the goal.

The Second Meal is somewhere in between, the place where one stands between the enthusiasm of the beginning and the anticipation of completion. It is the celebration of the process.

The middle is a challenging place to be. It is while traveling along the road, toward a goal, that people can get confused, convincing themselves that it is too much effort and ultimately giving up.

> *One should enjoy* **Shabbat** *by eating, drinking, and resting—the more, the better. Even if one cannot be certain that his enjoyment is for the sake of fulfilling God's will, the very pleasure that he derives from* **Shabbat** *is a great* **mitzvah** *itself, beyond measure.*
>
> Rabbi Levi Yitzchak of Berditchov

70

We see that in many aspects of our lives: career, marriage, friendship. We have a sense at the beginning of what we want to achieve, but along the way we get weighed down by the effort and abandon the journey. The goal seems too far in the distance, growing unclear.

Judaism says that *effort* is joyful. The Second Meal is there to remind us that it is important to keep on track after the initial burst of beginnings and before the achievement of the ends; that anything worth achieving involves a certain amount of struggle, challenge, and energy.

That which takes the most effort will, in the end, yield the greatest pleasure. Marriage, children, work for our community . . . they can be viewed as burdens or as opportunities for growth and as sources for our greatest joys.

Be aware of the middle ground, where ideals and goals can sometimes get lost. Take pleasure in your efforts and celebrate the process.

KIDDUSH—SHABBAT MORNING

In the dark and spiritual time of Friday night, it was easy to leave work and the hustle and bustle of the week behind us. But now it is daylight—midday. How easy it would be to get up and do . . . how challenging it is to stay and continue the experience of *Shabbat*.

And so in the *kiddush* that we recite at this time, there is a message for us to keep us on track and to remind us what we are all about.

"It is a sign . . ."

Shabbat is a sign: between ourselves and God, between the Jewish people and the world, and between us and our unique selves.

And, like any sign, it is a statement, a symbol of what we represent. When you see a sign for a store, the typeface, colors, and style all give hint to what is inside. It is the first and strongest form of advertising, something that is up before the store is even built—"Coming Soon to This Site . . ." And, once in business, it is the statement of purpose and the reflection of what the store is all about.

It is also the marker by which you find that something inside. Without it, you would all but pass it by.

And so it is with *Shabbat*.

This special day is our sign. We are advertising that God created the world, and just as He stopped creating for one day, *we* stop creating for one day. To be like God, to emulate the Almighty, is to come close to His essence and to experience the ultimate in transcendence. And, as we have spoken about, this recognition of God as Creator of the world brings forth a tremendous appreciation of what He has done for us in all aspects of our lives.

That is the sign between us and God.

Becoming a nation and being asked to be a "light" unto the other nations of the world means a certain responsibility. This "Jewish Sabbath" is one of the ways we fulfill this responsibility as we set an example of values that are eternal: family, community, and relationship to our Creator.

That is the sign between the Jewish people and the world.

> **Shabbat** *is a sign: between ourselves and God, between the Jewish people and the world, and between us and our unique selves.*

In the light of day, the temptation to get back on that treadmill is there. Thus we stop and make **kiddush** *once again.*

And this sign, this banner, this billboard that we call *Shabbat* is up there to remind ourselves who we are as individuals; that we were created not just with body, but with soul. This special 24 hours is to get in touch with that truth and to use it to realize our potentials as unique beings.

In the light of day, the temptation to get back on that treadmill is there. Thus we stop and make *kiddush* once again. Yet, this time, we insert a wholly different idea from that of the previous night.

This time we speak of *Shabbat* as a sign, hung for all to see, including ourselves. It beckons us in, and it is there so that we can find it, lest we pass it by.

How To

1. The Second Meal of *Shabbat* begins sometime after morning services at *shul* (approximately lunchtime).

2. *Kiddush* is usually made in *shul* after the Morning Service. Be sure to hear it from whoever is reciting it (often it is the rabbi). Afterward, you should eat some cake or cookies equal in volume to a slice of bread.

3. *Kiddush* can also be said at home prior to the "lunch" meal.

4. The procedure for *kiddush* is more relaxed during the day than it is at night. The person making *kiddush* on behalf of others may stand or sit (optional, but be consistent from week to week). The others should do the same.

5. *Kiddush* in the morning can be made on wine, grape juice, or beer (or any "important" drink whose makeup is not primarily water, for example, concentrated juice and the like).

6. The amounts to be used and drunk are the same as on Friday night (see page 24), except that others included in the blessing need not actually taste the wine, as long as a "meal" is eaten.

The following blessing is recited by the person making *kiddush*:

Shabbat Day–Second Meal *Kiddush*

Ve-shamru venei Yisrael	וְשָׁמְרוּ בְנֵי־יִשְׂרָאֵל
et ha-Shabbat, la'asot	אֶת־הַשַּׁבָּת, לַעֲשׂוֹת
et ha-Shabbat le-dorotam berit	אֶת־הַשַּׁבָּת לְדֹרֹתָם בְּרִית
olam. Beini u-vein	עוֹלָם. בֵּינִי וּבֵין
benei Yisrael ot hi	בְּנֵי־יִשְׂרָאֵל אוֹת הִיא
le-olam, ki sheishet yamim	לְעוֹלָם, כִּי שֵׁשֶׁת יָמִים
asah Adonai et ha-shamayim	עָשָׂה יְיָ אֶת־הַשָּׁמַיִם
ve-et ha-aretz uva-yom	וְאֶת־הָאָרֶץ וּבַיּוֹם
ha-shevi'i shavat va-yinafash.	הַשְּׁבִיעִי שָׁבַת וַיִּנָּפַשׁ.

Zachor et yom ha-Shabbat	זָכוֹר אֶת־יוֹם הַשַּׁבָּת
le-kadesho. Sheishet yamim	לְקַדְּשׁוֹ. שֵׁשֶׁת יָמִים
ta'avod ve-asita kol	תַּעֲבֹד וְעָשִׂיתָ כָּל־
melachtecha. Ve-yom ha-shevi'i	מְלַאכְתֶּךָ. וְיוֹם הַשְּׁבִיעִי
Shabbat ladonai Elohecha, lo	שַׁבָּת לַיָי אֱלֹהֶיךָ, לֹא־
ta'aseh chol melachah atah	תַעֲשֶׂה כָל־מְלָאכָה אַתָּה
u-vincha u-vitecha avdecha va-amatcha	וּבִנְךָ וּבִתֶּךָ עַבְדְּךָ וַאֲמָתְךָ
u-vehemtecha ve-geircha asher	וּבְהֶמְתֶּךָ וְגֵרְךָ אֲשֶׁר
bi-she'arecha. Ki sheishet yamim	בִּשְׁעָרֶיךָ. כִּי שֵׁשֶׁת־יָמִים
asah Adonai et ha-shamayim	עָשָׂה יְיָ אֶת־הַשָּׁמַיִם
ve-et ha-aretz et ha-yam	וְאֶת־הָאָרֶץ אֶת־הַיָּם
ve-et kol asher bam, va-yanach	וְאֶת־כָּל־אֲשֶׁר־בָּם וַיָּנַח
ba-yom ha-shevi'i,	בַּיּוֹם הַשְּׁבִיעִי,
Al kein beirach Adonai et yom	עַל־כֵּן בֵּרַךְ יְיָ אֶת־יוֹם
ha-Shabbat va-yekadsheihu.	הַשַּׁבָּת וַיְקַדְּשֵׁהוּ.

The children of Israel should keep *Shabbat*, observing *Shabbat* throughout their generations, as an everlasting covenant. It is a sign between Me and the children of Israel for all time, that in six days the Lord made the heavens and the earth, and that on the seventh day He was finished and He rested.

Be mindful of *Shabbat*, to make it holy. You should labor for six days and do all your work, but the seventh day is *Shabbat* for the Lord your God. You may not do any creative work—neither you nor your son, nor your daughter, nor your male or female worker, nor your cattle, nor the stranger who dwells among you. Because it was in six days that the Lord made the heavens and the earth, the sea, and all that they contain, and He rested on the seventh day.

That is why the Lord made *Shabbat* and made it holy.

Savri maranan ve-rabanan ve-rabotai:	סָבְרִי מָרָנָן וְרַבָּנָן וְרַבּוֹתַי:

With the permission of the distinguished people present.

For wine:

Baruch atah Adonai,	בָּרוּךְ אַתָּה יְיָ,
Eloheinu melech ha-olam,	אֱלֹהֵינוּ מֶלֶךְ הָעוֹלָם,
borei peri ha-gafen.	בּוֹרֵא פְּרִי הַגָּפֶן.

You are blessed, Lord our God, the sovereign of the world, creator of the fruit of the vine.

For other drinks:

Baruch atah Adonai,	בָּרוּךְ אַתָּה יְיָ,
Eloheinu melech ha-olam,	אֱלֹהֵינוּ מֶלֶךְ הָעוֹלָם,
she-hakol nihyeh bi-devaro.	שֶׁהַכֹּל נִהְיֶה בִּדְבָרוֹ.

You are blessed, Lord our God, the sovereign of the world, through whose word everything came into being.

The children of Israel should keep **Shabbat,** *observing* **Shabbat** *throughout their generations, as an everlasting covenant.*

THE SECOND MEAL

How To

After *kiddush* is said and everyone has had a taste of the wine, the procedure is the same as at the Friday night meal:

Washing—In preparation for eating the *challah* (see page 31).

Ha-motzi—The blessing and eating of the *challah* (see page 36).

Zemirot—Songs for *Shabbat* day. Any of the songs listed in the Friday Night section can be sung at this time (see page 40). For even more songs, refer to a NCSY *bentcher* (see Appendix B: For Further Reading, page 167).

Devar Torah—A word of Torah (see page 44).

Shir Ha-Maalot—Song preceding Grace after Meals (see page 49)

Mayim Acharonim—Cleansing fingertips before Grace after Meals (see page 50).

Birkat Hamazon (*Bentching*)—The saying of Grace after Meals (see page 51).

Reflections

I like the meal on *Shabbat* day because I'm so much more rested than on Friday night. Friday night is the end of a day of preparation, and the kids get tired in the evening. But *Shabbat* day we've all slept a little late, and everything's already done, so it's just a meal to enjoy.

I'm a bachelor, so Friday nights I have friends over for the meal, or go out to friends' homes. I never used to put a lot of effort into the *Shabbat* day meal, because it was kind of a letdown from Friday night. Leftovers were served, and I didn't even get dressed up.

But I've been changing, and I've tried to use the day as an opportunity to really make it *Shabbat*. Friday night seems so easy to achieve, but in the day I guess I'm more . . . distracted.

So now I dress up, even if I'm alone, and I try and do some Jewish reading. By the end of *Shabbat* I try to read through the Torah portion in English, but I must admit that it's also a time to read the paper.

It's my only day that I can relax. My friends know not to phone, and the peace and quiet is priceless.

Sitting at the table by myself is rare, because I'm either out at a friend's house sharing the meal or having friends or family over. But the times that I am the only one at the table are nice too. I sing some *Shabbat* songs without embarrassment (my voice is just so-so) and practice saying the *kiddush* and *ha-motzi* in my slow, just-learning Hebrew.

I'm getting better, and one day, when I have a wife and kids of my own, I'll be ready.

———

My *Shabbat* day meal is much simpler than Friday night. Usually I just make a big *cholent*, use cantaloupe as an appetizer, and cut up a salad. The *cholent* is like one big stew, so if my husband brings home surprise guests from *shul*, there's no problem just setting some more places.

The atmosphere is also different. Friday night is much more formal, while *Shabbat* day is laid back and relaxed. The focus is much more on the kids during the day, because we're not trying to get them to bed, and they're not tired like the night before.

My husband always tells a story at the table just for them with some lesson in it, and we go over their *parshah* sheets from school (see page 81).

———

To me the big difference between Friday night and *Shabbat* day is guests. Friday night we try to have people who have never been over as guests, while *Shabbat* day is a time to renew old friendships. I guess it's because you've got to be a good friend to enjoy the noise of the kids running around!

———

Friday night is so spiritual to me. It has that dark and deep quality to it that just infuses the atmosphere with meaning. It also reminds me of my childhood, because although we weren't as traditional as I am now with my own family, we always had some sort of Friday night celebration.

Shabbat day is much more free and easy. Perhaps not as spiritual, but a lot more fun. The kids come home from *shul* all excited, and we have a tradition that before we begin the meal we sing and the girls dance in a circle doing the *horah*. It's so cute.

At the table we usually have guests with kids and the focus is on the little ones. We ask them what they've been learning in school and try and make the *Shabbat* experience fun and meaningful for them on their level.

Friday night is much more formal, while **Shabbat** *day is laid back and relaxed.*

———

Friday night is so classy, with everything fresh and so *Shabbosdik* (in the spirit of *Shabbos*). I love the way the table looks with all the best china,

75

crystal, and linen napkins. We always invite two or three couples over to share the evening with. It's a "no kids" night, because for most of the year, the kids are in bed after *ha-motzi*.

Shabbat day is family. We invite friends with their children, and the meal and atmosphere are much more down-to-earth. I use disposable plates and napkins so I don't have to fret over the kids at the table, and it also makes cleanup a snap. That inspires me to have more guests, which I love.

Sometimes the atmosphere can get a little wild, what with all the children running around, but everyone seems very good-humored about it.

Sometimes the meal goes on and on, and before you know it, it's time to back to *shul*!

CHAPTER THREE

Shabbat Afternoon

WHAT TO DO *SHABBAT* AFTERNOON

It's actually a mitzvah *to nap on* Shabbat!

In the winter, when *Shabbat* ends so early, there is very little time for activity or rest after the lunch meal. But the balance of the year affords the opportunity to use *Shabbat* afternoon for true pleasure.

The *Shabbat* Nap

It's actually a *mitzvah* to nap on *Shabbat*! In fact, it's not so unusual for the whole family to sleep a good hour or so after the *Shabbat* midday meal. It may not be possible if there are kids around with varied sleeping schedules, but if parents take turns, a *Shabbat* nap can usually be had by all. Keep this tradition in mind if you plan on doing any visiting in the afternoon. If your knocking on the door yields no reply, chances are the household is snoozing.

Learning

Just because it's a *mitzvah* to nap on *Shabbat* doesn't mean you should sleep this important day away. Many people make a point of learning something from our tradition at this time, by reading Jewish books or by meeting with friends for formal or informal discussion. Most communities organize lectures at *shuls* or homes. If yours does not, why not start it! Get some people together and ask a rabbi or teacher to give a talk on a specified subject.

Socializing

This is a great time for connecting with friends and family. The phones are still not ringing, and the televisions are silent. Use this time to spend quality moments with the people you care most about. Visit, go for a walk, get to the local park or playground, read stories. Enjoy these last hours before the hectic pace of the weekday is upon you again.

SHABBAT AND KIDS

Shabbat for kids can either be hours of don'ts and can'ts . . . or hours of fun, excitement, family, and activity.

The challenge, for parents, is to convey all that makes *Shabbat* special and enjoyable, while teaching in a positive way anything that might be construed as a restriction. When properly done (and it takes practice), *Shabbat* should become the best day of the week for kids, something they anticipate with excitement all week long.

It is the parents' responsibility to educate their children about what it means to be a Jew, and of course this includes *Shabbat*. The process of education begins when children are at the age of understanding. You'll find that they slowly begin to absorb it and will want to participate in *Shabbat* as much as they can. (They love to rhyme off the laws: "We don't drive on *Shabbat*, we walk!" . . . "We don't cook on *Shabbat*, we have Shabbat treats!" . . . "Mommy and Daddy don't work on *Shabbat*, they play with us!")

Here's some tried-and-true ways to make *Shabbat* great for kids:

• You set the example. If they see you enjoying the preparation and fulfillment of *Shabbat*, that will be the greatest influence on them, bar none.

• Make everything special for *Shabbat*
  —special *Shabbat* clothes for them
  —special *Shabbat* shoes
  —special *Shabbat* hair ribbons, *kippot*, bows, and so forth.

• Save treats for *Shabbat* (a good way of getting out of it during the week—"Treats are for *Shabbat*!").

• Make their favorite foods on *Shabbat*.

• Get them involved in the *Shabbat* preparations: cooking, setting the table, tidying, shopping. Even the smallest child can place napkins at each place setting. Find what they like to do and give them a task within their means.

• Have special *Shabbat* toys—*just* for *Shabbat*. Let them put away the ones they can't use on *Shabbat* (musical instruments, crayons, modeling clay and so forth (see page 157) and take out the new ones.

• Adapt games for *Shabbat*—for example, you can play the standard Scrabble or other board games, but of course, you can't write down the scores. So assign everyone his or her own bookmark and keep score by using a large book and inserting the markers accordingly (10 points moves the marker to page 10, next turn is 7 points, move the marker to 17, and so on.) It really works!

• Read special *Shabbat* books (with Jewish themes, which can be purchased at Jewish book stores).

• Do family activities such as going to *shul*, visiting neighbors, going to the park (a nice *Shabbat* afternoon outing), taking walks, and so forth. *Shabbat* should be family focused, which is easier to achieve in the *Shabbat* atmosphere of no phones, TV, cars, and the like. (See *Halachah* and Beyond, page 153.)

• If you are having guests, get the kids involved in the *mitzvah* by having them make handmade place-setting cards, making up the guest room with fresh sheets, towels, flowers, and so forth. Explain to the children

It is the parents' responsibility to educate their children about what it means to be a Jew, and of course this includes **Shabbat.**

who is coming and encourage them to learn the guests' names ahead of time so they can greet them properly.

• At candlelighting, small children like to stand beside their mother to help say the blessing and enjoy the whole *mitzvah*.

• Children love to have a special place at the *Shabbat* table. (Try sitting them right up front so they can watch *kiddush*, *ha-motzi*, and so on.)

• Children like to imitate by saying their own *kiddush*.

• Have little inexpensive wine glasses for the kids, so they can feel special and grown-up.

• Let the week lead into *Shabbat*—"Only three more days 'til *Shabbat!*" . . . "Tomorrow is *Shabbat!*"

• Arrange to have their friends stay over for *Shabbat* or to visit on *Shabbat* afternoon.

• If your children attend Jewish schools, they often bring home *Parshah* sheets with questions on the Torah portion of the week. Ask these questions at the table—the guests love to get into the action! Have special treats as prizes for right answers or "good tries."

    If they don't have such sheets, tell them about what happened in the *parshah* and get them asking questions.

• Don't forget that *Shabbat* is for them too. So encourage their involvement at the table with talk, singing *Shabbat* songs, and assigning special *Shabbat* responsibilities. (One child can be the "dessert waiter" and help serve the dessert, another can be the "towel person," handing the hand towels to the guests after they wash for bread, and so on.)

• Do things on *Shabbat* that you don't do during the week—play games with them, cuddle up and read the comics, have uninterrupted talks.

• A lot of *shuls* have special programs for boys and girls held on *Shabbat* afternoon. Some are run by older teens for all ages. They are fun and educational and are offered as standard programs throughout North America. Make inquiries through the international contacts listed in Appendix C.

• Just in case the children do feel a little restricted on *Shabbat*, when *Shabbat* is over plan a *Melaveh Malkah* party (see page 96), with hot cocoa, popcorn, and a special tape. Bring out the crayons they couldn't use on *Shabbat* and let them color to their heart's content.

• In *shul* on *Shabbat* morning, bring little bags of snacks for each of them, juice boxes, and a book or quiet toy. If your *shul* doesn't have babysitting, organize the other parents and get some. Many *shuls* also have programs for older children. Again, if yours doesn't, organize some!

• After *Shabbat* is over, when you're tucking them into bed, review all the highlights of *Shabbat*—"Remember how yummy the *challah* tasted?" . . . "Oh, you were so quiet while Daddy made *kiddush!*" . . . "Wasn't our *Shabbat* outing fun?"

    They'll hardly be able to wait for next *Shabbat*.

SEUDAH SHELISHIT—THE THIRD MEAL

The Holy One, Blessed be He, said to Moses: I have [in my treasure house] a special gift, called Shabbat, and I wish to give it to the people of Israel. Go and tell them!

Talmud Bavli

We began *Shabbat* with a meal, with the determination that the physical gifts of life—food, silver, crystal, wine—would be elevated to a higher level. Through our actions and words, we brought new meaning to things such as eating and drinking.

Yet, with the two previous meals, which are often elaborate and festive, it can sometimes be easy to get caught up in the tasty dishes and forget the higher purpose of this celebration.

Seudah Shelishit, the Third Meal, being the last meal, is there as a completion. It is also a simple reminder of what the meals of *Shabbat* were all about and what they have contributed to our personal development over *Shabbat*.

It is by far the smallest of the meals, often just some tea and bread, perhaps a small piece of fish.

This is not just because we are full from previous meals. It is a statement that, for the past 24 hours we have lived a *Shabbat*, and that experience has made us hypersensitive to the world that we live in.

We have stepped away from the complex and flash of weekday living and entered a space where we identify not just as a body, but as a soul.

This simple meal of tea and *challah* becomes just as enjoyable as the sumptuous meal of Friday night, for we have retrained ourselves to get rid of the excess and have instead begun to focus on all that is important: family, friends, wisdom.

The *Shabbat* songs, the words of Torah, the blessings and the sharing of time were all integral parts of the meal, as tasty as the soup and the dessert. The time spent at the *Shabbat* table was precious.

It is the final meal. The sun is setting, and the cycle is complete.

How To

It is proper to have three meals at which bread is eaten on *Shabbat*: the Friday night meal, the *Shabbat* midday meal, and one meal toward the end of the day just prior to sunset. This last meal is called *Seudah Shelishit*, or the Third Meal.

1. You should try to leave room for this meal when eating lunch that day so you have an appetite for this third meal. However, if eating bread is very difficult to do, then eating cake (the equivalent amount of a slice of bread), or even just fruit will do.

2. No *kiddush* is recited before this meal.

3. The Third Meal must be started before sunset but can end well afterward. Grace after Meals (if bread was eaten) should include the special paragraph regarding *Shabbat*, as the meal officially began while *Shabbat* was still here.

4. It is common for *shuls* to have this meal available for people attending the *Minchah-Maariv* (afternoon-evening) service. The fare is usually quite simple, consisting of bread, herring, fruit, and the like.

      If no such meal is provided at *shul*, one can attend the afternoon service, return home for the Third Meal, and then return again to shul for *Maariv* and the end of *Shabbat*.

5. After finishing the meal, no food should be eaten until after the *Havdalah* ceremony (page 89).

Traditional Songs for the Third Meal

      The mood is much more solemn now, and we turn to the slower, more reflective songs.

Mizmor Le-David

Mizmor le-David. Adonai ro'i, lo echsar. Bi-ne'ot deshe yarbitzeini, al mei menuchot yenahaleini. Nafshi yeshoveiv, yancheini ve-magelei tzedek le-ma'an shemo. Gam ki eileich be-gei tzalmavet lo ira ra, ki atah imadi, shivtecha u-mishantecha, heimah yenachamuni.

מִזְמוֹר לְדָוִד. יְיָ רֹעִי, לֹא אֶחְסָר. בִּנְאוֹת דֶּשֶׁא יַרְבִּיצֵנִי, עַל מֵי מְנוּחוֹת יְנַהֲלֵנִי. נַפְשִׁי יְשׁוֹבֵב, יַנְחֵנִי בְמַעְגְּלֵי צֶדֶק לְמַעַן שְׁמוֹ. גַּם כִּי אֵלֵךְ בְּגֵיא צַלְמָוֶת לֹא אִירָא רָע, כִּי אַתָּה עִמָּדִי, שִׁבְטְךָ וּמִשְׁעַנְתֶּךָ, הֵמָּה יְנַחֲמֻנִי.

Ta'aroch lefanai shulchan, neged tzorerai, dishanta va-shemen roshi, kosi revayah. Ach tov va-chesed yirdefuni kol yemei chayai, ve-shavti be-veit Hashem le-orech yamim.

תַּעֲרֹךְ לְפָנַי שֻׁלְחָן, נֶגֶד צֹרְרָי, דִּשַּׁנְתָּ בַשֶּׁמֶן רֹאשִׁי, כּוֹסִי רְוָיָה. אַךְ טוֹב וָחֶסֶד יִרְדְּפוּנִי כָּל־יְמֵי חַיָּי, וְשַׁבְתִּי בְּבֵית יְיָ לְאֹרֶךְ יָמִים.

      A psalm of David. The Lord is my shepherd; I shall not want. He makes me lie down in green pastures; He leads me past still waters. He restores my soul; He leads me in the path of righteousness, for His name's sake. Even though I walk in the valley of the shadow of death, I will fear no evil, for You are with me. Your rod and Your staff, they comfort me.

      You set a table before me in the presence of my enemies. You have scented my head with oil; my cup overflows. Surely goodness and mercy will follow me all the days of my life, and I will dwell in the house of the Lord forever.

Surely goodness and mercy will follow me all the days of my life, and I will dwell in the house of the Lord forever.

Yedid Nefesh

Yedid nefesh av ha-rachaman meshoch avdecha el retzonecha,

יְדִיד נֶפֶשׁ אָב הָרַחֲמָן מְשׁוֹךְ עַבְדְּךָ אֶל רְצוֹנֶךָ,

83

yarutz avdecha kemo ayal,

יָרוּץ עַבְדְּךָ כְּמוֹ אַיָּל,

yishtachaveh el mul hadarecha,

יִשְׁתַּחֲוֶה אֶל מוּל הֲדָרֶךָ,

ye'erav lo yedidotecha, mi-nofet

יֶעֱרַב לוֹ יְדִידוֹתֶךָ, מִנֹּפֶת

tzuf ve-chol ta'am.

צוּף וְכָל־טָעַם.

Hadur naeh ziv ha-olam,

הָדוּר נָאֶה זִיו הָעוֹלָם,

nafshi cholat ahavatecha,

נַפְשִׁי חוֹלַת אַהֲבָתֶךָ,

ana Eil na refa na lah,

אָנָּא אֵל נָא רְפָא נָא לָהּ,

be-harot lah noam zivecha,

בְּהַרְאוֹת לָהּ נֹעַם זִיוָךְ,

az titchazeik ve-titrapei,

אָז תִּתְחַזֵּק וְתִתְרַפֵּא,

vehaytah lah

וְהָיְתָה לָהּ

simchat olam.

שִׂמְחַת עוֹלָם.

Vatik yehemu na rachamecha,

וָתִיק יֶהֱמוּ נָא רַחֲמֶיךָ,

ve-chusah na al bein ahuvecha,

וְחוּסָה נָא עַל בֵּן אֲהוּבֶךָ,

ki zeh kamah nichsof

כִּי זֶה כַּמָּה נִכְסֹף

nichsafti, lirot

נִכְסַפְתִּי, לִרְאוֹת

be-tiferet uzecha, eileh

בְּתִפְאֶרֶת עֻזֶּךָ, אֵלֶּה

chamdah libi, ve-chusah na

חָמְדָה לִבִּי, וְחוּסָה נָא

ve-al titalam.

וְאַל תִּתְעַלָּם.

Higaleh na u-fros chavivi

הִגָּלֶה נָא וּפְרוֹשׂ חֲבִיבִי

alai, et sukat shelomecha,

עָלַי, אֶת־סֻכַּת שְׁלוֹמֶךָ,

ta'ir eretz mi-kevodecha,

תָּאִיר אֶרֶץ מִכְּבוֹדֶךָ,

nagilah ve-nismechah bach, maheir

נָגִילָה וְנִשְׂמְחָה בָּךְ, מַהֵר

ahuv ki va mo'eid,

אָהוּב כִּי בָא מוֹעֵד,

ve-chaneinu kimei olam.

וְחָנֵּנוּ כִּימֵי עוֹלָם.

Beloved of my soul, merciful Father, draw Your servant toward You. Let Your servant run as a hind to bow before Your glory. Let Your affection for him be sweeter than a honeycomb or any other delicacy.

Glorious One, most beautiful splendor of the world, my soul is sick with love for You. Please God, heal it by revealing the delight of your splendor. Then it will be invigorated and healed, enjoying everlasting happiness.

Ancient One, let Your mercy be aroused and have pity on Your beloved son. For I have yearned for so long to see Your mighty splendor. This is the desire of my heart—have pity and do not hide Yourself.

Reveal Yourself and spread over me, beloved One, the shelter of Your peace. Let the earth sparkle with Your glory; we will rejoice and be happy with You. Be quick, beloved, for the time has come, and favor us as in days of old.

Let the earth sparkle with Your glory; we will rejoice and be happy with You.

Reflections

In the summer, *Shabbat* afternoon is l-o-n-g, especially with the kids, so a group of us got together to form "The *Shabbat* Club." It was originally five families, but grew to about twenty because it was such a hit.

Every *Shabbat* afternoon families would gather for *Seudah Shelishit* (the Third Meal), hosted in someone's backyard. The location would rotate, with everyone getting a turn to host throughout the summer. Food was kept really light—*challah* rolls, pita bread, salads, tuna fish, chopped egg, brownies. It really didn't matter, because the main thing was that we were all together, and the kids played, and *Shabbat* was spent as a community.

The person hosting would give a little talk on the Torah portion of the week, and the only other rule was that there should be beer—nice on a hot summer's day.

It really helped fill the day, and by the time you got home, your kids would be wiped out, so it was just a matter of putting them to bed, curling up on the couch, and reading until the stars came out.

———

I hate to admit this, but the Third Meal just doesn't exist here. O.K., maybe it does, but it's basically peanut butter and jam, and that's it.

I do try and use the time to just be with the kids, because we never have guests for this meal. I started a thing where I tell them a story from history, so that they learn how wars began, how nations are ruled, and how laws are made. I get them to talk and ask questions.

———

By that time of the day, I've had my *Shabbat* nap and it's my wife's turn to catch some sleep too. I'm not the most creative cook, so the Third Meal for me and the kids is usually cereal and milk.

When the older ones are finished, I try and learn with them a little before it's time for *Minchah-Maariv* at *shul*.

———

My kids are kind of bored by the end of the day, so I try to be really creative at the Third Meal. I "cater" and make up my own trays of egg salad, tuna, and salmon, with salads and healthful goodies they haven't seen all *Shabbat*. I want them to eat at this meal, because otherwise it's just lost, and they're hungry later that night, when they should really be sleeping.

The Third Meal is a *mitzvah*, and sometimes it's hard to achieve, so we make it as much fun as possible, with one of the kids giving a *devar Torah* instead of us. It makes them feel so important, and they come up with some wonderful ideas that are really very wise!

———

A friend of mine came up with something terrific—the Third Meal is for women only. We all leave our kids home with our husbands and gather

Any dish however small, if it is prepared in honor of the Sabbath, is considered a delight.

Talmud Bavli

together at her house early afternoon for a light meal and lots of singing. It's so nice to be together, and I've met some wonderful women this way. I hope it continues.

SYNAGOGUE (*SHUL*)—*SHABBAT* AFTERNOON-EVENING (*MINCHAH-MAARIV*)

People tend to lead their lives in mountain-valley patterns. We work hard to achieve our goals. When the goal is achieved—when it is all over—we often experience a letdown, a drop in energy and excitement.

If we are not careful, *Shabbat* could become just that—an achievement that ends, followed by a "fall."

As we enter *shul* for the final time, or as we pick up our *siddur* at home, we are making a physical and spiritual statement that, yes, this ultimate experience known as *Shabbat* is not an end, but a beginning.

In *shul*, there is a Torah reading. The first part of next week's Torah portion is read, a sample of what will be read in full next *Shabbat* morning.

Yes, even before this *Shabbat* is over, we begin preparing for the next.

Maariv—the Evening Service—begins when *Shabbat* ends. Thus we begin the week with prayer, asking God for wisdom, light, health, understanding . . . all that is important in life.

We have made it. We are not sinking. *Shabbat* may be over, but it is a new day and we are bringing the understanding and growth from *Shabbat* right into it, and already we are preparing for the *Shabbat* to come.

The week in between is not a time to forget, just a time to pause. We fill it with the knowledge and strength we have gained from *Shabbat* and use it to lead to the next *Shabbat* that will be that much greater; that much more an opportunity for the realization of personal potential.

---

*As we enter **shul** for the final time, or as we pick up our **siddur** at home, we are making a physical and spiritual statement that, yes, this ultimate experience known as **Shabbat** is not an end, but a beginning.*

How To

1. *Shul* on *Shabbat* afternoon consists of *Minchah* (the Afternoon Service) and *Maariv* (the Evening Service). It usually begins approximately a half hour before sunset. There is a break between services for a light meal (see page 82), and/or some learning (in the form of a short talk or private study).

2. There is a special section added to the Evening Service ("May the pleasantness . . .") toward the end, before *Aleinu*. This is said with the specific intention of instilling the holiness of *Shabbat* into the rest of the week.

CHAPTER FOUR

Shabbat Comes to a Close

HAVDALAH

Rabbi Simeon ben Lakish said: "On the eve of the Sabbath, the Holy One, Blessed be He, gives everyone an additional soul, and at the termination of **Shabbat**, withdraws it from him."

Talmud Bavli

The word *Havdalah* means to differentiate, to distinguish. The entire ceremony is to distinguish between the *Shabbat* that we have just experienced and the week that we are about to enter, both as an existence in time and as a feeling of existence.

Three blessings are said:

First on the wine, again a symbol of joy. Now we take pleasure in what we have accomplished, and hope that it will continue to grow into the week.

Then on the spices, whose fragrance we inhale to comfort our soul at the loss of *Shabbat*.

And finally on the flame, which symbolizes light and darkness and the ability to see the difference in a very deep way.

The greatest tool we have for appreciating anything is the ability to distinguish and differentiate. When we see things as rare and unique, they stand out as special, and somehow have their own place in the world.

Yet, all too often, we have a hard time utilizing this tool and seeing things for their own uniqueness. Masses of people just become ordinary beings. Beautiful sunsets start to look all the same.

Our challenge is to discern and see the minute differences that exist in the world in order to appreciate their rare and unique qualities and thus take pleasure in their existence.

It takes effort to refine this ability.

In the *Havdalah* ceremony, we set a braided candle aflame and hold up our fingers to see the light and shadows dancing upon them. This light and darkness symbolizes wisdom and confusion, and we hold our hands before the flame in order to see the difference.

When we contrast understanding with the tragedy of confusion, we differentiate and gain a deep appreciation for wisdom.

Shabbat is over. We mark the ending with *Havdalah* and recognize the beginning of a week. But we also mark the difference in how we will live the week.

Shabbat is a rare and unique gift. Appreciating its beauty and understanding the depths of its wonder sometimes means seeing it in contrast to the rest of the week.

And *Shabbat* is a different plane. When it ends, it is not just that the clock has ticked away, it is that the level that we have enjoyed has also come to an end. For the week is not *Shabbat*. If we have used the *Shabbat* properly however, we may be able to infuse some of it into our week.

The custom of lighting two additional candles, after the ceremony with the *Havdalah* flame, is just one way we can try and stretch out that light that we have gained just a little bit longer.

How To

What You'll Need:

- braided candle (or two candles held with flames together)
- cup of wine or grape juice
- spices (cloves work well)
- piece of foil to drip candle on and extinguish flame in

1. *Shabbat* ends when three medium-sized stars are visible in one glance in the evening sky. This time varies according to location and season.

In North America for a quick way to calculate when *Shabbat* is over, just add 1 hour and 10 minutes to candle-lighting time. (For example, Friday night candlelighting was 5:14 P.M., *Shabbat* ends approximately 6:24 P.M., Saturday night.) Many Jewish calendars list when *Shabbat* is over.

2. During the evening service, there is a special insertion in the *Shemoneh Esrei* (Silent *Amidah*) that acts as a preliminary *Havdalah*. A person who recites this paragraph should still come home and perform the *Havdalah* ceremony over wine.

However, if *Shabbat* is officially over, yet *Havdalah* has yet to be done (either in *davening* or over wine), one can recite the following words and then begin to do "post *Shabbat*" activities (using hot water, and the like):

Baruch ha-mavdil bein kodesh le-chol.

Blessed is the one Who divides between the sacred and the secular.

3. One should not eat or drink until the *Havdalah* ceremony is complete. This ceremony is made up of five sections: an introductory paragraph; the blessing over the wine, spices, and light; and the concluding paragraph. The procedure is as follows:

Fill a *kiddush* cup with either wine, grape juice, or beer until the liquid overflows the top onto the plate below. This is symbolic of our desire for blessings to overflow into the week.

Light the *Havdalah* candle (a braided candle with at least two wicks, or two candles held with their flames together). Someone other than the person making the blessings should hold the candle. If alone, place candle in a holder.

Fill a **kiddush** *cup with either wine, grape juice, or beer until the liquid overflows the top onto the plate below. This is symbolic of our desire for blessings to overflow into the week.*

90

Anyone included in the blessings for *Havdalah* should either sit or stand (as does the person leading) and should not speak until the ceremony is completed.

Holding the wine cup in the palm of the right hand (or left for "lefties"), the first paragraph is said:

Havdalah

*Hineih Eil yeshuati, evtach
ve-lo efchad, ki ozi
ve-zimrat Yah Adonai, va-yehi li
lishuah. Ushe'avtem mayim
be-sason mi-ma'ainei ha-yeshuah.
Ladonai ha-yeshuah, al amcha
birchatecha selah. Adonai tzeva'ot
imanu, misgav lanu Elohei
Ya'akov selah. Adonai tzeva'ot,
ashret adam botei'ach bach, Adonai
hoshiah, ha-melech ya'aneinu
ve-yom kareinu. La-yehudim
haytah orah ve-simchah,
ve-sason vikar. Kein tihyeh
lanu. Kos yeshuot esa,
uve-sheim Adonai ekra.*

הִנֵּה אֵל יְשׁוּעָתִי, אֶבְטַח
וְלֹא אֶפְחָד, כִּי עָזִּי
וְזִמְרָת יָהּ יְיָ, וַיְהִי לִי
לִישׁוּעָה. וּשְׁאַבְתֶּם מַיִם
בְּשָׂשׂוֹן מִמַּעַיְנֵי הַיְשׁוּעָה.
לַיְיָ הַיְשׁוּעָה, עַל עַמְּךָ
בִרְכָתֶךָ סֶּלָה. יְיָ צְבָאוֹת
עִמָּנוּ, מִשְׂגָּב לָנוּ אֱלֹהֵי
יַעֲקֹב סֶלָה. יְיָ צְבָאוֹת,
אַשְׁרֵי אָדָם בֹּטֵחַ בָּךְ, יְיָ,
הוֹשִׁיעָה, הַמֶּלֶךְ יַעֲנֵנוּ
בְיוֹם קָרְאֵנוּ. לַיְּהוּדִים
הָיְתָה אוֹרָה וְשִׂמְחָה,
וְשָׂשׂוֹן וִיקָר. כֵּן תִּהְיֶה
לָנוּ. כּוֹס יְשׁוּעוֹת אֶשָּׂא,
וּבְשֵׁם יְיָ אֶקְרָא.

Behold God is my salvation, I will trust and not be afraid. Indeed, the Lord is my strength and my song and He has become my salvation. You shall draw water with joy from the wells of salvation. Salvation belongs to the Lord; may Your blessings be upon Your people, Selah. The Lord of Hosts is with us, the God of Jacob is a refuge for us, Selah. Lord of Hosts, happy is the man who trusts in You. Lord, save us; may the King answer us on the day we call. "The Jews had radiance and happiness, joy and honor"—so may it be for us. I will lift up the cup of salvation and call upon the name of the Lord.

(Continue with the blessing over the wine.)

Savri maranan ve-rabanan ve-rabotai: :סָבְרִי מָרָנָן וְרַבָּנָן וְרַבּוֹתַי

For the wine:

*Baruch atah Adonai,
Eloheinu melech ha-olam,
borei peri ha-gafen.*

בָּרוּךְ אַתָּה יְיָ,
אֱלֹהֵינוּ מֶלֶךְ הָעוֹלָם,
בּוֹרֵא פְּרִי הַגָּפֶן.

(Those present respond, "Amen.")

You are blessed, Lord our God, the sovereign of the world, creator of the fruit of the vine.

DO NOT DRINK THE WINE YET . . .

"The Jews had radiance and happiness, joy and honor"— so may it be for us.

You are blessed, Lord our God, the sovereign of the world, who makes a distinction between sacred and secular, between light and darkness, between Israel and the other nations, between the seventh day and the six working days.

The cup is then passed to the left hand. The spice box (usually cloves or sweet pepper, not cinnamon since it is edible in spice form) is picked up with the right hand and the following blessing is recited:

For the spices:

Baruch atah Adonai,	בָּרוּךְ אַתָּה יְיָ,
Eloheinu melech ha-olam,	אֱלֹהֵינוּ מֶלֶךְ הָעוֹלָם,
borei minei vesamim.	בּוֹרֵא מִינֵי בְשָׂמִים.

("Amen")

You are blessed Lord our God, the sovereign of the world, creator of various kinds of spices.

The leader then smells the spices and passes them around for all to do the same.

With the wine cup still in the left hand, the blessing over the fire (candle flame) is said:

For the flames:

Baruch atah Adonai,	בָּרוּךְ אַתָּה יְיָ,
Eloheinu melech ha-olam,	אֱלֹהֵינוּ מֶלֶךְ הָעוֹלָם,
borei me'orei ha-eish.	בּוֹרֵא מְאוֹרֵי הָאֵשׁ.

("Amen")

You are blessed, Lord our God, the sovereign of the world, creator of the lights of fire.

Everyone should now extend their arms toward the flame to create shadows and light on their hands (to take advantage of the light of the candle).

The cup of wine is now passed back to the right hand for the concluding blessing:

Baruch atah Adonai,	בָּרוּךְ אַתָּה יְיָ,
Eloheinu melech ha-olam,	אֱלֹהֵינוּ מֶלֶךְ הָעוֹלָם,
ha-mavdil bein kodesh le-chol,	הַמַּבְדִּיל בֵּין קֹדֶשׁ לְחֹל,
bein or le-choshech, bein	בֵּין אוֹר לְחשֶׁךְ, בֵּין
Yisrael la-amin, bein	יִשְׂרָאֵל לָעַמִּים, בֵּין
yom ha-shevii le-sheishet	יוֹם הַשְּׁבִיעִי לְשֵׁשֶׁת
yemei ha-ma'aseh.	יְמֵי הַמַּעֲשֶׂה.
Baruch atah Adonai,	בָּרוּךְ אַתָּה יְיָ,
ha-mavdil bein kodesh le-chol.	הַמַּבְדִּיל בֵּין קֹדֶשׁ לְחֹל.

("Amen")

You are blessed, Lord our God, the sovereign of the world, who makes a distinction between sacred and secular, between light and darkness, between Israel and the other nations, between the seventh day and the six working days.

You are blessed, Lord, who makes a distinction between the sacred and the secular.

The leader, if standing, is then seated, to drink at least 2 ounces of the liquid.

The balance of the wine is used to extinguish the flame. Try pouring some into a dish and immersing the flame until the fire is out. However, some have the custom, before extinguishing, to light two new candles (or more), so that the "light" of *Shabbat* continues into the week.

Unlike *kiddush*, the cup is not passed around for others to drink.

Question and Answers

Why Do We Use a Candle with More Than One Flame?

It says that as *Shabbat* enters, each one of us is given an extra soul. In Judaism, candles represent soul; that is why we light a *yartzeit* candle to remember someone who has passed away.

When *Shabbat* comes in, we light a simple candle; yet, when *Shabbat* is leaving, we light a larger flame of intertwined lights, for now we have had the experience of living with an additional soul and living the opportunity that that soul provides.

Reflections

I was spending *Shabbat* in Safed in the northern part of Israel with a girl friend. We were both going to the same school for women in Jerusalem, but needed a getaway, and so we chose this quasi-mystical *Shabbaton* as our *Shabbat* adventure.

We met two girls there who were studying to be rabbis at a very nontraditional school in Jerusalem. Our school? Well, let's just say that our curriculums probably had very little in common.

Anyway, despite our philosophical differences, we all became fast friends during *Shabbat*. When *Shabbat* was over, we had just a few minutes to catch the only bus to Haifa where we could get a connection to Jerusalem, so there was no time to linger and make *Havdalah*.

But, as Egged bus has been known to do, there were some traveling delays, so by the time we arrived in Haifa, it was 11:30 at night, and there were no connecting buses to Jerusalem.

All four of us were traveling together, and the consensus was to grab a bus to Tel Aviv and from there get to Jerusalem. So we did.

By now we were getting kind of hungry, and though we had

In Judaism, candles represent soul; that is why we light a yartzeit candle to remember someone who has passed away.

To our dismay, we had missed the last bus to Jerusalem.

brought snacks along, you are not allowed to eat until you hear the *Havdalah* ceremony. I guess it keeps you from jumping back into your week without a properly honored separation from *Shabbat*.

Our two colleagues were not as traditionally observant as we were, but refrained from eating, as they knew the *halachah*—law—just as we did.

O.K., so now we're four young single girls getting off the bus in Tel Aviv very late at night. If you don't know, I must tell you that this is not exactly the nicest neighborhood to be in, day *or* night. And this was 1:00 A.M. We stuck close together.

To our dismay, we had missed the last bus to Jerusalem. By now we were all definitely in the realm of hunger, so first things first—let's make *Havdalah*!

My friend from school led the way, and we all followed her into this sleazy-looking shish kabob/falafel place filled with men drinking and speaking in quick, loud spurts, punctuated by bursts of laughter. Feel the mood? Believe me, we did.

My friend walked confidently up to the counter and announced to the owner of the "establishment" that we wanted to make *Havdalah*.

If I hadn't been there I wouldn't have believed what happened next. The guy lit up, got so excited, and announced to everyone there that we were about to make *Havdalah*! Men, who, believe me, looked far from religious, left their cards and cigarettes and came over to the counter.

Without missing a beat, my friend ordered an Israeli fruit juice (as you can make *Havdalah* over a social drink, not just wine or grape juice), borrowed some matches from someone in the crowd, and asked the owner if he had some sort of spice for the *besamim* part of the ceremony.

He came up with some chicken soup powder,[1] and we figured it was close enough.

Two matches were struck and held together in place of a braided candle, my friend made the *brachah* over the fruit juice, and the chicken soup powder was passed around for all to smell.

(Please note that the two rabbinical students were standing back with their mouths open, utterly shocked at what they were seeing.)

She said all the *brachot*, drank down the juice, and when the fire was extinguished, everyone in the place clapped.

We thanked them, waved good-bye, and grabbed a taxi to Jerusalem.

On route, we broke open our snacks and laughed about our *Havdalah* adventure. But I was struck with something much deeper, as my original negative assessment of the Israelis we encountered turned to one of appreciation that every Jew, religious or secular, has a spark of something inside.

We were attending an out-of-town wedding and stayed in a hotel over *Shabbat*. It went pretty smooth until the end when we made *Havdalah*.

---

[1] Not proper to do, but still a great story.

We lit the big, braided *Havdalah* candle that we had brought along and held it up. Halfway through the *brachahs* we heard the hotel fire alarm go off and a lot of commotion outside. We looked up to see that the candle was creating a lot of smoke and realized that must be what set off the alarm!

Quickly we extinguished the flame and went out into the hall to see people running this way and that. We were so unbelievably embarrassed that we just pretended not to know where the fire was, like everyone else.

Eventually the alarm stopped and everyone went back to their rooms. We finished *Havdalah* using two matches for a tiny, tiny, TINY flame.

To be honest, sometimes *Havdalah* is a very spiritual time, and sometimes it's just a relief because *Shabbat* is over and I can get the kids to sleep, take a hot shower, and *shmooze* on the phone to my sister in the States.

My three little girls love *Havdalah*. When I get home from *shul* they're all waiting around the table with my wife, and I can see the fight over who will hold the candle has already been won by someone.

We have our own little *Havdalah* custom that I started when my wife was pregnant with our first. When it comes time to smell the spices, I hold the container of cloves for my wife to smell, and then for her tummy.

Now when we do it there are lots of giggles from the ones who used to be inside but are now looking up to me all wide-eyed and real, anticipating the next baby brother or sister to join our family one day.

We always try to lower the lights during *Havdalah* so that the flame glows over all of us. It's so beautiful as our daughter holds the candle so carefully, watching it drip on a sheet of newspaper. My husband recites the *brachahs*, and we smell the sweet cloves.

Such a bittersweet moment. *Shabbat* is leaving, so it's kind of sad, but the week of events beckons with excitement.

Yes, I love *Havdalah*, from the first strike of the match, so forbidden to do over *Shabbat*, to the sizzle of the candle, as it's extinguished into the last of the wine.

We always end with *Shavua Tov*—"a good week"—and then sing "*Eliyahu*" slowly and quietly. Before long, everyone is in jammies and in bed, the dishes are done, and the lights are out.

What will I do until NEXT *Shabbat* . . .?

*Throughout the Jewish world we sing of Eliyahu HaNavi at the close of the Sabbath, since he is the harbinger who will precede the Messiah. We have been promised that Eliyahu will not come on the eve of a Sabbath or holiday because people are so preoccupied . . . rather, this bearer of good tidings will come to us after a **Shabbat**, since in the merit of **Shabbat**, the Lord will send our Redeemer.*
Sefer Ha-Manhig

MELAVEH MALKAH

Rabbi Elimelech of Lizensk advised women especially to partake of **Melaveh Malkah,** *saying out loud that they are eating in order to fulfill the mitzvah of* **Melaveh Malkah.** *This is deemed conducive to easy childbirth.*

Or Ha-Shabbat

There is a custom in the Jewish world that when someone finishes a complete section of Talmud study, a party, called a *siyyum,* is held.

In the secular world, if an insurance salesman surpasses the million-dollar mark, a party of honor is also held.

Why this need to have parties? Aren't the accomplishments of study, material wealth, and the like, suitable pleasures in themselves?

It seems not, for this custom of celebration is too prevalent to ignore. We see it all the time, at the end of the game that was clinched or the election that was won.

The party celebrates the reality of what has been accomplished and inspires one to accomplish again.

Melaveh Malkah means "the Escorting of the Queen," the *Shabbat* "Queen." She entered Friday night in all her glory, and now we usher her out in similar regal fashion.

We have a party.

I suppose you can call it the *Shabbat* "Awards Banquet," for its existence says that, hey, we've accomplished something here. It was incredible.

And we want to do it again.

How To

1. Prepare the *Shabbat* table as it was when *Shabbat* came in, with a nice tablecloth and fine dishes.

2. Light new *Shabbat* candles (see *Havdalah* for custom of lighting them at the end of the *Havdalah* ceremony).

3. Many have a *Shabbat*-like meal, albeit with leftovers, though it is said that it is praiseworthy to have a special dish for this meal too.

4. Music is played (sometimes with live instruments), songs are sung, and the soul is comforted by this joyful way of saying good-bye to *Shabbat.*

Reflections

The Lord said to Israel: If you succeed in observing the Sabbath, I will consider it as though you have kept all the commandments of the Torah.

Midrash Rabbah

In the winter, when *Shabbat* ends early, there's time to really do something social Saturday night, so a group of us started a "*Melaveh Malkah* Club." There are about twelve couples involved, and we pair up to put on a *Melaveh Malkah* every three weeks. So you have two couples sharing the responsibility of picking a theme (Italian, Israeli, and so forth) and assigning the food.

Every couple brings a homemade dish in keeping with the theme. For example, if it's Italian, then people can make pizza, spaghetti sauces, garlic bread and the like. With everyone pitching in, it's easy, delicious, and a lot of fun.

The family hosting it in their home that week is responsible for a short *devar Torah* (a "word" of Torah), and providing the paper goods— plates, cups . . . .

It's something we all look forward to, and it makes the long winters in Canada a heck of a lot more fun.

―――――――

My husband is a teacher and works most evenings during the week. What with caring for the kids and our work, it's hard to find time to just be together. That's why we made *Motza'ei Shabbat* (the end of *Shabbat*) our "date" night.

We have a babysitter booked every Saturday night who watches the kids and does my *Shabbat* dishes! We get dressed up and go out for dessert and coffee at a nice restaurant and just . . . talk. I love it.

―――――――

What do we do Saturday night? Walk. I know it sounds weird, but the most enjoyable time we spend together as husband and wife is after *Shabbat*. After I clean up and my husband tucks the kids in bed, our neighbor's teenage daughter comes over for an hour or so we head out for a delicious, leisurely walk. It's just around the neighborhood, but it's our time.

We have a babysitter booked every Saturday night who watches the kids and does my Shabbat dishes! We get dressed up and go out for dessert and coffee at a nice restaurant and just . . . talk.

―――――――

My children have taken it upon themselves to make *Melaveh Malkah* an integral part of our *Shabbat* experience. That means every Saturday night in the winter we all go ice skating, pick up a pizza and a tub of ice cream, go home and party. It's really a terrific night—bedtimes are unofficially suspended (except for the littlest ones), while we all indulge in good family fun.

It's a real treat, even for us. Because *Shabbat* is so home-based, it's nice to get out afterwards and do something a little different and physical.

―――――――

Our *Melaveh Malkah* goes like this: My wife and I clean up the dishes and tidy up after *Shabbat* while simultaneously putting our three year old and our baby to bed. Once done, my wife walks out to the corner store, buys some chocolate bars, diet Cokes, a newspaper, and a *Time* magazine, and comes home.

In the meantime, I've made some microwave popcorn; so all that's left is pouring the Cokes into large glasses with ice, moving into the living room, and cozying up for an evening of reading and munchies.

In the winter we sometimes substitute hot chocolate for diet Cokes, but it's basically the same routine. Nice and quiet.

———

I learned that even though our souls love *Shabbat*, our bodies sometimes feel as if they did without. So *Melaveh Malkah* is to make up to the body any feeling of loss it may have experienced over the past 24 hours.

One of my teachers said a hot shower could be someone's *Melaveh Malkah*, if that's what they missed, or a hot snack.

Mine is cheese melts. I take crackers and melt cheese on them in the toaster oven . . . yummmmm!

———

When I was first keeping *Shabbat*, I couldn't wait for it to be over so I could run out on Saturday night with my friends. I used to count the minutes.

But now I don't have that same desire to go downtown, or to a party. For me, it's just a leisurely cleanup and maybe a pizza after *Shabbat* is out. I don't feel as if I'm missing out, because now I see that I have so much more.

———

The secret's out—we just got rid of our TV. What does that have to do with *Melaveh Malkah*? Well, it used to be that Saturday night was movie or TV night, but my wife and I made a decision to chuck the TV because it really was a poor influence on our kids.

So instead of a passive *Melaveh Malkah* in front of the tube, my wife and I talk for two hours, just the two of us! It is great, and we both know it is because of the "no television" decision.

Some of our friends think it's strange, but we're going to hold to it . . . for now, anyway.

CHAPTER FIVE

What They Say about *Shabbat*

THE BEST THING ABOUT *SHABBAT*

Here is what some people said when I asked, "What is the best thing about *Shabbat*?"

• It's so much less distracting, so you can focus on what you really want to do.

• The nights . . . they are so contemplative.

• Coming home Friday night, seeing the candles burning, singing *Shalom Aleichem*, and giving the blessings to my children. It's so beautiful.

• The relaxation. As soon as *Shabbat* comes in, I relax. I don't keep the whole *Shabbat*, but that feeling Friday night really gives me a taste of what rest is really all about.

• Family. Friday night is the one night that we are all together, and the meal is so special because we all take our time eating!

• The feeling you get after lighting candles: Whew! I made it! Now it's time for 24 hours of peace—24 hours where I'm the queen, ready to enjoy what I've worked for. You know, I don't even remember that I cooked the food!

• We get to see so much of each other. There are no meetings, no phones, no appointments. Just us.

• The nap . . . not the physical sleeping, but the idea of what it represents—I don't have to go anywhere!

• Sitting around the table and discussing things for hours, interrupted only by the singing.

• It's a holiday!

• It subtracts you from the rest of the world for one day, and gives you enough energy for at least three.

• *Shabbat* carries the week; the week does not carry *Shabbat*.

• I feel so much closer to community; there's a real "togetherness" about it.

• I really feel I'm in another world on *Shabbat*. It makes me feel separate, in a very positive way, from everyday life—not an escape in the running-away sense, just, well . . . an oasis.

• It's the focus of my life that leaves me completely charged.

> *All the days of the week draw sustenance from* **Shabbat**; **Shabbat** *is the day on which the wheel of the six weekdays turns. It is a kind of root for the other days and will shed some of its sanctity on every day. . . . Some of the influence of* **Shabbat** *is present in each and every weekday.*
> Reishit Chochmah

• Friday night. It's the time I feel most protected.

• When *Shabbat* comes in, I feel a qualitative difference—an opening to something much more spiritual.

• Walking. We take long, long walks on *Shabbat*. It gives me a feeling of control over my environment and an appreciation of our own physical resources.

• You can eat and sleep . . . and it's a *mitzvah*!

THE MOST CHALLENGING THING ABOUT *SHABBAT* AT FIRST

I asked the same group, "What is the most challenging part of *Shabbat*?" Many gave two different answers; one was the challenge they felt when they were first beginning.

• Keeping *Shabbat* at home with your parents who don't keep *Shabbat*.

• Trying to separate the business week and the *Shabbat*. I had to sit down on Friday night and really concentrate on leaving the work behind.

• Using your time wisely. There is so much more uninterrupted time on *Shabbat*; no phones; no shopping. It was hard to use it in a meaningful way so it's not wasted.

• The *davening*. It's so long, especially *Shabbat* morning.

• Going to other people's homes every *Shabbat* and having to observe it the way they did it.

• *Gefilte* fish. For a Sephardi girl, it's a real adjustment.

• Friday nights. I used to always go out to a movie with the guys, or a party. So having a *Shabbat* dinner at home was a real adjustment at first.

• Those long *Shabbat* afternoons. I didn't know what to do with myself.

• *Shabbat* afternoon naps. I hadn't napped since before kindergarten!

• All that food!

• Learning to slow down.

• The lack of people to keep it with. You really need a core group for camaraderie.

• It was hard meeting people I didn't know at *shul*, at people's homes. Yet, later, these people became my closest friends.

• Not turning on the TV to entertain my kids.

• Not smoking! Yikes!

When Shabbat comes in, I feel a qualitative difference— an opening to something much more spiritual.

102

THE MOST CHALLENGING THING ABOUT *SHABBAT* NOW

What is the true spirit of **Shabbat?** *How can I be a witness to this taste of Creation?*

And some reflected on the challenges they still face:

• Learning all of the laws of *Shabbat*. The basics you can pick up pretty quick, but the rest is kind of hard.

• Trying to make it meaningful and fun for my kids, my guests, and myself, all at the same time.

• Keeping focused on what *Shabbat* is all about. I have to think beyond the nice clothes, the guests, and the food and ask myself: What is the true spirit of *Shabbat*? How can I be a witness to this taste of Creation?

• Keeping going; progressing. I know logically I should be consistently observing every *Shabbat*, but it's hard to make the final commitment.

• Trying to convince others about how great *Shabbat* is!

• Too much *davening* . . . but I do it!

• Using it to really elevate me.

• Bringing it in on time, with *everything* prepared: food, house, me, and so forth.

• Infusing it with spirituality.

• Not being able to smoke and trying to be nice about it.

CHAPTER SIX

Shabbat-on-the-Go

I t's bound to happen. There are going to be times when *Shabbat* must be spent by choice, or not by choice, away from your home environment. Examples include

- Hospital stay

- Hotel

- Camping

- Cottage

- Family or friends

- Traveling abroad

These can be opportunities to explore *Shabbat* creatively, but they can also be fraught with a certain amount of concern and challenge. When you've managed to pull it off and keep *Shabbat* under these circumstances, you feel as if you've really accomplished something! The whole thing can be a big adventure and a refreshing change of pace, as long as everyone has a positive attitude and a certain amount of preparation is done ahead. Some do's, don't's and helpful hints follow.

THINGS YOU'LL NEED WHEN GOING AWAY FOR *SHABBAT*

1. Candles—Even if you light several at home, the custom when away is to light two. There are special traveling candlesticks that compactly screw together (can be purchased at most Jewish book and gift stores), or just melt the candles on some foil. Don't forget the matches! (See Hospital Stay for lighting alternatives.)

2. Small bottle of wine or grape juice—Grape juice can also be found in "*tetra*" packs" that need no refrigeration—great for camping or traveling abroad.

3. *Kiddush* cup—It's nice to have a special cup, but in a pinch, any cup will do as long as it's not something disposable. (See page 24 for size requirements.)

4. *Challahs*—Remember, you can use buns, bagels, *matzot*, and the like (two whole "loaves" times three meals equals six "loaves"—maximum! You can get by with four, using one as the rotating "second loaf" at each meal).

5. *Challah* cover—It's nice to have something appropriate like a real cover, but a nice doily or napkin is just as good. In a pinch, use a paper napkin, tissue, and so forth.

6. *Salt*—To dip the *challah* in after *Ha-motzi*. Use little packets supplied in restaurants.

7. Knife to cut the bread—Or just tear it!

8. Hot plate or one-burner stove—To keep the food warm (may not be allowed in hotels). Bring extra foil paper to fashion a small *blech* (see page 147). It's nice to have hot food, but one "cold" *Shabbat* never hurt anyone. Try having something hot Friday night (heating it up, then turning the source of heat off just before candlelighting); and a cold meal *Shabbat* day—cold cuts, or dairy.

9. Vacuum-packed food—Most *kosher* restaurants can supply this upon request.

10. Facial Tissues—(See page 156).

11. A "curly scrubber"—For washing dishes.

12. Appropriate reading material—It's nice to have something in the spirit of *Shabbat*, especially since being in a strange environment can distract you from the feeling that this is *Shabbat*.

13. *Havdalah* candle—Or simply use two regular candles held together.

14. Plastic cutlery.

15. Masking tape—To tape lights on or off.

16. "Zipper" baggies—For leftovers (get the kind that are not attached, since you may not tear the perforations and separate them on *Shabbat*) (see page 156).

17. Thermos—To hold hot water (a pump type keeps water hot throughout *Shabbat*).

18. Small packages of powdered nondairy creamer—Open them before *Shabbat* to avoid tearing letters (see page 157).

19. Paper napkins or pretorn paper towels—For easy cleanups.

THINGS TO REMEMBER WHEN OUT-OF-TOWN

1. Check with a local rabbi or Kashrut Council regarding reliable regional kosher symbols you have to watch for on food packages (for example, CRC in Chicago, COR in Toronto).

2. There is usually a network of families who keep *Shabbat* in every town. Contact the local Jewish organizations to plug into it if you need home hospitality or just have questions. (See list of international contacts, page 171.)

HOSPITAL STAY

These are the general rules for observing *Shabbat* in a hospital. However, in case of a *life or death* situation, the laws of *Shabbat* are, of course, put aside.

1. Most hospitals will not let you light candles in your room. Some who have a large Jewish clientele will provide candlesticks that light up when you plug them in. This is perfectly acceptable, just say the blessing after you "light" them, as usual.

     If there is no such service, use an electric light. Just turn it on and say the blessing. Your nurse can shut it off for you before you retire.[1]

2. It is a good idea to let hospital staff know that you are observing the Jewish "Sabbath." Either they will be aware from past experience what to expect or they will be fascinated and be open to your explaining what it all means (we hope!).

3. Choose your food menus ahead of time (*kosher* is almost always available).

     Ask for extra rolls with your meals for *Ha-motzi* and have on hand (if you planned ahead) grape juice for *kiddush* (otherwise ask a friend or family member to bring you some before *Shabbat*).

4. Let your roommate know about the "sabbath" and that you will not be answering the phone until Saturday night. Be as light about it as possible, so as not to scare anyone. Again, experience shows that people are more than respectful.

> *It is a good idea to let hospital staff know that you are observing the Jewish "Sabbath."*

5. Anything that requires your signature, unless it is a life-or-death situation, can almost always be done before *Shabbat* or postponed until afterwards. Do not be afraid to be assertive when you are given "these are the rules" objections.

6. Make sure you have reading material to pass the day away, as TV and radio might be missed if you are confined to bed.

     A Jewish book, especially something on *Shabbat*, will help you focus on the fact that this is *really Shabbat*. Don't forget a *bentcher* with all of the blessings for *kiddush*, and so forth (see page 148).

7. Ask your roommate if it is all right to keep the bathroom light on during the "sabbath" as you would like to refrain from turning lights on and off, and so forth.

8. Make sure tissues are on hand in the bathroom (see page 156).

9. If you have had a baby or have had surgery within the last 72 hours, you are considered in the category of a "critically ill" patient and thus are

---

[1]If you have had a baby or have had surgery in the past 72 hours, you can ask the nurse to do it directly. If not, you can ask indirectly—for example, "It's hard for me to sleep with the light on." They usually catch on.

allowed to do *melachah*, (non-Shabbat activities such as turning on lights) *if* necessary in order to fully care for yourself medically. If at any time from 72 hours until 7 days after birth a doctor or patient feels a definite need for medical care, then the patient remains in the critically ill category.

10. Let the nurse know that you will not be able to buzz for her assistance unless it is an emergency. They are usually very agreeable to dropping by periodically to check to see if you need anything.

11. In any case of danger of life, you can do *anything*—drive, phone, buzz a nurse—*anything*!

12. Ask questions of your rabbi ahead of time, and speak to your doctor regarding your desire to observe *Shabbat* while in the hospital.

13. If your husband or wife lives out of walking distance, find out through your rabbi or local Jewish organization if a *Bikkur Cholim*[2] apartment is available near the hospital. These are apartments equipped with food and *Shabbat* items (candlesticks, and so forth) that are made available for situations such as these.

   If there is no such service, find out if there are *shomer Shabbat*[3] families living within walking distance with whom your spouse can stay. People are usually more than happy to open their homes to guests.

HOTEL

Hotel stays present some unique challenges:

1. Beware of hotels that use electric "pass keys" to open room doors. These are prohibited on *Shabbat*, as they function through electrical connections. Choose a place with good old-fashioned keys.

2. Many doorways in and out of the hotel, as well as within the hotel, open and close electrically (for example, automatic sliding glass doors). Avoid these, as they are also prohibited on *Shabbat*.

3. When booking, request a room on a *low* floor so that the elevator can be avoided.

4. Do any signing ahead of time (when registering, and the like).

5. Escalators may be used as they run automatically.[4] Elevators and electric doors require you to start and stop them, and thus are to be avoided on *Shabbat*.

---

[2]Literally, "Visiting the Sick"—These are local support groups that make sure people who are ill, or recovering from childbirth, receive food, help, and so on.
[3]Those who observe *Shabbat*.
[4]"Many very reliable authorities say that this is permitted," according to Rabbi Yaakov Weinberg, Dean, Ner Israel, Baltimore.

6. Inform the front desk that you will be observing the Jewish Sabbath. Ask them to take all phone messages and not to call your room for wake-ups, and so forth.

VISITING FAMILY OR FRIENDS

Here are a few helpful hints to make your visit even more pleasurable:

1. You may want to bring your own personal *siddur* (prayer book) for *davening* (prayer).

2. Inform your hosts of any dietary requirements important to you or members of your family (allergies, vegetarianism, and so forth) ahead of time.

3. Bring a gift—flowers, a bottle of wine, small gifts for the kids that can be played with on *Shabbat*, and the like.

4. Bring a traveling clock for your room.

WHEN YOUR HOSTS DO NOT OBSERVE *SHABBAT*

This is always a challenge. But, it is bound to happen, so let's approach it the best way we know how.

1. Try to avoid being in this situation (unless it is family).

2. If there is no alternative, decide to make it the most positive experience for you and your hosts (*especially* if it's family!)

3. Bring all the necessary *Shabbat* items with you (see list page 107).

4. Discuss unscrewing the light bulb ahead of time so that you can access the refrigerator (see page 156).

5. Try to involve those around you in *Shabbat* without imposing anything on them (a neat trick). Hints include making a nice Friday night meal with *kiddush*, and so forth. If people are open to it, help them wash for bread, and so on. *Don't* make anyone do anything that would make him or her feel negative or uncomfortable.

   Shabbat day, those around you may be watching TV, answering the phone, going shopping, and so on. *Don't* lecture them on the evils of breaking *Shabbat* (you wouldn't want anyone to do it to you). Just be positive in your own level of observance, and, chances are, they will notice, ask questions, and want to join you in certain things.

6. Let them know in advance that you appreciate their concern, but you would prefer if they don't do things for you such as turn on or off lights, make you a coffee, and so forth.

Bring a gift—flowers, a bottle of wine, small gifts for the kids that can be played with on Shabbat, *and the like.*

7. Make sure you have some Jewish reading material to help you remember that it is *Shabbat*.

8. Walk to a *shomer Shabbat* family on *Shabbat* day if it's not too far—either for a meal or just for a visit.

9. Go to *shul* if possible. Ask others to join you if you think they'd like it.

Remember—minimize the discomfort of your hosts while bringing the special spirit of *Shabbat* to their home. Countless people have done it with great success. After a few visits, you'll see a big difference in how they react and how much they would like to participate.

Shabbat *in the hospital? How would we do it?*

Reflections

It was our first baby, and it ended up being an emergency Caesarean, so my stay in the hospital was longer than we had expected. That meant I had to be there over *Shabbat*.

Shabbat in the hospital? How would we do it?

Well, we did, and it was great. First my mom (who doesn't observe *Shabbat*), came to visit me Friday afternoon and put some kosher food in the communal fridge located on my floor. I was worried about how I would get my food over *Shabbat* without turning the fridge's light on and off by opening and closing it. But my mom, who has—what I guess you would call—*chutzpah*, solved it. After she kissed me good-bye, she opened her coat and with a wink showed me the fridge bulb tucked neatly into her inner pocket.

"Good *Shabbos*!" she said, and then, in a whisper, "I'll put it back Saturday night." With that she turned and strolled confidently to the elevator.

My husband arranged to spend *Shabbat* at a home as near to the hospital as possible, which was still many miles away. Friday night wasn't a problem, because he drove to the hospital before sundown and left his car in the parking lot for the remainder of *Shabbat*.

Our Friday night meal was so special. My best friend had brought a scrumptious chicken dinner with homemade *challah*, fish, and soup . . . so much better than the frozen kosher dinners they were serving.

The best part of the evening was when it was time for the blessing of the children. It was the first time we were doing it! For years I had seen other people's children at the *Shabbat* tables getting their blessings, with their mother and father placing their hands on their heads.

But our baby wasn't with us because she was in an incubator in the nursery. She was quite jaundiced and had to be under the special lights.

After my husband sang *Eishet Chayil*, he excused himself and said he'd be back in a minute. A few minutes later he returned and told me

112

he had gone to the nursery and had placed his hands on the incubator and had given our little daughter her blessing.

I cried, picturing my husband doing this. I loved him so much at that moment, it's hard even to describe.

I once had a "*Shabbat*-on-the-Go," but it wasn't exactly by choice. My wife and I were on our way to a youth convention in Los Angeles, where I was supposed to entertain—I'm a singer.

It was Friday afternoon, and we were driving through the mountains, when, suddenly, there was an avalanche and the road right ahead was totally blocked!

Although we were only a 15-minute drive from our destination, without this road we were virtually stuck. Walking was out of the question, as we would never arrive in time. Turning back was our only option, yet there was very little to turn back to—just a valley with a small town, and beyond it more mountains.

The town was Ontario, California, and believe me, we were the first *Shabbat*-observing Jews they had seen in a while.

Quickly, we assessed the situation. While my wife checked us into a motel, I ran to the general store to try and buy some supplies. The closest thing I could find for *Shabbat* candles were those long, red, tapered Christmas candles. Kosher wine was out of the question, but I was able to buy some liquor so that I could make *kiddush* on the next day.

Now for *challah*—of course there was no *kosher* bread, but how about a box of *matzoh*? No way. Frantically I ran up and down the aisles, time running out. I grabbed the only *kosher* thing I could find—bread sticks. They would have to do.

Well, we lit our "*Shabbat*" candles on time and settled in for 26 hours of watermelon, vegetables . . . and lots and lots of breadsticks.

Ever since that *Shabbat*, whenever we travel, we carry not only a first-aid kit, but an emergency *Shabbat* kit—candles, canned food, and some bottled grape juice. We haven't been stranded like that since then, but if we ever are, we'll be prepared!

It was in the middle of the week of Passover when a sore on my lower back that had been hurting really began to feel painful. I was at work, and my friend said I'd better go see a doctor about it. It was Friday morning, and I figured I shouldn't put it off through *Shabbat*; better have it looked at now.

So I went to the doctor, and he said I'd better go to the hospital right away. I did, and they said it was a cyst that had to be removed immediately. They did the surgery with just a local anesthetic and said I could go home right away.

It was Friday afternoon, and we were driving through the mountains, when, suddenly, there was an avalanche and the road right ahead was totally blocked!

By now it was late in the afternoon and I was feeling kind of weak from it all, so I called my father to drive me home.

But what about *Shabbat*? My parents didn't observe *Shabbat*, and they didn't keep *kosher*, and on top of all that, it was Passover, so food was going to be a problem.

We thought we had left plenty of time for travel, but we forgot one thing: it was Friday of New Year's weekend. The traffic was unbelievable; it was midafternoon, and time was running out.

When I got home, I called the family that I had planned to go to for *Shabbat* and explained the situation. The wife insisted that if I had to stay home to recuperate, she was going to send me food for *Shabbat*. Quickly she dispatched her husband with a box full of food for me.

In the meantime, I was trying to figure out how to spend *Shabbat* at home, which I had never done because I didn't want to impose on my folks. But they were terrific. They asked me what they needed to do to help me keep *Shabbat*.

It really didn't take much doing. We decided which lights would stay on and which would remain off—they even let me unscrew the light in the fridge. My mom heated some food up for her and my dad, so she wouldn't have to cook after sundown. The only other question was the TV.

I knew I couldn't ask them not to watch it all *Shabbat*, so we compromised and set it on a favorite channel that would remain on until *Shabbat* was over.

O.K., so I watched TV on *Shabbat* . . . but no laws were broken. And I got to spend *Shabbat* with my parents, who were amazing and totally tried to accommodate me by keeping *Shabbat* with me.

Oh—and I almost forgot—about a half hour before candlelighting, I got a call from the woman whose home I was supposed to spend *Shabbat* at, and she said that her husband couldn't find my house, so he left the box of *kosher*-for-Passover-*Shabbat* food at a donut shop, which was about a half mile away! He was sorry, but he wouldn't have made it home in time if he had kept driving around.

My father was so nice about it and volunteered to drive over and pick up the food at the donut shop. He made it there and back in time for *Shabbat*.

Even though all of this setting lights, leaving on the TV, and frantically rushing to get the food on time must have seemed weird to them, they never let on that they thought it was anything but important and necessary.

A friend and I were on our way from Manhattan to New Jersey, where we planned to spend *Shabbat* with friends. Yes, just two girls ready for a *Shabbat* "out," but, as they say, "The best laid plans of mice and men . . ."

We thought we had left plenty of time for travel, but we forgot one thing: it was Friday of New Year's weekend. The traffic was unbelievable; it was midafternoon, and time was running out.

Somewhere in the Lincoln Tunnel we realized that we were not going to make it there on time. We were frantic. By the time we got to the toll booth we were almost crying, and told the policeman there our dilemma.

He calmed us down and said he would be glad to escort us to New Jersey on the shoulder of the freeway. So off we went with a police escort for *Shabbat*! Is that style, or what?

———

We had just gotten married in Toronto and were on our way to Scranton, where my parents lived. They, along with my new in-laws, had planned a gala *Sheva Berachot* (post-wedding party) for about a hundred people, which was to be held that night, Friday night.

Perhaps it was the excitement of getting married just days before, or maybe I wasn't cut out to be a navigator. What I'm trying to say is, we got lost. Somewhere along the way we went the wrong way on a freeway and didn't realize it . . . for a few hours.

When we drove into Hornell, New York—which isn't exactly near Scranton—we concluded that, yes, we were definitely lost; and, no, we were not going to make it to Scranton for *Shabbat*.

We quickly phoned my parents with the bad news, who by now were just happy to hear that we were O.K.—(the embarrassment of having the bride and groom absent for their own *Sheva Berachot* would certainly sink in later).

Then we had to get practical. We found a motel and a small grocery store where we purchased our honeymoon feast: two cans of kosher tuna, some vegetables, and a bag of pita bread.

It sounds like a real fiasco, but, after our parents forgave us (they had the *Sheva Berachot* anyway with their hundred guests), the whole thing seemed rather, well, romantic. In fact, we came very close to returning to that motel for our first anniversary.

———

My wife and I traveled to Rumania in the hope of adopting a baby. We came prepared for weeks of waiting, and that meant a few out-of-the-ordinary *Shabbats*.

There was little to no food in the country, so it was a good thing we had brought some along.

There was a Jewish community center in town that provided us with *challah*, if we were able to brave the Rumanian blizzard to get there to get it. One time they even provided some *matzoh*.

But there was more than one *Shabbat* when we had to make *Ha-motzi* on bagel chips or *matzoh* crackers from home.

It sounds like deprivation, but it was really an uplifting experience, for it drove home the idea that as a Jew, no matter where you are, the action and meaning is the same. *Ha-motzi* in Bucharest or *Ha-motzi* in New York . . . it's still *Shabbat*.

Perhaps it was the excitement of getting married just days before, or maybe I wasn't cut out to be a navigator. What I'm trying to say is, we got lost. Somewhere along the way we went the wrong way on a freeway and didn't realize it . . . for a few hours.

At one point we invited another North American Jewish couple who were also staying in the hotel waiting to adopt to join us for Friday night festivities.

They were blown away. They couldn't believe that we were celebrating *Shabbat* here . . . or anywhere for that matter.

After we washed and made *ha-motzi*, they started asking us a lot of questions as to the meaning and significance of everything.

It was as if we were able to pass the light on, even so far away. And it made me realize that the actions within Judaism *are* important, for the action itself perpetuates Judaism. It is a constant.

CHAPTER SEVEN

Recipes

CLASSIC MENUS

Friday Night Dinner

The classic *Shabbat* Friday night dinner goes something like this:

challah
fish (as a separate course)
soup
chicken
kugel
vegetable dish(es)
dessert

But, you have to make it your own. In other words, make the food that you like best, for *Shabbat* is supposed to be a pleasure, and if your pleasure is brown rice and stir-fried veggies with sautéed tofu, eat and enjoy.

Shabbat Day

The classic *Shabbat* lunch goes something like this:

challah
fish (as a separate course)
cholent
cold meat (chicken, beef, tongue . . .)
salads (pasta, green, veggie . . .)
dessert

Again, serve what you prefer. Many have the custom of serving *milchigs*—dairy—at lunch. Bagels, lox, cream cheese, salad, cold soup . . . great on a hot summer's day!

Seudah Shelishit

The classic Third Meal, *Shabbat* afternoon, goes something like this:

challah (rolls)
tuna fish
salmon salad
egg salad
leftover fish

Once the Emperor of Rome questioned Rabbi Yehoshua ben Chananiah, "Why does the Sabbath food smell so delicious?" "We have a special spice, called 'Shabbat' that we put into the dishes that makes them so appetizing," was Rabbi Yehoshua's reply.
Talmud Bavli

119

This is the lightest of the three meals and can be as simple as peanut butter and jam on bread. It is said to be praiseworthy to have bread at this meal, so that one washes and *bentches*. However, any type of "meal" is fine, even if it's just a piece of fruit or some cake.

SHABBAT RECIPES

CHALLAH

Our Sabbath bread is called *challah* because it is a *mitzvah* to "separate *challah*" from bread dough, when it is made in a certain quantity. This is considered a special *mitzvah* for women, with its source and significance dating back to the Torah itself.

Bread, being considered the sustenance of life, was prepared, and, before being baked, a portion of the dough (called *challah*) was separated after reciting a blessing recognizing the act. It goes like this:

Baruch atah Adonai,   בָּרוּךְ אַתָּה יְיָ,
Eloheinu melech ha-olam,   אֱלֹהֵינוּ מֶלֶךְ הָעוֹלָם,
asher kideshanu be-mitzvotav   אֲשֶׁר קִדְּשָׁנוּ בְּמִצְוֹתָיו
ve-tzivanu lehafrish challah   וְצִוָּנוּ לְהַפְרִישׁ חַלָּה
min ha-isah.   מִן הָעִסָה.

A *kezayit* (approximately 1/2 ounce/15 gm.) of dough is separated after reciting the *brachah*, and, since we do not have a Temple to which we bring the separated dough, we destroy it and dispose of it in a dignified manner. The most common way is to burn it in a piece of foil under the broiler, wrap it in some more foil, and throw it away. Do not eat it.

This blessing and separation applies *only* when you are using a recipe whose quantities are more than 3 pounds, 12 ounces (1.680 kg.)— approximately 12.4 cups of flour.[1]

It is noted in each recipe at what point *challah* should be separated. If one decreases or increases a recipe, check the preceding paragraph to see if the new volume of flour requires the *mitzvah* of separation of *challah*.

If you forgot to separate *challah*, and the bread is already baked, simply place all the loaves together on one pan, say the blessing, and cut off a piece of one.

---

[1]*Challah* is also separated *without* a blessing if the quantity is 1.248 kg., approximately 9 to 10 cups (but less than the 1.680 kg. discussed earlier). In this case, the size of the separation does not have to be a *kezayit*. Is was confusing for me at first too.

Please note that bread should not be eaten if *challah* was not separated. Take a look at the side panel of most boxes of *matzoh* and you will see the words *"Challah* Taken." Now you know what it means.

Take a look at the side panel of most boxes of **matzoh** *and you will see the words "Challah Taken." Now you know what it means.*

Always Successful *Challah*

8–9 cups flour	2 1/2 cups lukewarm water
1/4–1 cup sugar	1/2 cup oil
1 Tbsp. salt	1/4 cup raisins (optional)
1–2 oz. (50 gm.) yeast	5 eggs

Mix together 2 1/2 cups flour with sugar, salt, yeast (no need to dissolve first), water, and oil. Mix in 4 eggs. Beat in 1 1/2 cups flour very well. Add 4–5 cups flour until a very soft dough is formed. Add raisins (optional). Knead. Separate *challah*, if necessary. Refrigerate overnight. In the morning, let warm to room temperature, 1–2 hours. Make balls, roll them into ropes, and braid (see illustration, page 122). Let rise, covered, for 1/2–1 hour. Make egg wash by beating 1 egg. Brush on *challah*. Bake in preheated oven at 325 degrees F. (160 degrees C.) for 30 minutes. Apply egg wash once more and bake another 30 minutes at 350 degrees F. (175 degrees C.). Makes 4 medium-sized *challahs*.

Sweet Half-and-Half *Challah*

2 oz. (60 gm.) yeast	4 eggs
2 cups warm water	4 cups whole-wheat flour
1–1 1/2 cups honey	5–6 cups white flour
3/4 cup oil	

Mix together yeast, water, honey, oil, and eggs. Add the sifted flour. Knead until dough does not stick to fingers. Cover dough with a damp cloth and let rise in a warm place for 2 hours. Separate *challah*, if necessary. Divide the dough into 6 balls. Divide each ball into thirds and braid (see illustration, page 122). Let rise for 1 hour. Bake in preheated oven at 350 degrees F. (175 degrees C.), for 30–45 minutes. Do not overbake. Makes 6 loaves.

Eggless or "Water" *Challah*

2 oz. (60 gm.) yeast	1/2 cup oil
9 cups flour	1/2 cup plus 2 tsp. sugar
3 cups water	2 tsp. salt

FOUR-STRAND BRAIDED CHALLAH

Figure 1

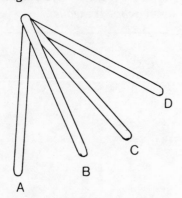

Figure 1: Separate and roll dough into 4 equal strands approx. 10 inches long, and pinch together at one end. Place a knife on top of the pinched end to hold it down and allow for easy maneuvering.

Figure 2

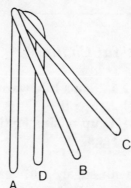

Figure 2: Align strands as in Figure 1 and move strand D under strands C and B.

Figure 3

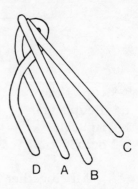

Figure 3: Place D over A.

Figure 4

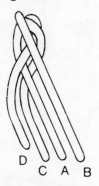

Figure 4: Move C under B and A.

Figure 5

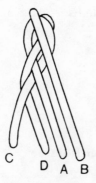

Figure 5: Place C over D.

Figure 6

Figure 6: Move B under A and D.

Figure 7

Figure 7: Place B over C.

Figure 8

Figure 8: Move A under D and C.

Figure 9

Figure 9: Place A over B.

Figure 10

Figure 10: Continue the under-two, over-one pattern until you reach the end of the strands. Tuck final strand under all and seal.

Dissolve yeast and 2 tsp. sugar in 1/2 cup warm water. Sift flour into a very large bowl. Make a well in middle of flour. Add 2 1/2 cups water, oil, 1/2 cup sugar, salt, and yeast mixture. Mix until a soft dough is formed. Knead. Separate *challah*, if necessary. Place dough in a greased bowl. Cover with a towel. Let dough rest until double in bulk. Punch down. Knead. Divide into 9 balls. Let dough rest 10 minutes. Roll into ropes and braid (see illustration, page 122) into 3 loaves. Let rise 20–30 minutes. Bake at 350 degrees F. (175 degrees C.), for 45 minutes to 1 hour. Makes 3 *challahs*.

Whole-Wheat *Challah*

2 oz. (60 gm.) yeast	1/3 cup honey
3 cups warm water	2 eggs
1 tsp. sugar	1 Tbsp. salt
10 cups whole-wheat flour	poppy, caraway, or sesame seeds
1/3 cup oil	1 egg yolk

The following "sponge method" gives whole-wheat *challah* a lighter texture. Activate yeast in 1/2 cup water with sugar. Beat in remaining 2 1/2 cups of water, 5 cups flour, oil, honey, 2 eggs, and salt. Dough should now resemble a cake batter. Let rise 30–60 minutes. Punch down. Add the rest of the flour slowly, while kneading, until dough no longer sticks to fingers. Separate *challah*, if necessary. Cover with damp towel. Allow to rise again until double in size. Punch down. Shape into loaves and braid (see illustration, page 122). Place in well-greased loaf pans. Beat egg yolk and brush over loaves. Pat on poppy, caraway, or sesame seeds. Let rise for 30 minutes. Bake in preheated oven at 350 degrees F. (175 degrees C.) for 30 minutes. Makes 4 medium *challahs*.

Variation: Substitute 1 cup wheat germ for 1 cup flour and/or 1 cup soy flour for 1 cup flour.

Meira's Famous *Challah*

3 Tbsp. yeast (or 3 pkgs.)	2 1/4 cups warm water
"soup bowl" of warm water	salt
1 Tbsp. brown sugar	raisins
4 eggs	7 cups white flour
3/4 cup oil	7 cups whole-wheat flour
3/4 cup brown sugar	sesame seeds (optional)

Dissolve yeast in "soup bowl" of warm water with 1 Tbsp. brown sugar. Set aside to "bubble-up." In a large bowl or pot, put in eggs, slightly beaten, add oil, brown sugar, 2 1/4 cups warm water, about a tablespoon of salt, a couple of handfuls of raisins (white raisins work best). Add the yeast mixture that has started to "bubble-up" a bit. Stir together. Add flour, alternating a couple of cups of white, then whole wheat. Use your hands and keep adding flour (you may need a little more), until the dough doesn't stick to your hands. Remove the dough and knead just a couple of minutes. Add some oil to the bowl or pot and place dough mixture back in, turning it over so that all sides are coated with oil. Take a towel dampened with warm water and cover the container. Let rise at least 1 hour. Punch down. Separate *challah* with a *brachah*, roll, and braid (see illustration, p. 122). Brush with egg wash (using 1 whole egg slightly beaten) and sprinkle with sesame or poppy seeds if desired. Bake in preheated 350 degree F. (175 degrees C.) oven for approximately 20 minutes, or until *challahs* are golden brown and sound hollow when tapped. Makes about 6 loaves.

FISH

Sweet *Gefilte* Fish

In the animal world, fish are the most pure. The flood that destroyed all forms of life in the time of Noah did not destroy the fish, for they alone had remained uncorrupted. Fish require no ritual slaughter or salting before eating. . . . Because of its elevated position among the animal species, fish is deemed proper food for the Jew on Shabbat.

Or Ha-Shabbat

1 lb. (500 gm.) ground fish or 2 lbs. (1 kg.) whole fish (carp, silver carp, or whitefish and pike)	1/2 cup *matzoh* meal
	black pepper to taste
	4 Tbsp. salt
	6 Tbsp. sugar
1 carrot	2 eggs
3 onions	oil

Slice 2 onions. Sauté a small amount of oil in frying pan over a small flame, until soft and translucent, but not brown. If using whole fish, clean and grind fish. Grind the fried onions. Mix fish well with the onions. Add *matzoh* meal, eggs, 3 Tbsp. sugar, 2 Tbsp. salt, and black pepper. Let set 15 minutes. Fill a medium-sized pot halfway with water. Add sliced carrot, 1 sliced onion, 2 Tbsp. salt, 3 Tbsp. sugar, and black pepper. Bring to a boil. Make fish balls with wet hands, place the balls into the simmering stock. Cook for 3/4 hour. When it has cooled, pour the sauce into a jar and refrigerate until it jells. Use the gel as garnish. Serves 15.

Variation: Spicy Baked *Gefilte* Fish: Combine 1/2 cup tomato sauce, 1/2 cup water, salt and pepper to taste. Pour over cooked *gefilte* fish pieces. Bake 1/2 hour at 350 degrees F. (175 degrees C.)

Claire's Food-Processor *Gefilte* Fish

2 medium onions	6 Tbsp. cold water
1 large carrot	1 1/4 tsp. salt (or less)
1 1/2 pounds ground fish	1/2 tsp. pepper
3 eggs	3/4 tsp. sugar (or less)

This is a fast and easy recipe where the fish is baked instead of boiled, avoiding that "fishy" smell.

Grate onions and carrot in food processor until well mixed, approximately 10 seconds. Add fish (a mixture of white and pike is nice—fast and easy if you buy it already ground at your local fish store—stores catering to a Jewish clientele will have it on hand Wednesday to Friday), and process 20 seconds. Then add and process the rest of the ingredients for 15 seconds, scraping the sides of the bowl if necessary. Pour into oiled pan (8″ × 11″), and bake at 325 degrees F. (165 degrees C.) for 1 1/4 hours, covering with foil for the last 1/2 hour to avoid its drying out. When done, it should be slightly brown, and a knife inserted in the middle should come out clean. When cool, cut into rectangular pieces and serve cold

Garnish *gefilte* fish with sprigs of parsley, place on a bed of lettuce, or add some cherry tomatoes on the plate for color. Instead of just horseradish, try filling a 3-compartment pickle dish with red horseradish, white horseradish, and some spicy mayonnaise (recipe to follow).

By eating fish on the Sabbath we gain a triple blessing. During creation, God conferred three blessings: on the fifth day fish were blessed; on the sixth day man was blessed; and on the seventh, the Sabbath itself was blessed. Thus, when fish is eaten by man on the Sabbath, he benefits from a threefold blessing.

Bnei Yissaschar

Spicy Mayonnaise

regular or light mayonnaise	paprika
mustard	pepper
garlic powder	

Add all spices to mayonnaise and stir until well blended. Serve cold with fish.

Curried Fish

1 lb. (500 gm.) frozen fish	Any or all of the following:
1/2 tsp. curry powder	(but not more than 2 cups in all)
1 tsp. garlic powder	onions, carrots, tomatoes,
2 apples	zucchini, corn, string beans,
1/2 cup raisins	mushrooms
2–4 Tbsp. oil	
salt to taste	

Preheat oven to 350 degrees F. (175 degrees C.) and bake fish until done. In the meantime, dice and stir-fry the vegetables and fruit in a small amount of oil. Sprinkle with curry powder, garlic powder, and salt. Pour over cold fish. Serve hot or cold. Serves 5.

Moroccan Fish

2 onions, finely chopped	6 hake (bakala) fillets
oil	dash sweet paprika
3 tomatoes, finely chopped	2 crushed garlic cloves
1 Tbsp. turmeric	or 1 Tbsp. garlic salt
chili powder, chili pepper	pepper (optional)
juice of 1/2 lemon	olives (optional)

Place onions in pan with a little oil and fry over low flame until soft. Add tomatoes, cover, and simmer for a few minutes. Add spices and lemon juice. Place fish on top, sprinkle with paprika, and baste with onion-tomato-spice mixture. Cover and cook over low flame for 1/2 hour. Garnish with olives. Serves 6.

SOUP

Old Jerusalem Chicken Soup

1/2 cup white beans	2 onions
2 zucchini	2 tomatoes
2 carrots	1 chicken, cut into serving pieces
2 potatoes	

Soak beans 6 to 12 hours. Cut zucchini, carrots, and potatoes into large pieces. Put all the vegetables and beans into a large pot. Place the chicken pieces on top, cover with water, bring to a boil and simmer 2–3 hours. Take out the tomatoes before serving. Add *kneidlach* (see page 128) or *kugelach*. Serves 6.

Yemenite Soup

1 chicken cut into serving portions or 2 lbs. (1 kg.) meat, cubed	1 squash
	1 tomato
	2 celery stalks
5 medium carrots	2 Tbsp. *hawaich* (Yemenite
5 medium onions	spice mixture) or 2 tsp. curry
5 medium potatoes	powder plus 1 tsp. pepper plus
	2 tsp. paprika

Boil water in a large pot. Add chicken or meat pieces. Skim off brown foam with spoon. When soup is clear, add vegetables and *hawaich* (a traditional Yemenite spice, which gives this soup its characteristic deep-yellow color). Simmer chicken soup for one hour on a low flame. Meat soup should simmer 3–4 hours. Meat and vegetables are served together in a soup bowl. Served with pita, this soup is the traditional Friday night meal of many Yemenite families. Serves 5.

"Its tasters merit life." One should sample every dish prepared for the Sabbath before the candles are lit to ensure that everything is perfectly seasoned.

Mishnah Berurah

Chicken Soup

1 whole chicken	1 onion
2 carrots	salt
3 stalks celery	pepper
1 Tbsp. chicken soup powder (optional)	

Clean chicken and cut into pieces. Cover with water (8–10 cups). Bring all ingredients to a boil, then simmer for 2 hours. Cool. Take out chicken pieces to serve separately. Strain soup. Serves 6.

Vegetable Soup

2 Tbsp. oil	string beans, cooked
1 large onion, sliced	chick-peas, peeled
4 medium carrots	tomatoes, pumpkin (optional)
4 potatoes	1/2–1 cup oatmeal
4 squash	water
	salt
	pepper

Sauté onion in oil until transparent. Cut carrots, potatoes, and squash into chunks. Add remaining ingredients and enough water to cover, plus 3 cups. Season to taste. Cook soup for 1 hour. The oatmeal in this recipe disappears, leaving the soup nice and thick. Serves 6–8.

Variation: Pour into blender or food processor and blend until just chunky or smooth, as desired.

Thick Tomato Soup

1 large onion, chopped	1/4 cup brown rice
2 celery stalks, chopped	1 potato, grated
2 Tbsp. margarine	salt
4–5 cups boiling water	pepper
2 lbs. (1 kg.) ripe tomatoes	garlic powder

Sauté onion and celery in margarine until soft. Pour boiling water over tomatoes to skin, saving water for soup. Skin tomatoes and slice. Add all ingredients except for potato. Cook until rice is almost tender. Add grated potato and continue cooking 15 more minutes. Serves 4–6.

Variation: Save rice to add with grated potato. Cook other ingredients about half an hour. Then puree entire mixture in blender. Pour back into pot and add rice and grated potato. Cook 1/2 hour or more.

Matzoh Balls (*Kneidlach*)

1 cup coarse *matzoh* meal	salt
1/2 cup water	pepper
4 beaten eggs	garlic powder (optional)
1/3 cup oil	

Mix all ingredients together well. Refrigerate at least 1 hour. Wet hands, form balls and drop into rapidly boiling soup, or salted water. Cook for 20 minutes. After cooking and cooling, *matzoh* balls can be drained and frozen. Boil again for 15 minutes before serving. Makes 12–20 *kneidlach*, depending on size.

CHICKEN

Tangy Roast Chicken

1 chicken	2 Tbsp. brown sugar
4 large onions, sliced	1/4 cup ketchup
2 Tbsp. oil	2 Tbsp. soy sauce
1/2 cup water	

Roast chicken uncovered for 1 hour at 350 degrees F. (175 degrees C.). Sauté onions. Add water, brown sugar, ketchup, and soy sauce. Pour over chicken, cover, and bake an additional 1/2 hour or more. Serve hot or cold.

Baked Chicken with an Assortment of Sauces

Cut chicken into quarters or smaller pieces (some cooks remove the skin). Sprinkle each piece lightly with paprika or garlic powder and/or black pepper. (Do *not* salt.)

Arrange pieces in a single layer in a roasting pan. Then choose a sauce from the sauce selections, following the directions carefully.

Amounts are intended for 2 medium-sized chickens.

All are baked (covered, or uncovered, as per instructions) at 350 degrees F. (175 degrees C.) and are done when brown and fork-tender. Chicken prepared this way can be served hot at the evening meal and cold at the midday meal.

Honey-Garlic Sauce

Combine:

6 Tbsp. honey	1 tsp. garlic powder
6 Tbsp. soy sauce	1 tsp. ginger

Coat chicken pieces with mixture; bake uncovered, basting often, for 1 hour.

A l'Orange

Combine:

2 onions, sliced and fried in oil	1 tsp. black pepper
2 tsp. paprika	juice of 2 oranges

Pour over chicken pieces. Bake uncovered for 45 minutes or longer, basting often.

Coffee Sauce

Combine:

3/4 cup strong hot coffee (about 1 Tbsp. instant coffee to 3/4 cup boiling water)
1/3 cup ketchup
3 Tbsp. soy sauce

2 Tbsp. lemon juice
2 Tbsp. wine vinegar (or other vinegar)
1 Tbsp. oil
1/4 cup brown sugar

Pour over chicken and cover pan for first 1/2 hour. Baste and continue baking for another 1/2 hour, uncovered.

Apricot Sauce

Combine:

1/2 cup apricot jam
1/2 cup mayonnaise

1/2 tsp. black pepper
1 tsp. garlic powder

Spread on chicken pieces. Bake for 45 minutes covered, then for about 1/2 hour uncovered.

Barbecue Sauce

Combine:

1 cup canned tomato sauce
1 medium onion, chopped
1 clove garlic, minced
1/2 cup soy sauce

2 Tbsp. sugar
1 tsp. mustard
1/8 tsp. paprika

Pour over chicken and bake uncovered for about 1 hour, basting occasionally.

Shabbat in a Pot

oil to cover pan
1 onion, diced
1 carrot, diced

1 cup brown rice
1 chicken cut in serving pieces
1/4 cup tomato paste

1 zucchini, diced
3–5 cloves garlic, minced
sesame seeds (optional)

1 3/4 cup water
1 Tbsp. soy sauce
salt to taste

In a large frying pan, sauté onion, carrot, zucchini, garlic, and sesame seeds in oil till soft. Add rice. Place chicken on top of rice mixture and pour liquid over it. Bring to the boil and cover. Lower heat. Simmer about 45 minutes or until liquid is absorbed. With soup and salad, you have a complete meal. The rice takes on the flavor of the chicken. Delicious! Serves 4.

Baked Chicken with Honey-Orange Sauce

1 3–4 lb. (1 1/2–2 kg.)
  chicken cut into pieces
2 eggs, beaten
2 cups bread crumbs
salt

pepper
1 cup orange juice
1/2–1 cup honey
1/2 cup water

Preheat oven to 350 degrees F. (175 degrees C.). Combine bread crumbs, salt, and pepper. Roll chicken pieces in egg, then in bread crumbs, and place in pan. Cover and bake for 15 minutes. Mix orange juice, honey, and water. Pour over chicken. Bake for additional 30–45 minutes, until tender. Serve hot or cold.

BEEF

Cathy's Sweet and Sour Meatballs

2 lbs. ground beef
2 cloves garlic (or powder)
1/2 tsp. salt
1/4 tsp. pepper
1 egg

1/4 cup *matzoh* meal
2 14-ounce cans cranberry sauce
2 8-ounce cans tomato-mushroom
  sauce
1/2 tsp. cinnamon

Mix all ingredients except sauces and cinnamon. Combine sauces and cinnamon in a medium-sized saucepan, stir together over low heat until well-blended. Roll meat mixture into balls and drop into sauce. Bring to boil and simmer on low for 1/2 hour.

CHOLENT

Known by many different names in the world's Jewish communities, *cholent* is nonetheless the dish that is universally unique to the Sabbath. If you've never seen or tasted one, the best description is: a Jewish stew that comes in many flavors and styles.

Since cooking is prohibited on *Shabbat*, but hot food is appropriate, some dish had to be devised that could be left to simmer on a covered fire or hot plate, untouched from before sunset on Friday until the following day, when it is usually served for "lunch."

It became a matter of principle to serve hot food at *Shabbat* midday in the time of the Saduccees some two thousand years ago. Seeking to differ from the God-given interpretation of the Torah in our Oral tradition, they redefined the verse "You shall kindle no fire . . . on the Sabbath day," to mean that no fires might burn at all (even if kindled before the Sabbath).

So, while the Saduccees sat in darkness, partaking of cold foods, loyal Jews filled their homes with light each Sabbath eve and prepared dishes to be kept warm so that *Shabbat* might be enjoyed in the manner intended by the Creator.

Beef *Cholent*

3 Tbsp. oil	1 onion
2 Tbsp. sugar	1 or 2 lbs. (1/2 to 1 kg.)
6–7 potatoes	meat (chuck or flanken)
1/2 cup barley	2–3 tsp. salt
1/2 cup lima beans	1/2 tsp. pepper
1/2 cup kidney beans	Gravy from roasted chicken or
(optional)	meat for added flavor (optional)
meat bones	water

In large pot, brown the sugar in oil. Immediately add 1 cup water. Peel and cut potatoes into chunks and add to water. Rinse beans and barley and add to pot. Add remaining ingredients. Add water just to cover mixture. Bring to a boil. Cook covered on a low flame for 1–2 hours. Add water to cover and bring to boil. Place on covered fire (*blech*—see page 147) before *Shabbat* and keep close to flame overnight but not directly over it. It should simmer gently. Serves 6–10.

Variation: Substitute 1 chicken for meat.

Chicken *Cholent*

3 onions	1/2 cup lima beans
oil	1/2 cup barley
1 chicken, cut in serving pieces	water
5 potatoes	

Slice onions. Fry in a little oil until golden brown. Add pieces of chicken and cook until the skin browns (about 10 minutes). Add potatoes, peeled or unpeeled, cut in large pieces. Add beans and barley. Add water to cover, plus 1 additional cup and cook for at least 1 hour. Before putting the cholent on a covered fire (*blech*), add another cup of water. Cover *cholent* and keep it on a low–medium covered flame.

Variation: For extra *Shabbat* flavor, add *kneidlach* and some additional water after you have cooked the cholent for 1/2 hour.

Vegetarian *Cholent*

1 large onion, sliced	5 Tbsp. onion soup powder
2 Tbsp. oil	4 carrots, cut in chunks
1 cup barley, soaked for several hours	4 medium potatoes, cut in chunks
1 cup split peas, soaked for several hours	water

Sauté onion in oil in pot until soft, then add rest of ingredients with water to cover. Bring to a boil and cook for at least 1 hour, adding water as needed to keep a soupy consistency. Place cholent on covered fire (*blech*). Variations:

1. Add *kishke* (see below) and simmer 20 minutes before putting on covered fire.

2. Chunks of meat substitute may be added for extra texture and to make it more interesting.

3. Well-washed raw eggs may be carefully immersed in the *cholent* before putting it on the covered flame. At serving time, remove eggs and peel. They turn brown. Serve them separately.

Vegetable *Kishke*

2 stalks celery, *or* 1 medium zucchini	1/2 tsp. salt
1 large onion	1/8 tsp. pepper
3 carrots	1 tsp. paprika
1 small potato	3 cups sifted flour
	3/4 cup oil

Shred vegetables. Add remaining ingredients and mix well. Form into a loaf, wrap in aluminum foil. Roast with chicken or place directly into boiling cholent for at least 1 hour before *Shabbat*. Let it remain in cholent on covered fire (*blech*) until serving the next day. Freezes well raw. A few loaves may be prepared in advance and frozen in aluminum foil.

SHABBAT IN AN HOUR (OR SO)

Some people make big, elaborate meals for *Shabbat* and enjoy making one thing every day in preparation for the Friday festivities. Others (like myself), prefer the Thursday-night or Friday-morning whirl of activity.

For those interested, I have found the following formula for making a yummy, nutritious *Shabbat* in no time flat—(even with a whole pile of guests coming!).

It goes something like this:

Friday Night Menu

Challah
Grape juice/wine
Soup (chicken or vegetable)
Duck-sauce chicken
Roast potatoes and onions
Spicy string beans
Salad
Dessert

Shabbat Day Menu

Challah
Grape juice/wine
Soup (from Friday night)
Teriyaki chicken and roasted veggies
Salad
Dessert

In an hour?? Well, kind of . . .

Challah—I use Meira's Famous *Challah* recipe (see page 123—never fails, and people love it! We even auctioned off eight loaves at a fund-raising auction for the *shul*, and it brought in a tidy sum). I make enough for two weeks at a time. Or, buy some at your local *kosher* bakery, warm up a loaf before *Shabbat* for the Friday night meal, and it tastes practically homemade (see page 150).

(O.K., so I didn't include baking your own *challah* in the hour, but who's counting?)

Wine and grape juice and other beverages—a good thing to ask guests to bring, or include it in your grocery shopping.

Soup—I alternate between chicken soup and vegetable soup, depending on whether our guests are vegetarians or not.

O.K., so I didn't include baking your own challah *in the hour, but who's counting?*

Chicken Soup

1 chicken, skinned, cut in tenths (have your butcher do this)	chicken soup powder (1 or 2 pkgs.)
carrots (lots)	salt
onions (lots)	garlic powder
	parsley flakes

Start with a large pot of boiling water, add everything, spice it up with some salt, garlic, and parsley flakes (to taste). Cook FOREVER, simmering on low. I start it Friday morning, add *matzoh* balls in the afternoon (use the boxed mix, it's great!), skim the fat from the top occasionally, and by Friday night, voilà! I always make a big potful, and keep it on the stove all Friday night and serve it the next day for lunch. It gets even tastier and takes on a darker look. Even the *matzoh* balls are better on *Shabbat* day!

Vegetable Soup

4 packages dried soup mix (comes in long clear plastic-tube packages). Any kind will do, lima bean, barley, vegetable . . . you can have any, or combine them

sweet potatoes, peeled	salt
onions	pepper
carrots	garlic powder
2 handsful of oatmeal	

Add everything to a big pot of boiling water and simmer all day Friday. The oatmeal helps make this soup very thick. Add salt, pepper, and garlic powder to taste.

You can also serve this Friday night (great with homemade whole-wheat *challah*), keep it on the stove, and serve the next day for lunch. It's a hit, even if you're not vegetarian!

Duck-Sauce Chicken

1–2 chickens, skinned and
   cut in tenths
1 jar of duck sauce (sweet-and-
   sour or hot-and-spicy)
1 can of peach slices
    (or pineapple rings)

garlic powder
paprika
pepper

Place chickens in a roasting pan (make sure your butcher skins and cuts them for you, a real time-saver!). Sprinkle with spices. Cover and bake at 350 degrees F. (175 degrees C.) for one hour. Uncover, pour on sauce, continue baking another 30 minutes or so, basting occasionally until golden brown. Remove from oven, place fruit on top. Yummm!

Spicy String Beans

1–1 1/2 lbs. string beans
1 tsp. salt
1/2 tsp. basil
1/2 tsp. thyme (or allspice)

dash garlic powder
1 Tbsp. minced onion
1/4 cup water
2 Tbsp. oil

Break string beans into 1-inch pieces. Put all ingredients into a medium-sized pot. Cover and cook over medium heat 20 minutes or until tender. Good hot or cold. Serves 6 to 8. If serving Friday night, don't forget to undercook them because of the warming period.

Leora's Roast Potatoes and Onions

potatoes
onions
oil
garlic powder

salt
pepper
paprika

Cut up lots of potatoes (leave skins on) and onions and place in a large oiled pan. Sprinkle liberally with spices. Bake uncovered for about an hour, stirring occasionally until golden brown.

Shabbat Day Teriyaki Chicken and Veggies

1–2 chickens, skinned and cut in tenths	**onions**
teriyaki sauce	**carrots**
ketchup	**potatoes**
garlic powder, pepper, paprika	**sweet potatoes**

Place vegetables in large chunks at the bottom of a roasting pan. Put pieces of chicken on top, and sprinkle liberally with spices. Shake on teriyaki sauce (comes in a bottle), and squeeze a little bit of ketchup over it all. Cover and cook at 350° F. (175° C.) for 30 minutes and place in 200° F. (100° C.) oven overnight, never opening up the pan until you serve it *Shabbat* day. Serve the chicken on a platter and the vegetables in a large bowl. Pour some juices over the chicken. Serve with a salad. It's a whole meal!

Dessert—When pressed for time, try one or all of these:

1. Have a guest bring dessert from a kosher bakery.

2. Serve a nondairy "ice cream" in pretty dishes and pour some liqueur on top.

3. Serve it all with a tray of dried fruit, candies, and dark chocolate.

Putting It All Together

Friday morning (or Thursday night)

1. Your *challah* has been bought, or you take the loaves you baked earlier in the week out of the freezer.

2. Put the water on for your soup. Preheat the oven for the chicken and potatoes.

3. Make your *Shabbat* Day Teriyaki Chicken, cutting up extra carrots and onions that you will use in your soup. (Takes about 10 minutes to put together.) Put the pan in the fridge, because you will put it in later that day before *Shabbat* begins.

4. Water should be boiling, so add chicken and veggies for chicken soup (or veggie soup mixes and veggies for vegetable soup). Cover and simmer all day.

5. Make roasted potatoes and onions (takes another 10 minutes because you leave the skins on, also more nutritious). Pop into oven, which is now hot.

6. Make Duck Sauce Chicken (takes 5 minutes), put in oven too.

7. Now snap together the Spicy String Beans, cook them now, or wait until just before *Shabbat*.

8. Green salad . . . and you're done!!

CHAPTER EIGHT

Getting Organized

PREPARING FOR *SHABBAT*

The week does not carry Shabbat . . . Shabbat *carries the week.*

This is not just about preparing the *Shabbat* meals; it is a statement encompassing all sorts of things one should do in honor of *Shabbat*. It all comes down to—you get out of *Shabbat* what you put into *Shabbat*; a statement covering everything, from the clothes you wear to the sheets on which you sleep.

Preparing is part of *Shabbat*, to the point where even if one has help to do all the cooking, cleaning, and so forth, one must still personally prepare something in honor of the day.

If you are a guest at someone's home and arrive Friday night, you will probably notice things sparkling and shining, from the silver to the smiles on the children's faces (on a good night). How did it all happen, and why is it all for this day?

The Talmud asks: ". . . One who takes time to plan erev Shabbat *(before Shabbat), will eat on* Shabbat. *But one who does not, from where will they eat?*

How To

Part of preparing for *Shabbat* means knowing what is permissible to do on *Shabbat* and what is not. It is a matter of learning and experience, which, in time, become as natural as breathing. Hang in there, find the rhythm that is best for you and a system that works, but be flexible! Just when you think you've got preparing down pat, another kid is born, or a family of seven moves in for the weekend.

Roll with the changes, and enjoy the feeling of making the week lead to the day we've all been waiting for: *Shabbat*.

1. Since the *Shabbat* is supposed to be a "delight," make sure your home is comfortable. Sufficient light should be available, so decide which lights will be left on and which off.

2. If one does not wish to leave a light (or a fan, and the like) on throughout *Shabbat*, a timer may be used, preset before *Shabbat*, to regulate usage on *Shabbat* (see page 156).

3. The Talmud says that one should make a point of tasting food prepared for *Shabbat* before it begins, to make sure that it will be prepared to everyone's liking.

4. Cooking is not allowed on *Shabbat*, but keeping cooked food warm during *Shabbat* and, in some cases, warming up cooked food that is cold, is not only permissible, it is considered part of the *mitzvah* of making *Shabbat* a delight.

However, since there is a possibility that one may adjust the controls to regulate the degree of heat reaching the food, a

141

reminder that this is not permissible on *Shabbat* is required. Thus a *blech* (a thin sheet of metal covering; even aluminum foil is acceptable) must cover the source of heat and, ideally, the controls as well (see page 147).

5. Some make a point of covering the table with a special *Shabbat* tablecloth early in the day, as well as placing the candles and *challah* on the table in advance to usher in a *Shabbat* atmosphere.

6. One should shower, don special *Shabbat* clothing, and even change the bed sheets—all in honor of *Shabbat*.

Try to do as much as possible beforehand (within reason), which in turn will enhance one's own personal *Shabbat*.

How does one fulfill the requirement of **oneg**—*Sabbath pleasure? Our Sages recommended preparing an especially rich dish and an aromatic beverage—more or less, in accordance with one's means. The more a person spends on the* **Sabbath**, *and the more one prepares delectable foods—the more praiseworthy is such a person!*
Maimonides
Twelfth Century

Reflections

When I first started getting into *Shabbat*, preparing was very stressful, as I would too often leave everything until Friday. Big mistake. It made the whole "coming into *Shabbat*" such a rush.

Now I've learned to plan ahead. On Monday I decide what I'll be serving on *Shabbat*, make my menus, and figure out what I need to buy. On Wednesday I shop.

Thursday is the day I cook. I get home from work and first make the desserts, because I like baking best. Then I do all the meats and hot side dishes like *kugels*. Fresh salads and the like wait until Friday.

I like to make everything ahead, even though you can make salads on *Shabbat*, because for me it's not *Shabbat* if I'm stuck in the kitchen. I'd much rather go to *shul* or enjoy time with my family.

I suppose I've come a long way since those first *Shabbats*—most dishes I can do with my eyes closed. But I still wonder if everyone will like what I make, so it's nice to be extra creative every once in a while.

My first *Shabbat* that I made myself was a nightmare. I had left everything until Friday—you just can't imagine the scene.

So now I've spread it out for the week. On Monday my cleaning lady comes to give the place a good scrubbing. On Wednesday I think of menus and shop, and usually make my chicken soup so I know that it's done.

Thursday I cook most everything, so Friday is only small last-minute items.

Some weeks I'm really "into it" and cook up a storm, but other weeks I'll just throw something together and keep it simple.

I make sure everyone gets a bath before *Shabbat*; the little ones I do Thursday night, the older ones do themselves Friday after school.

142

Before *Shabbat* comes in they get a choice of wearing either their *Shabbat* clothes or pj's. And I always get dressed up, even if there's no company. My husband says, "You don't get dressed for guests, you get dressed for *Shabbat.*"

I used to set the table Thursday night to make the place feel *Shabbosdik* all day Friday, but more often than not the kids do it Friday afternoon.

When I was single and first experiencing *Shabbat*, it was never hard to stop everything for *Shabbat*. I liked leaving the material plane and entering the spiritual. The table was always filled with such meaningful talk.

My challenge now is to try and make it fun for the kids.

I used to work for a non-Jew, and the more observant I became, the harder it was to take off early on Friday in the winter (when *Shabbat* comes in early) and for the holidays.

At first I would be apologetic and make excuses, but then I realized that he would never understand, saying things like "just stay late this one time." Finally, I just said I had to go, period.

The whole situation was a good incentive to leave and branch out on my own. Now that I'm my own boss, the pressure of preparing for *Shabbat* has lifted, and I don't have to worry about not making it in time. I remember a couple of times when it was so close, I thought I'd have to pull over on the road and walk the rest!

Maybe it's because I'm Sephardi, but to me preparing for *Shabbat* is a total sensory experience: particular attention to colors, smells, textures. This is what *Shabbat* is all about. You just can't serve any old meal; it has to look alive, beautiful, inviting . . . special.

My challenge is to finish up all my work in order to get away on time to be a help to my wife before *Shabbat*.

Before I leave work on Friday, I phone home to see if there are any last-minute items that need to be picked up at the grocery store or cleaners.

When I get home I set all the lights, making sure the one in the fridge is always turned off, and go through the bathrooms, swapping facial tissues for toilet paper.

Then I rip the lettuce. Don't ask me how I got that job, but somehow it's become mine, so unless I do it there's no salad.

*This is what **Shabbat** is all about. You just can't serve any old meal; it has to look alive, beautiful, inviting . . . special.*

143

Before I grab a shower, I put away all the *muktzah* (non-*Shabbat* items like money and pens).

This whole routine takes about an hour, so I make sure I'm home at least an hour before lighting.

Looking back, before I was more committed, I wonder what used to keep me going. I suppose it was the fact that, unless I got home in time for *Shabbat*, my wife would kill me!

I started getting into *Shabbat* in Israel, where I ran my own aerobics business.

Friday was my busiest day, as I taught about seven classes all over Jerusalem. Then I would rush back to my dorm before the buses stopped running, run in totally panicked, and yell, "I'm never going to make it!"

There was always this same girl who lived in our flat who would calmly answer, "Yes, you will," and then help me do what I had to do.

Shower . . . makeup . . . wine for my hosts . . . lights off in my room . . . (which I unfortunately would leave in a mess) . . . and then grab a taxi to whatever neighborhood I was spending *Shabbat* in.

Sometimes it was so tight that I thought I'd be stranded, but I always seemed to get in just under the wire—exhausted, but there.

It's funny, today I have my own family and have so much more to do to prepare for *Shabbat*. When my guests arrive I sometimes envy them the leisure of going out for *Shabbat*, and then I remember my days in Israel, and realize, married or single, it's still a challenge to be on time.

My teacher always said that Friday is not a time for frantic physical preparation for *Shabbat* but rather unhurried, spiritual preparation for this important day.

She had a rule: no cooking on Friday. What's done is done, and that's it! Instead of cooking she would gather up all the children and go on an outing. Then she would take time to do some reading and thinking about the whole concept of *Shabbat*.

How I envied her attitude and organization! And yet some of it seems to be finally rubbing off on me.

It used to take me the whole week to make *Shabbat*, with Friday being jam-packed. But now I've gotten pretty good at the whole thing, with recipes that are easy and yet impressive to serve and helpful hints that make the whole process a breeze.

The main thing is to make the time-consuming stuff ahead. That means *challah* has to made and frozen by Wednesday or Thursday.

I make a double batch every time so that I only have to make it for every other *Shabbat*. I suppose I don't have to make my own, but once you start doing it, the family gets spoiled, including me. So it isn't *Shabbat* without homemade bread.

She had a rule: no cooking on Friday. What's done is done, and that's it!

144

I get my groceries delivered to save a lot of time, even though it might cost me a little bit more. But I figure my time is worth something, and running around to a million stores to save a few dollars just isn't worth it.

So this is the way it goes—Monday I try and secure all of my guests, so I know how many I am feeding and what their dietary needs are (vegetarian, and so forth). Tuesday night I think about menus and make my grocery list, which I call in Wednesday morning.

My food arrives Wednesday afternoon, but I don't start cooking until Thursday (except for *challah*). I try and do everything before I go to bed Thursday, even if I stay up late, because it makes a big difference in my day Friday to wake up, knowing that I just have to put the soup on or stir-fry some veggies.

Once you get into a routine, it's a snap. And that means Friday I can take the kids to the park and enjoy.

I couldn't do it without my husband. He's the last-minute shopper for those things that I've forgotten. He's the one who makes sure the lights that are to be left on are on, and the ones to be off, off.

Friday afternoon he gets home early enough, he takes over the kids so I can just smooth out the rough edges of the house, take a shower, put on my makeup, and get dressed.

My goal is to try and provide a Shabbat atmosphere as early as possible, so that when he comes home, things are in order, with the table set, the kids dressed and bathed, and me in my finest *Shabbat* attire.

The goal isn't always achieved, but, hey, I do my best.

I like to make things on *Shabbat* that I never make during the week—to make it special. Even a fruit salad can be extra nice by using only tropical fruits. Things should be different and in the spirit of *Shabbat*. If something cost a little extra, that's O.K. It's for *Shabbat*!

Shabbat preparations start when I invite my guests at the beginning of the week. I try to prepare things with them in mind, even when it comes to the inviting. Who will mix well at the table? Who would enjoy so-and-so? And so forth.

I used to go to a woman's house for *Shabbat* when I was single, and she never let me make my own bed. "That's *my mitzvah*," she would say. "Don't take it away from me." I've tried to incorporate her philosophy with my own guests now, so I'm careful to make their beds ahead of time, lay out fresh towels for them, and try to think about the things I used to like when I was a guest, then duplicate them in my own home.

145

*I used to go to a woman's house for **Shabbat** when I was single, and she never let me make my own bed. "That's my mitzvah," she would say. "Don't take it away from me."*

My husband had a terrific idea that we have followed: Try to think about interesting questions to ask at the *Shabbat* table that will make people feel comfortable, as well as stimulate the conversation. The best is when you can think of questions that will bring in Jewish themes, such as Israel or the Torah portion of the week. Now *that's* a *Shabbat* table!

———

For us, it's not *Shabbat* without guests, so part of my preparation is making sure there are clean sheets on the beds, fresh towels in the bathrooms, and a flowering plant in the guest room.

I find it's small touches that make people feel at home, so you should always show them the house (especially the bathrooms), so they know where everything is. If they are overnight guests, putting out coffee mugs by the hot-water urn and special treats like brownies or cookies for the morning seems to make the difference.

I want people to enjoy *Shabbat* and want to come back, often.

———

We do not keep *Shabbat* . . . yet. But I guess it's fair to say that it is our goal. So preparing for *Shabbat* is a real part of our life every week, even though we are still doing things like driving on Saturday and cooking.

Every Friday I get into *Shabbat* "mode" and always make sure I leave early from work, especially in the winter when it comes in so early. And I try to pick up flowers for my wife.

We are very precise about lighting the candles on time, and my wife prepares the Friday night meal in advance.

It's funny, even though I may not be keeping *Shabbat* strictly, I am unbelievably conscious of it, to the point where I get bothered if I see a Jew performing on TV on a Friday night—even though I'm sitting there myself watching TV!

But I find that just thinking about *Shabbat* is making a difference in my life. It's become the rhythm of the week.

Right now I'm kind of at a crossroad—I enjoy the things I do that are in the spirit and law of *Shabbat* and feel guilty when I do the things that aren't. But, as a friend always says: "It's a level."

THINGS YOU'LL NEED TO HAVE FOR *SHABBAT*

1. TIMERS—You can use timers so that lights will come on and off automatically throughout *Shabbat*. Simple timers that your lamps plug into can be picked up at most hardware or department stores and are

*Each man's income for the entire year is determined between Rosh HaShanah and Yom Kippur—with the exception of **Shabbat** and festival expenses, and the cost of Torah education for one's children. These are granted in accordance with one's outlay. If one spends little for these, little will be given; if one spends more, one will be given more.*

Talmud Bavli

quite affordable. Set them to go off Friday night about 11:30 or so (depending on your own sleeping schedules), and have them come on in the late afternoon *Shabbat* day, perhaps around 4 or 4:30, or whenever it begins to get dark.

For overhead lighting such as chandeliers, wall timers can be easily installed in your light switches.

2. *BLECH*—Sounds like something unpleasant (as in yuch!), but is really the name for the stove-top cover that allows you to keep things warm over *Shabbat* without transgressing the prohibition of cooking.

It is a simple piece of sheet metal that is cut to cover your stove top (usually available in standard sizes). It is placed, before *Shabbat*, over the four burners. Usually one or two of the burners are left on fairly low underneath, and the food that you wish to serve hot that evening or the next day is placed on the *blech* to remain at a warm-to-low simmer until it is ready to be eaten.

The burners must be covered so that you will not come to turn them up or down during *Shabbat*, which would in fact be considered cooking.

The beauty of a *blech* is that you can move the food around on top, either closer or farther away from the source of heat, depending upon how hot you wish that dish to be. For example, if you have a vegetable soup in a pot on the *blech* that you served soup from for the Friday night meal, and you wish to serve it the next day for lunch, you simply leave it on the *blech* slightly off the area of immediate heat. That way, it will stay hot without boiling away. For more detailed laws, you may want to consult the book *Laws of Cooking on the Sabbath and Festivals* (see page 170).

3. SLOW COOKER—This can be used instead of, or in addition to, a *blech*. Your soup or stew can simmer effortlessly overnight in these slow cookers, which can be purchased from a catalog or at a department store. Use them by simply plugging them into any electrical outlet. As a reminder that we don't cook on *Shabbat*, it is proper to cover the controls with foil.

4. HOT-WATER URN OR LARGE THERMOS—Because you can't boil water (which is cooking) on *Shabbat*, you must have either a hot-water urn, such as the kind you see at parties, which is plugged in before *Shabbat* and will keep the water hot the whole *Shabbat*; or a large thermos that was filled with hot water before *Shabbat*; or a large pot that will keep warm on the *blech*.

With the hot-water urn, making coffee and tea is quite simple. Just fill a clean, dry cup or mug with the hot water and pour that water into a second mug where you will add instant coffee, tea, and so forth.

The reason for the intermediary mug is to cool the water down slightly so that again you don't transgress the law of refraining from cooking on *Shabbat*.

If you choose to use the thermos, no intermediary mug is needed, as the water was already poured from the kettle to the thermos, an act that serves the same purpose.

5. CANDLESTICKS—It's nice to have special candlesticks to light candles on, especially if they were candlesticks handed down in the family.

But, in a pinch, melt the candles on the back of a plate! (See story, page 8.) It's nice to have extra candlesticks for guests to light as well.

6. KERCHIEFS—When a married woman lights candles, it is proper for her to cover her head when saying the blessing. So have pretty kerchiefs available for yourself and for guests.

7. *KIPPOT*—Men and boys should wear *kippot* at the *Shabbat* table, so it's nice to have some extras around, in case your guests didn't come with their own. (BYOK—Bring Your Own *Kippah*.) Also called *yarmulkas* (in Yiddish).

8. *KIDDUSH* CUP—It's nice to have a special cup to make *kiddush* with. This can be an expensive silver goblet, or an affordable yet attractive wine glass or anything in between (for size requirements see page 24).

9. SMALL *KIDDUSH* CUPS—After the blessing ". . . *borei peri ha-gafen*," which is said over the wine, the wine is poured into smaller glasses to be passed around to all those seated at the table. Sets of these can be purchased at local Jewish book or gift stores, or simply substitute small "shot" glasses or plastic cups (for "How To" see page 25).

10. WASHING CUP—Two-handled cups can be purchased at Jewish book or gift stores, or a quick substitute can be a large mug or glass (see page 32).

11. WASHING SIGN—You may find it helpful to purchase or make your own sign, with the blessing for washing your hands written on it in Hebrew and phonetics. It simplifies the washing process and helps those who may not know the *brachah*.

12. *CHALLAH* BOARD—There are bread boards and knives made especially for the *Shabbat* table, often made out of olive wood or stone, on which the *challahs* rest, or use any kind of cutting board.

13. *CHALLAH* COVER—This can be a pretty napkin, or it can be a specially made *challah* cover, which is draped over the *challah* before and during *hamotzi*. This is symbolic of the dew that covered the *mannah* that fell for the Jewish people in the desert (see page 37).

14. *MAYIM ACHARONIM*—This is the "final water" that is passed around to wash your fingertips with (see page 50). You can purchase a cup and saucer designed especially for this (they can get as elaborate as a wishing-well design, or something to that effect) or simply use a cup in a small bowl.

15. *BENTCHERS*—These are small books that contain blessings for such things as candles, wine, and *ha-motzi*, as well as the longer blessing following the meal (referred to as *bentching*, Yiddish for blessing). Many *bentchers* also contain songs to sing at the *Shabbat* table (see page 169 for recommended *bentchers* and page 52 for "How To"). It's good to have enough for each person to have his or her own. They are often handed out as gifts to the guests at a traditional wedding, so grab a few.

16. *HAVDALAH* CANDLE—This is a braided candle used for the *Havdalah* ceremony that officially ends *Shabbat*. They can be purchased at most

When a married woman lights candles, it is proper for her to cover her head when saying the blessing. So have pretty kerchiefs available for yourself and for guests.

Jewish bookstores or grocery stores and come in decorative colors and varied lengths. If you don't have one, simply use two candles, putting their wicks together while they burn.

17. SPICE BOX—Cloves or sweet pepper used in the *Havdalah* ceremony (see page 89) can be beautifully encased in decorative spice boxes made of silver, ceramic, wood, and other materials that can be purchased at most Jewish book and gift stores. If you don't have one, just use the bottle that the spice came in.

Complete *Havdalah* sets: *kiddush* cup, candle holder, and spice box, are often purchased together. Makes a terrific gift!

PRE-*SHABBAT* CHECKLIST

1. SET LIGHTS—Decide which lights will remain on and which will be off, including the level of the dimmer switch, which also can't be touched on *Shabbat*. Set timers if you have them.

The most important light is the one in the refrigerator and/or freezer. Unscrew the light bulb inside, so that it is off during the whole *Shabbat*. Otherwise, opening the fridge will be just like turning on a light, which is not permitted on *Shabbat*.

Many people put a piece of tape over the light switches in high-traffic areas such as bathrooms, so that there is no involuntary switching on and off. There are also specially made light-switch covers that can be purchased.

2. CHECK THERMOSTAT—Decide if the heat or air conditioning is set at the right temperature.

3. HUMIDIFIERS OR VAPORIZERS—If one will be needed over *Shabbat* in someone's room, fill it and plug it in before *Shabbat* begins.

4. FANS—They can be moved without unplugging them during *Shabbat*, but they can't be turned on or off, so set the levels before *Shabbat*.

5. COOKING—Is all cooking complete? Anything that will remain hot (on a *blech* or in a slow-cooker) should be cooked before *Shabbat* begins. Cold salads and such can be prepared on *Shabbat*, but it's often nice to have everything done ahead.

6. *BLECH*—If you will be using the *blech*, it should be on the stove top with the burners set at the required temperatures (usually low to medium low). It's a good idea to heat up your food 30 minutes to 1 hour before *Shabbat*, so that things are hot before placing them on the *blech* to simmer.

If you do not wish to utilize the *blech*, or you have too much to fit on the stove top, you can use the inside of the oven in the following way:

Heat up your prepared food ahead of time inside the oven (15 to 30 minutes, depending on temperature of food—did you take it out of the fridge, or is it room temperature?). If you are serving this food Friday night, you may have at least a 1-hour delay between the time you bring

*If one sees a fine object during the week suitable for **Shabbat**, and doubts whether or not he can afford it, he should buy it and save it for the Sabbath, as it is proper to thus honor **Shabbat**. One should continuously honor **Shabbat** this way all week long. The Creator will then show kindness to him and provide for all his needs in abundance. As he opens his hand for the Sabbath, so shall the heavens open for him and bless him with ample sustenance.*
Seder Ha-Yom

Whoever delights in the Sabbath—all his wishes are granted.
Talmud Bavli

Shabbat in (candlelighting) and the time you actually sit down and eat (to say nothing of the preliminaries: songs, *kiddush*, washing, appetizers, and so forth).

To be able to serve all of this hot, here's a good trick: Time the 15-to-30-minute reheating period to be just before candlelighting. At the last minute, put a *Challah* wrapped in foil into the oven with the rest of the food, close it up, and turn the heat up very high for one minute. Then turn it off. Do not open it again until you are ready to serve the food.

Everything inside should remain hot, if well wrapped to ensure minimal heat loss. It is also a good idea to make your meat with sauces, so that they won't dry out.

If you are serving hot vegetables, *undercook* them, because this warming period will do most of the cooking for you. (For more detailed laws, see *Laws of Cooking on the Sabbath and Festivals*, page 170).

Since you can't use the hot-water tap, here is a good trick to have hot water for washing dishes.

7. FACIAL TISSUES—Make sure there are cleansing tissues or pretorn toilet paper in all the bathrooms (see page 156).

8. *MUKTZAH* (literally, "set aside")—These are things that have no use on *Shabbat* and therefore shouldn't be handled, for example: money, pens, crayons, and the like. Place these items out of reach so you won't come to use them. Some people have a *muktzah* drawer, into which things get thrown at the last minute.

9. HOT WATER—If you are using an urn, make sure the water is hot, with the urn plugged in before *Shabbat*. If you are using a thermos, boil water before *Shabbat* and fill the thermos full.

10. HOT WATER FOR DISHES—Since you can't use the hot-water tap (falling under the prohibition of cooking, since hot water removed from the hot-water tank is replaced by cold water, which then becomes hot), here is a good trick to have hot water for washing dishes: Just before candlelighting, fill one kitchen sink with hot water. Squeeze in some dishwashing soap and cover the whole sink with foil. After dinner (even hours later), simply remove the foil, and, voilà, hot water to wash it all up!

11. PRETORN FOIL, PAPER TOWELS—You may want to pretear plastic wrap, foil, paper towels, and the like, if you think you will be needing them on *Shabbat* (see explanation, page 156). Foil can actually be purchased in pretorn sheets in a large boxed dispenser. For a neat paper-towel substitute, just use some cheap paper napkins.

12. NON-*SHABBAT* TOYS—Crayons, modeling clay, scissors, and so forth, shouldn't be used by children on *Shabbat*. Try to put them away to avoid any problems. (See "*Shabbat* and Kids," page 80).

13. MAKEUP—All makeup should be applied before *Shabbat* begins, as it falls under the prohibition of "dyeing." There is special *Shabbat* makeup now available that can be applied *on Shabbat* (very loose powders, eye shadows, and others).

14. SHOWERS—Is everyone bathed and showered?

15. FLOWERS IN WATER—If you have *Shabbat* flowers, place them in water before *Shabbat* begins (see page 156). Plants should also be watered, if necessary, ahead of time.

16. TV, RADIO, AND SO FORTH—Make sure they are off or set on timers (see "*Halachah* . . . and Beyond," page 153.

17. LAST-MINUTE PHONE CALLS—Call someone and wish them a "Good *Shabbos*!" "*Shabbat Shalom*!"

TERMS YOU SHOULD KNOW, OR GETTING DOWN THOSE *SHABBAT* "BUZZ" WORDS

Aliyah—To be "called up" to the Torah. Common usage: "I got an *aliyah*," or "This is the last *aliyah*." (Also refers to the act of moving to Israel—"The Cohens have decided to make *aliyah*.")

Amidah (also called *Shemoneh Esrei*)—The silent prayer said at home or in *shul* (see page 11).

Eishet Chayil—"The Woman of Valor," a song in praise of the Jewish woman, written by King Solomon. Traditionally sung Friday night, between *Shalom Aleichem* and the blessing of the children (see page 15).

Bentching—Yiddish, meaning "to bless." The Grace after the Meal recited at the conclusion of the three meals, if one has "washed" and eaten bread. Common usage: "Let's *bentch*" or "I already *bentched*" (see page 51).

Blech—The covering for the stove top, usually made of sheet metal (see page 147).

Brachah—Blessing. Common usage: "It's time for the children's *brachah*" or "This beautiful day is a real *brachah*."

Challah—Bread traditionally used on *Shabbat*, often braided. Can be white, whole-wheat, sweet, "water," or egg (see page 120).

Cholent—A *Shabbat* stew, usually served for lunch *Shabbat* day (Saturday after *shul*) (see page 132).

Davening—Prayer service, or, praying. Common usage: "I'm late for *davening*" or "It was so nice to *daven*."

Devar Torah—"A Word of Torah" (sometimes called a *vort*, Yiddish for a "word"). A short talk or discussion at the *Shabbat* table, usually centered on the Torah portion of the week. Common usage: "Shhh . . . David is giving a *devar Torah*" or "Do you have a *vort*?" (see page 44).

Erev—Eve. Common usage: "I'll drop the flowers off at our hosts *erev Shabbat*"—as in the hours just before *Shabbat*.

First Meal—Friday night dinner.

"Good Shabbos"—Traditional *Shabbat* salutation, said upon meeting or departing. Can be said as early as Thursday, meaning "Hope you have a 'Good *Shabbat*' " (see also "*Shabbat Shalom*").

Note: "Good *Shabbos*" is really from the Yiddish, "*Gut Shabbos*" and uses the Ashkenazi pronunciation, with the "s" sound at the end of *Shabbos*. *"Shabbat Shalom"* is Hebrew, using the Sephardi pronunciation, with the "t" sound at the end of *"Shabbat."*

"Gut Voch"—Yiddish, meaning "Good Week." Said to one another at the end of *Shabbat* (see also *"Shavua Tov"*).

Ha-motzi—The blessing over the bread (see page 36).

Havdalah—The ceremony that ends *Shabbat*. Performed with a braided candle, wine, and sweet scent (see page 89).

Kiddush—Blessing over the wine at the First Meal (Friday night), in *shul Shabbat* morning, and/or at home at the Second Meal (Saturday lunch) (see pages 23, 67, and 71).

Kippah (Yiddish, *"yarmulka"*)—Headcovering for a Jewish male.

Lechem Mishneh—"Two Breads," the two *challahs* used for *ha-motzi* (see *Ha-motzi*; see also page 36).

Maariv—The evening prayer service, said after sundown at the conclusion of *Shabbat* (Saturday evening) (see page 86).

Matzoh—Unleavened bread, resembles large crackers.

Mayim Acharonim—Literally, "final water," the washing of one's fingertips at the conclusion of the meal, so as to have clean hands for *bentching* (see *Bentching*; see also page 50).

Mazel Tov!—Congratulations! (Literally, "Good Luck!") Common usage: *"Mazel Tov* to the Greens on the recent birth of their daughter."

Melaveh Malkah—Celebration Saturday night after *Shabbat*.

Minchah—The afternoon prayer service, said just before sundown on *Shabbat* afternoon (Saturday) (see page 86).

Minyan—A quorum for prayer. Usage: "We need a *minyan*" or "I'm going to *minyan*," meaning, "I'm going to *shul*."

Mitzvah—A commandment. Also used to describe an act that is good or praiseworthy.

Motza'ei Shabbat—Saturday night, after *Shabbat* is over.

Muktzah (Literally, "to set aside")—Objects whose handling is subject to restrictions of various kinds on *Shabbat* and *Yom Tov*. Generally refers to things that have no use on *Shabbat* and therefore are prohibited (for example, money, pens, and so forth).

Parshah—Torah portion of the week (see page 45, footnote 14).

Second Meal—*Shabbat* "lunch," eaten Saturday after *shul*.

Sefer—A book containing words of Torah.

Sefer Torah—The handwritten scroll containing the Five Books of Moses.

Seudah Shelishit—The Third Meal of *Shabbat*, eaten late Saturday afternoon (also called *Shalosh Seudos*).

Shabbat Shalom—*Shabbat* greeting, meaning a "Peaceful Sabbath" (see also "Good *Shabbos*").

Shabbos—The Jewish Sabbath, also called *Shabbat*.

Shacharit—The morning prayer service, said in the morning. On *Shabbat*, usually followed by *kiddush* (see *kiddush*).

Shalom Aleichem—First song at the Friday night meal, welcoming the visiting "angels" (see page 13). Also a greeting, meaning "Peace be with you," answered with *"Aleichem Shalom,"* "And with you, peace."

Shalosh Seudos—The third meal of *Shabbat* in the late afternoon (also called *Seudah Shelishit*).

Shavua Tov—Literally, "Good week," said to one another at the end of *Shabbat* (see also *Gut Voch*).

Shir Ha-Maalot—The psalm sung before the *bentching*.

Shkoyach—A mashed together version of *Yasher Koach*, literally, "May your strength be straightened," but more effectively translated loosely as "Way to Go," or "More Power to Ya." Often said at the conclusion of the *devar Torah* (see *Devar Torah*) by those listening.

Shul—Yiddish for synagogue, house of prayer.

Siddur—Book containing formal prayer service.

Siyyum—A party held in celebration of the completion of something (for instance, learning an entire book of the Torah).

Synagogue—See *Shul*.

Tallit—Prayer shawl.

Third Meal—The last meal of *Shabbat*, always the smallest, eaten Saturday afternoon before sundown.

Torah—Five Books of Moses (see also *Sefer Torah*).

Washing—"We're washing," "Let's wash," or "Did you wash for bread?"—meaning the ritual cleansing of hands before the blessing over bread. Usually performed with a two-handled washing cup, pouring water over each hand, followed by a blessing (see page 31).

Yarmulka—See *Kippah*.

Zemirot—*Shabbat* songs (see page 40).

HALACHAH . . . AND BEYOND

When one learns the laws in a deep way and applies them within a Jewish life-style, ha-lachah becomes not a restriction, but a direction.

In one breath, God said, "*Guard* and *remember* the *Shabbat*."

Until this point, we have discussed many aspects of *Shabbat*, almost all pertaining to the latter—to *remembering* the Sabbath. Love of God, time with family, reconnecting with friends and with oneself—all fulfill the commandment to *remember*.

But these become merely a handful of beautiful concepts unless they are grounded in a foundation of strength, a structure that will provide the soil in which these ideas can take hold, root, and blossom.

This foundation is the commandment to *guard* the Sabbath, and it is referring to *halachah*, known as Jewish law.

Yet the word *halachah* does not literally translate as "law," for it comes from the root *halach*, which means "to go," "to walk." *Halachah* means "a path." It is not about cold do's and don't's, but about movement. When one learns the laws in a deep way and applies them within a Jewish life-style, *halachah* becomes not a restriction, but a direction. And, when paired with the beauty of *remember*, the coupling opens up a world without limitations—a world of endless depth and opportunity.

The two commandments, to *guard* and to *remember*, are said in one breath, for one without the other would be empty.

If you are in a relationship and you hear from the other person the words "I love you," there is a nice feeling. But suppose the person never

153

On **Shabbat** *we stop creating in order to recognize that there is a Creator. On* **Shabbat** *the world is complete. I am complete.*

did anything, never demonstrated the love in any way. Words without action are merely . . . words.

If you want to make real the idea that God is Creator, you must stop creating, it is as simple as that. Otherwise it is a beautiful concept that remains in the theoretical.

Judaism is not theoretical, it is experiential.

We have said, and it is worth repeating, that on *Shabbat* we stop creating in order to recognize that there is a Creator. On *Shabbat* the world is complete. I am complete.

Shabbat is the weekly reminder of this completeness. We recognize it, but the only way to make it happen is to live it, to emulate it.

When God says, "Six days a week you will do all your work . . . ," He is not just talking about making the office deadlines. He is talking about us, and how we strive to work on ourselves.

Shabbat is there, calling us to where we want to be: self-actualization; nature; oneness; completion. I am a happy human being. I am in touch with the things in which I want to be complete.

The ideas are within reach; grasping them means heading in the right direction. You are almost there—the path is *halachah*.

The Basics

Where do all these laws come from?

Remember the part in the movie *The Ten Commandments* when the Jewish people left Egypt and were wandering through the desert? At one point, God instructs them to build a *mishkan*, which was a portable sanctuary that would hold, among other things, the tablets of the Ten Commandments. This *mishkan* would be carried by the Jewish people throughout their journey.

Our tradition tells us that through understanding the *mishkan*, we will understand *Shabbat*.

This was to be the central dwelling place of God's presence. It would bring God's presence into this world. Any activity used in forming this house of the Creator would be considered acts of creation.

On *Shabbat* we also strive to bring God's presence into this world. We remove ourselves from creating in order to reaffirm that we do not have mastery over our lives. Someone else is in charge.

To learn what is considered "creating," we study the principles found in our original creation of the *mishkan*. Our tradition identifies thirty-nine categories.

There are many books (some listed in For Further Reading) that discuss these concepts and list the laws of *Shabbat* in detailed form. They cover almost any possible occurrence on *Shabbat* and how properly to deal with it (for example, "A framed picture falls from the wall. Am I allowed to rehang it on *Shabbat*?").

However, there are very basic areas of law that deal with action, or refraining from action, that occur in the vast majority of times over an average *Shabbat* (assuming you are not marooned on a desert island, or on a ship at sea).

Remember—this is the structure. Do not make the mistake of

154

taking them out of the context of the concepts we've been discussing throughout the book.

We've done *remember*. Now it's time for *guard*—time to learn what things we have to try to refrain from in order to create an environment where these ideas can take hold.

If on *Shabbat* the world is complete, then we must make sure that we are doing nothing to add to it, or to take away from it. We must stop creating.

The following are the everyday areas and principles you are likely dealing with and their application on *Shabbat*.

Cooking

We are not allowed to apply heat to things in order to change them in any way. Loaves of bread were formed and baked for the *mishkan*; thus we refrain from any sort of cooking on *Shabbat*.

How to approach it: For more information on keeping things warm throughout the *Shabbat*, see page 149. It's basically a matter of cooking ahead and keeping things warm, either by using a *blech* (cover for the stove top, see page 147) or by utilizing a slow cooker. Water is kept hot using an urn that is plugged in before *Shabbat*. To properly keep this important aspect of *Shabbat*, careful study is required (see page 170).

Driving

Fires cannot be started or extinguished on *Shabbat*, and driving (which sparks and burns fuel) falls under this category.

How to approach it: Walk! There is no greater feeling than just plain walking. It's a total slowdown, giving one time to think, look around, breathe. It's amazing what we miss, zooming by life in an automobile. Enjoy the break from having to go everywhere, and just enjoy *being*.

If your synagogue is a real hike away, you may want to drive there Friday night before *Shabbat* begins and park the car there until Saturday night. Then there is just the one-way walk back home Friday night. During the day, the walk to and from *shul* seems a pleasure.

Plan to visit friends and neighbors nearby or arrange to meet with them halfway, or at the park *Shabbat* afternoon.

Handling Money

On *Shabbat*, we avoid weekday activities such as shopping, and thus money becomes *muktzah*, among the objects that have no purpose on *Shabbat* and thus are not to be touched. Bills (which of course can't be paid) are also *muktzah*.

How to approach it: Put away wallets, purses, and loose change before *Shabbat* begins.

Telephones

There is a prohibition against completing things ("The final blow of a hammer . . ."), which includes the completion of circuits. Telephones fall under this category, as do radios, televisions, and items like them. It also happens to be one of the areas that, when observed,

It's a total slowdown, giving one time to think, look around, breathe. It's amazing what we miss, zooming by life in an automobile. Enjoy the break from having to go everywhere, and just enjoy being.

155

provides one of the most pleasurable aspects of *Shabbat*. The island of peace that you wish to reach can be achieved only through the beautiful silence of no ringing phones.

How to approach it: You may want family and friends to know that you will be unavailable by phone during *Shabbat*. People usually catch on quickly and just take it in stride that they must wait until Saturday night to call. If you really want a *Shabbat* atmosphere, unplug the phones so you won't be disturbed by the ringing.

Lights

This also falls under completing a circuit, as discussed under telephones.

How to approach it: Decide which lights should be left on and which left off before *Shabbat* begins. You may want to tape certain light switches in high-traffic areas, such as bathrooms, so they aren't inadvertently turned off or on. (Sleepy trips to the bathroom in the middle of the night often end in an automatic flip of the switch!)

Timers can be used to automatically turn lights on and off throughout *Shabbat*, as long as they are preset before *Shabbat* begins.

Toilet Paper

Things that are attached, through glue, sewing, or even perforation, cannot be unattached for a purpose on *Shabbat*. This would involve taking something in one form and carefully dividing it up into another for some use, thus creating something anew. Paper towels also fall into this category.

How to approach it: Pretear toilet paper before *Shabbat* or use tissues. For paper towels, pretear what you might use or use paper napkins.

Watering plants/picking flowers

If everything is complete on *Shabbat* and we are refraining from things that indicate that we have mastery over the world, then causing things to live (or in some cases causing things to die) would, of course, be avoided. Thus, once *Shabbat* begins, we do not water our plants. (Another related category does not allow cut flowers to be placed in water on Shabbat).

How to approach it: Make sure flowers are put in water ahead of time and that plants are watered before *Shabbat*. If someone happens to bring you cut flowers after *Shabbat* has begun, thank them and simply put them in a vase without water—they'll never know the difference (and they're usually fine. Just quickly add water once *Shabbat* is over).

PLEASE NOTE: When it comes to human life, *everything* is done to save it. Thus one can drive on *Shabbat* to bring someone in an emergency situation to a hospital. Phones can be used, and so forth. The laws of *Shabbat* are put aside to save a life.

> The island of peace that you wish to reach can be achieved only through the beautiful silence of no ringing phones.

Writing/erasing/tearing letters

Again, on *Shabbat* we are not the Creator, so writing, drawing, erasing, even tearing through letters on a package that you are opening are to be avoided. Pens, pencils, erasers, and the like, thus fall under the category of *muktzah* (see listing).

How to approach it: Put away pencils, markers, pens, and so forth, so you won't come to use them. Any packages or wine-bottle covers that are to be used on *Shabbat* should be preopened or carefully opened on *Shabbat* so as not to tear through any letters.

APPENDIX A: SUMMARY OF THE BLESSINGS

Blessing over the Candles

Arms are motioned three times, hands drawing over the flames as if to bring the light in toward you, at last covering your face as the special blessing is said:

Baruch atah Adonai,	בָּרוּךְ אַתָּה יְיָ,
Eloheinu melech ha-olam,	אֱלֹהֵינוּ מֶלֶךְ הָעוֹלָם,
asher kideshanu be-mitzvotav	אֲשֶׁר קִדְּשָׁנוּ בְּמִצְוֹתָיו
ve-tzivanu lehadlik neir	וְצִוָּנוּ לְהַדְלִיק נֵר
shel Shabbat.	שֶׁל שַׁבָּת.

You are blessed, Lord our God, the sovereign of the world, who made us holy with His commandments and commanded us to kindle lights for *Shabbat.*

After the recitation, many take special time to thank God for the many blessings of health, prosperity, and joy in their lives. There is also a special prayer composed by women, for women, which many include at this time:

Yehi ratzon mi-lefanecha, Adonai	יְהִי רָצוֹן מִלְּפָנֶיךָ, יְיָ
Elohai veilohei avotai,	אֱלֹהַי וֵאלֹהֵי אֲבוֹתַי,
she-techonein oti (ve-et	שֶׁתְּחוֹנֵן אוֹתִי (וְאֶת־
ishi ve-et banai) ve-et kol	אִישִׁי וְאֶת־בָּנַי) וְאֶת־כָּל־
kerovai vetashlim bateinu.	קְרוֹבַי וְתַשְׁלִים בָּתֵּינוּ.
ve-sashkein shechinat'cha beineinu.	וְתַשְׁכֵּן שְׁכִינָתְךָ בֵּינֵינוּ.
Ve-zakeini legadeil banim u-vnay	וְזַכֵּנִי לְגַדֵּל בָּנִים וּבְנֵי
vanim chachamim u-meirim	בָנִים חֲכָמִים וּמְאִירִים
et ha-olam ba-Torah	אֶת־הָעוֹלָם בַּתּוֹרָה
uve-ma'asim tovim veha'eir	וּבְמַעֲשִׂים טוֹבִים וְהָאֵר
neireinu she-lo yichbeh le-olam	נֵרֵנוּ שֶׁלֹּא יִכְבֶּה לְעוֹלָם
va-ed. Ve-ha'eir panecha ve-nivashei'a	וָעֶד. וְהָאֵר פָּנֶיךָ וְנִוָּשֵׁעָה.
Amein.	אָמֵן.

May it be Your will, Lord my God and of my fathers, to be gracious to me (and to my husband and children) and to all my family, crowning our home with the feeling of Your divine presence dwelling among us. Make me worthy to raise learned children and grandchildren who will dazzle the world with Torah and goodness, and ensure that the glow of our lives will never be dimmed. Show us the glow of Your face and we will be saved. Amen.

Make me worthy to raise learned children and grand-children who will dazzle the world with Torah and good-ness, and ensure that the glow of our lives will never be dimmed.

Blessing of the Children

For a son:

Yesimcha Elohim
ke-Efrayim vechi-Menasheh

יְשִׂמְךָ אֱלֹהִים
כְּאֶפְרַיִם וְכִמְנַשֶּׁה.

May God make you like Ephraim and Menasha.

For a daughter:

Yesimeich Elohim ke-Sarah,
Rivkah, Racheil ve-Lei'ah

יְשִׂמֵךְ אֱלֹהִים כְּשָׂרָה,
רִבְקָה, רָחֵל וְלֵאָה.

May God make you like Sarah, Rebecca, Rachel, and Leah.

For both continue:

Yevarechecha Adonai ve-yishmerecha.
Ya'eir Adonai panav eilecha viy-chuneka.
Yisa Adonai panav eilecha
ve-yaseim lecha shalom.

יְבָרֶכְךָ יְיָ וְיִשְׁמְרֶךָ.
יָאֵר יְיָ פָּנָיו אֵלֶיךָ וִיחֻנֶּךָּ.
יִשָּׂא יְיָ פָּנָיו אֵלֶיךָ,
וְיָשֵׂם לְךָ שָׁלוֹם.

May the Lord bless you and watch over you. May the Lord shine His face toward you and show you favor. May the Lord be favorably disposed toward you and may He grant you peace.

Afterward, it's nice to whisper something personal into each child's ear, praising some accomplishment in the week, like a good mark on a test or playing nicely with a kid brother. It's your moment with your child; use it as a way of connecting in your own personal way.

It's your moment with your child; use it as a way of connecting in your own personal way.

Friday Night *Kiddush*

(The first line is recited quietly to oneself.)

Va-yehi erev va-yehi voker
yom ha-shishi.

וַיְהִי־עֶרֶב וַיְהִי־בֹקֶר
יוֹם הַשִּׁשִּׁי.

Va-yechulu ha-shamayim ve-ha'aretz
ve-chol tzeva'am. Va-yechal
Elohim ba-yom ha-shevi'i
melachto asher asah,
va-yishbot ba-yom ha-shevi'i
mi-kol melachto asher
asah. Va-yevarech Elohim
et yom ha-shevi'i va-yekadeish
oto, ki vo shavat mi-kol
melachto asher bara
Elohim la'asot.

וַיְכֻלּוּ הַשָּׁמַיִם וְהָאָרֶץ
וְכָל־צְבָאָם. וַיְכַל
אֱלֹהִים בַּיּוֹם הַשְּׁבִיעִי
מְלַאכְתּוֹ אֲשֶׁר עָשָׂה,
וַיִּשְׁבֹּת בַּיּוֹם הַשְּׁבִיעִי
מִכָּל־מְלַאכְתּוֹ אֲשֶׁר
עָשָׂה. וַיְבָרֶךְ אֱלֹהִים
אֶת־יוֹם הַשְּׁבִיעִי וַיְקַדֵּשׁ
אוֹתוֹ, כִּי בוֹ שָׁבַת מִכָּל־
מְלַאכְתּוֹ אֲשֶׁר בָּרָא
אֱלֹהִים לַעֲשׂוֹת.

It was evening and it was morning, the sixth day. So the heavens and the earth were finished, with all their comple-

ment. Thus, on the seventh day, God had completed His work which He had undertaken, and He rested on the seventh day from all His work which He had been doing. Then God blessed the seventh day and made it holy, because on it He ceased from all His creative work, which God had brought into being to fulfill its purpose.

Savri maranan ve-rabanan ve-rabotai: סָבְרֵי מָרָנָן וְרַבָּנָן וְרַבּוֹתַי:

Baruch atah Adonai,   בָּרוּךְ אַתָּה יְיָ,
Eloheinu melech ha-olam,   אֱלֹהֵינוּ מֶלֶךְ הָעוֹלָם,
borei peri ha-gafen.   בּוֹרֵא פְּרִי הַגָּפֶן.

  (Those present respond, "Amen.")

  You are blessed, Lord our God, the sovereign of the world, creator of the fruit of the vine.

Baruch atah Adonai,   בָּרוּךְ אַתָּה יְיָ,
Eloheinu melech ha-olam,   אֱלֹהֵינוּ מֶלֶךְ הָעוֹלָם,
asher kideshanu be-mitzvotav   אֲשֶׁר קִדְּשָׁנוּ בְּמִצְוֹתָיו
ve-ratzah banu, ve-Shabbat kodesho   וְרָצָה בָנוּ, וְשַׁבַּת קָדְשׁוֹ
be-ahavah uve-ratzon hinchilanu,   בְּאַהֲבָה וּבְרָצוֹן הִנְחִילָנוּ,
zikaron le-ma'aseh vereishit.   זִכָּרוֹן לְמַעֲשֵׂה בְרֵאשִׁית.
Ki hu yom techilah   כִּי הוּא יוֹם תְּחִלָּה
le-mikra'ei kodesh, zeicher   לְמִקְרָאֵי קֹדֶשׁ, זֵכֶר
litziat mitzrayim. Ki vanu   לִיצִיאַת מִצְרָיִם. כִּי־בָנוּ
vacharta ve-otanu kidashta   בָחַרְתָּ וְאוֹתָנוּ קִדַּשְׁתָּ
mi-kol ha-amim, ve-Shabbat   מִכָּל־הָעַמִּים, וְשַׁבַּת
kodshecha be-ahavah uve-ratzon   קָדְשְׁךָ בְּאַהֲבָה וּבְרָצוֹן
hinchaltanu. Baruch atah Adonai,   הִנְחַלְתָּנוּ. בָּרוּךְ אַתָּה יְיָ,
mekadeish ha-Shabbat.   מְקַדֵּשׁ הַשַּׁבָּת.

  ("Amen")

  You are blessed, Lord our God, the sovereign of the world, who made us holy with His commandments and favored us, and gave us His holy *Shabbat*, in love and favor, to be our heritage, as a reminder of the Creation. It is the foremost day of the holy festivals marking the exodus from Egypt. For—out of all the nations—You chose us and made us holy, and You gave us Your holy *Shabbat*, in love and favor, as our heritage. You are blessed, Lord, who sanctifies *Shabbat*.

Blessing over the Washing of the Hands

Baruch atah Adonai,   בָּרוּךְ אַתָּה יְיָ,
Eloheinu melech ha-olam,   אֱלֹהֵינוּ מֶלֶךְ הָעוֹלָם,
asher kideshanu be-mitzvotav   אֲשֶׁר קִדְּשָׁנוּ בְּמִצְוֹתָיו
ve-tzivanu al netilat yadayim.   וְצִוָּנוּ עַל נְטִילַת יָדָיִם.

  You are blessed, Lord our God, the sovereign of the world, who made us holy with His commandments and commanded us in the washing of the hands.

Then God blessed the seventh day and made it holy, because on it He ceased from all His creative work, which God had brought into being to fulfill its purpose.

Ha-motzi—Blessing over the Bread

It is a sign between Me and the children of Israel for all time.

Baruch atah Adonai,
Eloheinu melech ha-olam,
ha-motzi lechem min ha-aretz.

בָּרוּךְ אַתָּה יְיָ,
אֱלֹהֵינוּ מֶלֶךְ הָעוֹלָם,
הַמּוֹצִיא לֶחֶם מִן הָאָרֶץ.

("Amen")

You are blessed, Lord our God, sovereign of the world, who brings forth bread from the earth.

Shabbat Day—Second Meal Kiddush

The following blessing is recited by the person making kiddush:

Ve-shamru venei Yisrael
et ha-Shabbat, la'asot
et ha-Shabbat le-dorotam berit
olam. Beini u-vein
benei Yisrael ot hi
le-olam, ki sheishet yamim
asah Adonai et ha-shamayim
ve-et ha-aretz uva-yom
ha-shevi'i shavat va-yinafash.

וְשָׁמְרוּ בְנֵי־יִשְׂרָאֵל
אֶת־הַשַּׁבָּת, לַעֲשׂוֹת
אֶת־הַשַּׁבָּת לְדֹרֹתָם בְּרִית
עוֹלָם. בֵּינִי וּבֵין
בְּנֵי־יִשְׂרָאֵל אוֹת הִיא
לְעוֹלָם, כִּי שֵׁשֶׁת יָמִים
עָשָׂה יְיָ אֶת־הַשָּׁמַיִם
וְאֶת־הָאָרֶץ וּבַיּוֹם
הַשְּׁבִיעִי שָׁבַת וַיִּנָּפַשׁ.

Zachor et yom ha-Shabbat
le-kadesho. Sheishet yamim
ta'avod ve-asita kol
melachtecha. Ve-yom ha-shevi'i
Shabbat ladonai Elohecha, lo
ta'aseh chol melachah atah
u-vincha u-vitecha avdecha va-amatcha
u-vehemtecha ve-geircha asher
bi-she'arecha. Ki sheishet yamim
asah Adonai et ha-shamayim
ve-et ha-aretz et ha-yam
ve-et kol asher bam, va-yanach
ba-yom ha-shevi'i,
Al kein beirach Adonai et yom
ha-Shabbat va-yekadsheiu.

זָכוֹר אֶת־יוֹם הַשַּׁבָּת
לְקַדְּשׁוֹ. שֵׁשֶׁת יָמִים
תַּעֲבֹד וְעָשִׂיתָ כָל־
מְלַאכְתֶּךָ. וְיוֹם הַשְּׁבִיעִי
שַׁבָּת לַיְיָ אֱלֹהֶיךָ, לֹא־
תַעֲשֶׂה כָל־מְלָאכָה אַתָּה
וּבִנְךָ וּבִתֶּךָ עַבְדְּךָ וַאֲמָתֶךָ
וּבְהֶמְתֶּךָ וְגֵרְךָ אֲשֶׁר
בִּשְׁעָרֶיךָ. כִּי שֵׁשֶׁת־יָמִים
עָשָׂה יְיָ אֶת־הַשָּׁמַיִם
וְאֶת־הָאָרֶץ אֶת־הַיָּם
וְאֶת־כָּל־אֲשֶׁר־בָּם וַיָּנַח
בַּיּוֹם הַשְּׁבִיעִי,
עַל־כֵּן בֵּרַךְ יְיָ אֶת־יוֹם
הַשַּׁבָּת וַיְקַדְּשֵׁהוּ.

The children of Israel should keep Shabbat, observing Shabbat throughout their generations, as an everlasting covenant. It is a sign between Me and the children of Israel for all time, that in six days the Lord made the heavens and the earth, and that on the seventh day He was finished and He rested.

Be mindful of Shabbat, to make it holy. You should labor for six days and do all your work, but the seventh day is Shabbat for the Lord your God. You may not do any creative work—neither you nor your son, nor your daughter, nor your male or female worker, nor your cattle, nor the stranger who

dwells among you. Because it was in six days that the Lord made the heavens and the earth, the sea, and all that they contain, and He rested on the seventh day.

That is why the Lord made *Shabbat* and made it holy.

Savri maranan ve-rabanan ve-rabotai: סָבְרִי מָרָנָן וְרַבָּנָן וְרַבּוֹתַי:

For wine:

Baruch atah Adonai, בָּרוּךְ אַתָּה יְיָ,
Eloheinu melech ha-olam, אֱלֹהֵינוּ מֶלֶךְ הָעוֹלָם,
borei peri ha-gafen. בּוֹרֵא פְּרִי הַגָּפֶן.

You are blessed, Lord our God, the sovereign of the world, creator of the fruit of the vine.

For other drinks:

Baruch atah Adonai, בָּרוּךְ אַתָּה יְיָ,
Eloheinu melech ha-olam, אֱלֹהֵינוּ מֶלֶךְ הָעוֹלָם,
she-hakol nihyeh bi-devaro. שֶׁהַכֹּל נִהְיֶה בִּדְבָרוֹ.

You are blessed, Lord our God, the sovereign of the world, through whose word everything came into being.

Havdalah

Holding the wine cup in the right hand (or left for "lefties") the first paragraph is said:

Hineih Eil yeshuati, evtach הִנֵּה אֵל יְשׁוּעָתִי, אֶבְטַח
ve-lo efchad, ki ozi וְלֹא אֶפְחָד, כִּי עָזִּי
ve-zimrat Yah Adonai, va-yehi li וְזִמְרָת יָהּ יְיָ, וַיְהִי לִי
lishuah. Ushe'avtem mayim לִישׁוּעָה. וּשְׁאַבְתֶּם מַיִם
be-sason mi-ma'ainei ha-yeshuah. בְּשָׂשׂוֹן מִמַּעַיְנֵי הַיְשׁוּעָה.
Ladonai ha-yeshuah, al amcha לַיְיָ הַיְשׁוּעָה, עַל עַמְּךָ
birchatecha selah. Adonai tzeva'ot בִרְכָתֶךָ סֶּלָה. יְיָ צְבָאוֹת
imanu, misgav lanu Elohei עִמָּנוּ, מִשְׂגָּב לָנוּ אֱלֹהֵי
Ya'akov selah. Adonai tzeva'ot, יַעֲקֹב סֶלָה. יְיָ צְבָאוֹת,
ashrei adam botei'ach bach, Adonai, אַשְׁרֵי אָדָם בֹּטֵחַ בָּךְ, יְיָ,
hoshiah, ha-melech ya'aneinu הוֹשִׁיעָה, הַמֶּלֶךְ יַעֲנֵנוּ
ve-yom kareinu. La-yehudim בְיוֹם קָרְאֵנוּ. לַיְּהוּדִים
haytah orah ve-simchah, הָיְתָה אוֹרָה וְשִׂמְחָה,
ve-sason vikar. Kein tihyeh וְשָׂשׂוֹן וִיקָר. כֵּן תִּהְיֶה
lanu. Kos yeshuot esa, לָנוּ. כּוֹס יְשׁוּעוֹת אֶשָּׂא,
uve-sheim Adonai ekra. וּבְשֵׁם יְיָ אֶקְרָא.

Behold God is my salvation, I will trust and not be afraid. Indeed, the Lord is my strength and my song and He has become my salvation. You shall draw water with joy from the wells of salvation. Salvation belongs to the Lord; may Your blessings be upon Your people, Selah. The Lord of Hosts is with us, the God of Jacob is a refuge for us, Selah. Lord of

Because it was in six days that the Lord made the heavens and the earth, the sea, and all that they contain, and He rested on the seventh day.

Hosts, happy is the man who trusts in You. Lord, save us; may the King answer us on the day we call. "The Jews had radiance and happiness, joy and honor"—so may it be for us. I will lift up the cup of salvation and call upon the name of the Lord.

(Continue with the blessing over the wine)

Savri maranan ve-rabanan ve-rabotai: סָבְרֵי מָרָנָן וְרַבָּנָן וְרַבּוֹתַי:

For the wine:

Baruch atah Adonai,   בָּרוּךְ אַתָּה יְיָ,
Eloheinu melech ha-olam,   אֱלֹהֵינוּ מֶלֶךְ הָעוֹלָם,
borei peri ha-gafen.   בּוֹרֵא פְּרִי הַגָּפֶן.

(Those present respond, "Amen.")

You are blessed, Lord our God, the sovereign of the world, creator of the fruit of the vine.

DO NOT DRINK THE WINE YET.

The cup is then passed to the left hand. The spice box (usually cloves or sweet pepper, not cinnamon since it is edible in spice form) is picked up with the right hand and the following blessing is recited:

For the spices:

Baruch atah Adonai,   בָּרוּךְ אַתָּה יְיָ,
Eloheinu melech ha-olam,   אֱלֹהֵינוּ מֶלֶךְ הָעוֹלָם,
borei minei vesamim.   בּוֹרֵא מִינֵי בְשָׂמִים.

("Amen")

You are blessed Lord our God, the sovereign of the world, creator of various kinds of spices.

The leader then smells the spices and passes them around for all to do the same.

With the wine cup still in the left hand, the blessing over the fire (candle flame) is said:

For the flames:

Baruch atah Adonai,   בָּרוּךְ אַתָּה יְיָ,
Eloheinu melech ha-olam,   אֱלֹהֵינוּ מֶלֶךְ הָעוֹלָם,
borei me'orei ha-eish.   בּוֹרֵא מְאוֹרֵי הָאֵשׁ.

("Amen")

You are blessed, Lord our God, the sovereign of the world, creator of the lights of fire.

Everyone should now extend their arms toward the flame to create shadows and light on their hands (to take advantage of the light of the candle).

The cup of wine is now passed back to the right hand for the concluding blessing:

Baruch atah adonai,	בָּרוּךְ אַתָּה יְיָ,
Eloheinu melech ha-olam,	אֱלֹהֵינוּ מֶלֶךְ הָעוֹלָם,
ha-mavdil bein kodesh le-chol,	הַמַּבְדִּיל בֵּין קֹדֶשׁ לְחֹל,
bein or le-choshech, bein	בֵּין אוֹר לְחֹשֶׁךְ, בֵּין
Yisrael la-amim, bein	יִשְׂרָאֵל לָעַמִּים, בֵּין
yom ha-shevii le-sheishet	יוֹם הַשְּׁבִיעִי לְשֵׁשֶׁת
yemei ha-ma'aseh.	יְמֵי הַמַּעֲשֶׂה.
Baruch atah Adonai,	בָּרוּךְ אַתָּה יְיָ,
ha-mavdil bein kodesh le-chol.	הַמַּבְדִּיל בֵּין קֹדֶשׁ לְחֹל.
("Amen")	

You are blessed, Lord our God, the sovereign of the world, who makes a distinction between sacred and secular, between light and darkness, between Israel and the other nations, between the seventh day and the six working days. You are blessed, Lord, who makes a distinction between the sacred and the secular.

The leader is then seated to drink at least 2 ounces of the liquid.

The balance of the wine is used to extinguish the flame.

APPENDIX B: FOR FURTHER READING

The Sabbath: A Guide to Its Understanding and Observance
Dayan Dr. I. Grunfield
Feldheim Publishers
200 Airport Executive Park
Spring Valley, NY 10977

Why is the Sabbath the only religious observance mentioned in the Ten Commandments?

A blend of the underlying ideas of the Sabbath, with insights and information about its practical observance. Easy and enjoyable reading.

Sabbath — Day of Eternity
Rabbi Aryeh Kaplan
NCSY Publications
Union of Orthodox Congregations of America
45 West 36th Street
New York, NY 10018

Why is the Sabbath the only religious observance mentioned in the Ten Commandments? Why does the Talmud call the Sabbath "a taste of the world to come"? What is the connection between the Sabbath, belief in God, the Exodus from Egypt, and the coming of the Messiah? These questions and more are answered in this concise, creative, practical as well as philosophical work, by one of the greatest Jewish minds of the twentieth century.

Shemirath Shabbath
Rabbi Yehoshua Y. Neuwirth
Feldheim Publishers
200 Airport Executive Park
Spring Valley, NY 10977

A detailed guide to the practical laws of Sabbath and Festival observance. Two volumes cover everything from Laws of Cooking to Laws Concerning Pets. An excellent reference manual for the, "Can I do this?" or, "Am I allowed to do that?" questions that arise on *Shabbat* and *Yom Tov*. Recommended for those who want more detailed laws regarding the observing of *Shabbat*.

The Living Torah
Rabbi Aryeh Kaplan
Moznaim Publishing Corp.
4304 12th Avenue
Brooklyn, NY 11219
(212) 438-7680/853-0525

Everything begins with the Torah. But there has never been a work like this. This is an *excellent* English translation of the Five Books of Moses, with relevant commentary, maps, and diagrams. Written without all the "thees and thous." A *must* for every Jewish home. Also makes a terrific *bar* or *bat mitzvah* gift.

The Nine Questions People Ask About Judaism
Dennis Prager and Joseph Talushkin
Simon & Schuster, Inc.
Rockefeller Center
1230 Avenue of the Americas
New York, NY 10020

"The intelligent sceptic's guide to Judaism"—Herman Wouk. Questions addressed include "Can one doubt God's existence and still be a good Jew?" "Why do we need organized religion?" "Why shouldn't I inter-marry?" "How do I start practicing Judaism?" Written in a concise and engaging style. It has become a classic introduction to Judaism.

Gateway to Happiness
Rabbi Zelig Pliskin
Aish HaTorah Publications
1742 East 7th Street
Brooklyn, NY 11223
(212) 376-5903

A practical guide to happiness and peace of mind, culled from the full spectrum of Torah literature.

Growth Through Torah—Relevant Thoughts on the Torah Portion of the Week
Rabbi Zelig Pliskin
Aish HaTorah Publications
1742 East 7th Street
Brooklyn, NY 11223
(212) 376-5903

Perfect for anyone looking for practical as well as inspirational thoughts on the weekly Torah portion. Great reference text for everyone when a *devar Torah* is being prepared. A must for every home.

Waking Up Jewish
Uri Zohar
Hamesorah Publications
5 Habakuk Street
P.O.B. 5656
Jerusalem
Israel

Uri Zohar was the Johnny Carson/Robert Redford of Israel, and he shocked the country by quietly becoming a Torah-observant Jew. This is his story, told with humor, insight, and thought-provoking argument. From media star to Torah scholar . . . a fascinating journey.

The Complete ArtScroll Siddur
Mesorah Publications, Ltd.
1969 Coney Island Avenue
Brooklyn, NY 11223
(718) 339-1700

One of the best prayer books available, with easy-to-follow explanations as to the hows and whys of daily, Sabbath, and Festival prayer. Complete English translation, commentary, and guidance. Available in Ashkenaz or Sephard. Special editions for the High Holidays. Whether you are a beginner or more advanced, this is the *siddur* for you. Available in paperback or hardcover.

The NCSY Bencher
National Conference of Synagogue Youth
45 West 36th Street
New York, NY 10018

A small, easy-to-follow booklet containing blessings from Candlelighting to Grace after Meals. Hebrew, English, and transliteration included. Also seventy-two songs for the *Shabbat* table. Stock up; everyone at the *Shabbat* table needs his or her own to follow the blessings and join in the singing.

The Taste of Shabbos: *The Complete Sabbath Cookbook*
Feldheim Publishers
200 Airport Executive Park
Spring Valley, NY 10977

Recipes perfect for the *Shabbat* meals, as well as *Melaveh Malkah*. Easy to follow, inspiring thoughts on *Shabbat* throughout; illustrations include "How to Braid *Challah*."

The Book of Our Heritage
Eliyahu Kitov
Translation by Nathan Bulman
Feldheim Publishers
200 Airport Executive Park
Spring Valley, NY 10977

The Jewish year and its days of significance. Three volumes guide you through each Jewish month, its holidays, meanings, and laws.

To Pray as a Jew: A Guide to the Prayer Book and the Synagogue Service
Rabbi Hayim Halevy Donin
Basic Books Inc., Publishers
10 East 53rd Street
New York, NY 10022

"A lucid and sensitive guide for those who would like to pray Jewishly but don't know how. . . ."—*Hadassah* Magazine. An excellent, detailed guide (in English) to Jewish prayer. From protocol in synagogue to in-depth understanding of each prayer, Rabbi Donin creates an easy-to-follow work that should be a prominent "member" of every Jewish home.

Laws of Cooking on the Sabbath and Festivals: A Pictoral Guide
Feldheim Publishers
200 Airport Executive Park
Spring Valley, NY 10977

A clear and comprehensive guide to all of the laws of cooking on *Shabbat*.
A good book to study with a partner. Charts throughout are invaluable.

Tapes that demonstrate the songs of *Shabbat*—as well as provide more
in-depth meaning—and explain the laws and customs can be ordered
through:

Aish HaTorah Tape Library
900 Forest Avenue
Lakewood, New Jersey 08701
Telephone: 201-370-9053
Fax: 201-364-7627

Ask for the "Songs for the *Shabbat* Table" tape, as well as the tape library
catalog, so that you can choose tapes that are of particular interest to you
and your family.

APPENDIX C: BEGINNER'S SERVICES

For those who don't feel comfortable in a regular traditional *Shabbat* service, there are special introductory services held across North America that are designed for the person who needs a little more explanation during the *davening*, and a lot more English.

NJOP—National Jewish Outreach Program—coordinates these services to ensure that both the quality and content of presentation is such that the novice worshiper can ease into prayer in a relaxed, enjoyable fashion, without pressure or formal commitment.

Contact any of the *shuls* listed to make sure the Beginner's Service is still in effect. If there is nothing listed from your community, contact NJOP and they'll be glad to help you. Perhaps one just began recently, or maybe you'd like to help start one yourself!

Both the quality and content of presentation is such that the novice worshiper can ease into prayer in a relaxed, enjoyable fashion, without pressure or formal commitment.

National Jewish Outreach Program,
485 Fifth Avenue, Suite 212
New York, NY 10017

CALIFORNIA

Chabad of the East Bay
Rabbi Yehuda Ferris
2643 College Ave.
Berkeley, CA 94704
(415) 540-5824/(415) 527-9074

Sunday, 9:30 A.M.

Congregation Beth Jacob of
  Beverly Hills
Rabbi Yitzchak Etz Shalom
9030 West Olympic Blvd.
Beverly Hills, CA 90211
(213) 278-1911/(213) 273-8314

Saturday, 9:30 A.M.

Congregation Beth Jacob of Irvine
Rabbi Daniel Epstein
3000 Parkview #1B
Irvine, CA 92715
(714) 786-5230

Sunday, 9 A.M.

Jewish Learning Exchange of LA
Rabbi Avraham Czapnick
7466 Beverly Blvd. #103
Los Angeles, CA 90036
(213) 857-0923

Saturday, 9:30 A.M.

The Aish Center
Rabbi Irwin Katsof
10100 Santa Monica Blvd.
Los Angeles, CA 90067
(213) 556-3054

Saturday, 9:20 A.M.

Beth Jacob Congregation
Rabbi Howard Zack
3778 Park Blvd.
Oakland, CA 94610
(415) 482-1147

One Saturday per month, 10 A.M.

Congregation Beth Jacob
Rabbi Eliezer Langer
College and Mesifta
San Diego, CA 92115
(619) 287-9890

Saturday, 9:30 A.M.

COLORADO

East Denver Orthodox
  Synagogue
Rabbi Yaakov Meyer
198 South Holly St.
Denver, CO 80224
(303) 629-8200

Sunday, 9:15 A.M.

CONNECTICUT

Young Israel of New Haven
Rabbi Michael Whitman
292 Norton St.
New Haven, CT 06511
(203) 776-4212

Saturday, 10 A.M.

WASHINGTON, DC

Congregation Kesher Israel
Rabbi Barry Freundel
2801 N St., NW
Washington, DC 20007

Saturday, 9 A.M.

GEORGIA

Beth Jacob of Atlanta
Rabbi David Silverman
1855 LaVista N.E.
Atlanta, GA 30329
(404) 321-4085

Saturday, 10 A.M.

MARYLAND

Etz Chaim Centre for
  Jewish Studies
Rabbi Shlomo Porter
3702 Fords Lane
Baltimore, MD 21215
(301) 764-1553

Sunday, 8:15 A.M.

NEW JERSEY

Congregation Sons of Israel
Rabbi Bernard Rothman
720 Cooper Landing Rd.
Cherry Hill, NJ 08002
(609) 667-9700

Saturday, 10:45 A.M.

Congregation Ahavath Torah
Rabbi Shmuel Goldin
240 Broad Ave.
Englewood, NJ 07631
(201) 568-1315

Saturday, 9:30 A.M.

Congregation Shomrei Torah
Rabbi Benjamin Yudin
19-10 Morlot Ave.
Fair Lawn, NJ 07410
(201) 791-7910

Saturday, 10 A.M.

Congregation Ahavas Achim
Rabbi Ronald Schwartzberg
216 South First Ave.
Highland Park, NJ 08904
(908) 247-0532

Every Saturday morning
Call for information.

Princeton University
Mr. Dan Jacobson
Stevenson Hall
Princeton, NJ 08544
(609) 258-8133

Friday at candlelighting

Congregation B'nai Yeshurun
Rabbi Michael Taubes
641 West Englewood Ave.
Teaneck, NJ 07666
(201) 493-0420/(201) 384-8704

Saturday, 9:30 A.M.

NEW YORK

Hebrew Institute of Riverdale
Rabbi Yosef Kanefsky
3700 Henry Hudson Parkway
New York, NY 10463
(212) 796-4730/884-0930

Saturday, 10 A.M.

Congregation Shaarei Emuneh
Rabbi Langsam/Rabbi Loeb
1583 40th St., 2nd Floor
Brooklyn, NY 11218
(718) 436-7331

Friday night, candlelighting
Saturday-morning
Call for information

Flatbush Minyan
Rabbi Meyer Fund
825 East 15th St.
Brooklyn, NY 11230
(718) 338-8442

Once a month
Call for information

Young Israel of Flatbush
Mr. Moshe Sorscher
1012 Ave. I
Brooklyn, NY 11230
(718) 377-4400

Saturday, 10 A.M.

Jewish Heritage Center
Rabbi Moshe Turk
68-54 Main St.
Flushing, NY 11367
(718) 575-3100

Sunday, 9 A.M.

Congregation Machane Chodo
Rabbi Manfred Gans
67-29 108th St.
Forest Hills, NY 11375
(718) 793-5656

Saturday, 10 A.M. (for Russians)

Havurat Yisrael
Rabbi David Algaze
106-20 70th Ave.
Forest Hills, NY 11375
(718) 261-5500

Saturday, 9:45 A.M.

Congregation Kehillath Jeshurun
Rabbi Mark Dratch
125 East 85th St.
New York, NY 10028
(212) 427-1000/517-5955

Saturday, 10 A.M.

Congregation Ohab Zedek
Rabbi Alan Schwartz
118 West 95th St.
New York, NY 10025
(212) 749-5150

Saturday, 10:30 A.M.

Lincoln Square Synagogue
Rabbi Ephraim Buchwald
200 Amsterdam Ave.
New York, NY 10023
(212) 874-6105

Saturday, 9:15 A.M.

Park East Synagogue
Rabbi David Gorelick
164 East 68th St.
New York, NY 10021
(212) 737-6900

Saturday, 11 A.M.

Sutton Place Synagogue
Rabbi Reuben Kahane
225 East 51st St.
New York, NY 10022
(212) 593-3300

Saturday, 9:30 A.M.

Young Israel of Fifth Ave.
Rabbi Israel Wohlgelernter
3 West 16th St., 4th Floor
New York, NY 10003
(212) 929-1525

Saturday, 9:30 A.M.

Young Israel of Woodmere
Rabbi Herschel Billet
859 Peninsula Blvd.
Woodmere, NY 11598
(516) 295-0150

Sunday, 10 A.M.

OHIO

Taylor Road Synagogue—
  Beechwood
Rabbi David Zlatin
25400 Fairmont Blvd.
Beechwood, OH 44122
(216) 321-4875/(216) 561-6512

Saturday, 9:45 A.M.

Taylor Road Synagogue
Rabbi David Zlatin
1970 South Taylor Rd.
Cleveland Heights, OH 44118
(216) 321-4875

Saturday, 9:45 A.M.;
Sunday, 9:30 A.M.

PENNSYLVANIA

Congregation Degel Israel
Rabbi Gavriel Weinberg
1120 Columbia Ave.
Lancaster, PA 17603
(717) 397-0183
Call for information

Congregation Shaarei Torah
Rabbi Boruch Poupko
2319 Murray Ave.
Pittsburgh, PA 15217
(412) 421-8855

Saturday, 10 A.M.

SOUTH CAROLINA

Brith Sholom Beth
  Israel Congregation
Rabbi Joel Landau
182 Rutledge Ave.
Charleston, SC 29403
(803) 577-6599

Once a month—call first

TENNESSEE

Baron Hirsch Congregation
Rabbi Marc Mandel
400 South Yates
Memphis, TN 38119
(901) 683-7485

Saturday at 9 A.M.

Congregation Anshei
  Sphard Beth E
Cantor Aryeh Samberg
120 East Yates Rd. No.
Memphis, TN 38119
(901) 682-1611

Sunday, 10 A.M.

TEXAS

Ohav Shalom
Rabbi Aryeh Rodin
6959 Arapaho Rd. #575
Dallas, TX 75248
(214) 991-6115/(214) 701-8433

Saturday, call for time

(Private Home)
Mr. & Mrs. David Lamm
228 Rainbow Circle
El Paso, TX 79912
(915) 584-3304
Call for information

Thursday, 8 P.M.

WISCONSIN

Lake Park Synagogue
Rabbi Ephraim Becker
Corner of Hampshire and Hack
Milwaukee, WI 53211
(414) 964-9487

Sunday, 9 A.M.

CANADA

The Aish Centre
Rabbi Aaron Hoch
296A Wilson Ave.
(Bathurst & Wilson)
Toronto, Ont.
M3H 1S8
(416) 636-7530

Saturday, 8:45 A.M.

Congregation Beth Israel
Rabbi Howard Finkelstein
116 Centre St.,
Kingston, Ont.
K7L 4E6
(613) 542-5012

Friday 6 P.M., Sunday, 1 P.M.

The Village Shul
Rabbi Yaakov Palatnik
884 Eglinton Ave. W.,
(Bathurst & Eglinton)
Toronto. Ont.
M6C 2B6
(416) 636-7530

Friday evening, candlelighting time (summer-7 P.M.); Saturday, 9 A.M.; Sunday, 8:30 A.M.; "Be Cool in *Shul*" Beginner's Program, 10 A.M. Saturday morning

Ohr Somayach/JEP
Rabbi Avraham Rothman
613 Clark Ave. W.
Thornhill, Ont.
L4J 5V3
(416) 886-5731

Saturday, 8:15 A.M.

B'nai Torah Synagogue
Rabbi Raphael Marcus
465 Patricia Ave.
Willowdale, Ont.
M2R 2N1
(416) 226-3700

Friday, 7:15 P.M.

APPENDIX D: FOR FURTHER LEARNING

Although the people interviewed for this book shared a wide variety of thoughts and feelings about *Shabbat*, there surfaced a common thread: the more learning, the more understanding; the more meaning, the more pleasure.

In other words, the reading they did and the classes and seminars they attended greatly enhanced their Jewish knowledge and thus added greatly to their own personal *Shabbat*.

Don't let this book be your only guide. Keep reading, ask questions, and seek out teachers in your community who can help you with the answers.

The following are branches of Aish HaTorah, the Jewish adult educational organization for which I teach, one that specializes in explaining traditional Jewish concepts to those with little or no formal Jewish background. Classes range from the mystical to the practical. Students from all walks of life choose from seminars on Love, Dating, and Marriage; Making the Holidays Meaningful; Philosophy; Why Be Jewish?; What Happens After You Die?; Judaism and Feminism; Raising Jewish Children in a Non-Jewish World, and more.

There are many other organizations offering educational programs, but since my familiarity is with Aish, I'll list their centers. If your community is not listed, please feel free to call any of the branches and ask what is available in your area.

The more learning, the more understanding; the more meaning, the more pleasure.

CALIFORNIA

Aish HaTorah
Director: Rabbi Irwin Katsof
9106 West Pico Boulevard
Los Angeles, CA 90035
Phone: 213-278-8672
FAX: 213-278-6925

WASHINGTON, DC

Aish HaTorah
Director: Rabbi Steve Baars
11727 Gainsborough Road
Potomac, MD 20854
Phone: 301-588-7187
FAX: 301-299-4370

FLORIDA

Aish HaTorah
Director: Rabbi Kalman
  Packouz/Rabbi Tzvi Nightengale
1606 NE 205th Terrace
North Miami Beach, FL 33179
Phone: 305-945-2155
FAX: 305-945-6790

MICHIGAN

Aish HaTorah
Director: Rabbi Alon Tolwin
32712 Franklin Rd.
Franklin, MI 48025
Phone: 313-737-0400
FAX: 313-737-0405

MISSOURI

Aish HaTorah
Director: Rabbi Elazar Grunberger
8149 Delmar Boulevard
St. Louis, MO 63130
Phone: 314-862-2474 (AISH)
FAX: 314-862-4643

NEW JERSEY

Aish HaTorah
Director: Rabbi Moshe Weisberg
900 Forest Avenue
Lakewood, NJ 08701
Phone: 201-370-9053
FAX: 201-364-7627

NEW YORK

Aish HaTorah
Director: Rabbi Chanan Kaufman
28 Park Avenue
New York, NY 10016
Phone: 914-425-8255
FAX: 914-425-8442

Discovery North America
Director: Rabbi Eric Coopersmith
1388 Coney Island Avenue
Brooklyn, NY 11230
Phone: 718-377-8819
FAX: 718-377-8978

OHIO

Aish HaTorah
Director: Rabbi Yehuda Appel
23312 Beachwood Blvd.

Beachwood, OH 44122
Phone: 216-691-1531
FAX: 216-371-9769

CANADA

Aish HaTorah
Director: Rabbi Ahron Hoch
296A Wilson Ave.
Downsview, Ont.
M3H 1S8
Phone: 416-636-7530
FAX: 416-636-7866

ENGLAND

Aish HaTorah
Director: Rabbi Shaul Rosenblatt
8 Henden House
Brent Street
Hendon, London NW4 2QL
England
Phone: 81-203-1457

Aish HaTorah
Director: Rabbi Chananya
   Silverman
53A Wellington Rd.
Enfield, Middlesex ENl 2PG
Phone: 81-363-2697

ISRAEL

Aish HaTorah College of
   Jewish Studies
70 Misgav Ladach St.
Jewish Quarter, Old City
Israel
Phone: 02-894-441
FAX: 02-273-172

INDEX

About the Author

Lori Palatnik is a writer and educator with Aish HaTorah, Toronto, an international Jewish adult-education organization. She has appeared on television and radio and has lectured, both in North America and abroad, illuminating traditional practices and life-styles for our contemporary world.